Safety Aspects of Computer Control

Safety Aspects of Computer Control

Edited by
Phil Bennett PhD, FEng, FIEE
Managing Director, The Centre for
Software Engineering Ltd, Flixborough, Scunthorpe

BUTTERWORTH
HEINEMANN

Butterworth-Heinemann Ltd
Linacre House, Jordan Hill, Oxford OX2 8DP

PART OF REED INTERNATIONAL BOOKS

OXFORD   LONDON   BOSTON
MUNICH   NEW DELHI   SINGAPORE   SYDNEY
TOKYO   TORONTO   WELLINGTON

First published 1993

© Butterworth-Heinemann Ltd 1993

All rights reserved. No part of this publication
may be reproduced in any material form (including
photocopying or storing in any medium by electronic
means and whether or not transiently or incidentally
to some other use of this publication) without the
written permission of the copyright holder except in
accordance with the provisions of the Copyright,
Designs and Patents Act 1988 or under the terms of a
licence issued by the Copyright Licensing Agency Ltd,
90 Tottenham Court Road, London, England W1P 9HE.
Applications for the copyright holder's written permission
to reproduce any part of this publication should be addressed
to the publishers

British Library Cataloguing in Publication Data
A catalogue record for this book is available
from the British Library

Library of Congress Cataloguing in Publication Data
A catalogue record for this book is available from
the Library of Congress

ISBN 0 7506 1102 2

Typeset by Vision Typesetting, Manchester
Printed and bound in Great Britain by
Redwood Press, Melksham, Wiltshire

Contents

Preface vii

List of contributors ix

1 Software in safety-related systems: basic concepts and concerns 1
   Bob Malcolm

2 Regulatory issues 19
   Diane Rowland

3 Legal liability 35
   Dai Davis

4 Standardization efforts worldwide 56
   J. M. Rata

5 Real-time software requirements specification and animation using extended Petri nets: theory and application 76
   Sandro Bologna

6 Independent software verification and validation in practice: methodological and managerial aspects 88
   Sandro Bologna

7 Formal methods: use and relevance for the development of safety-critical systems 96
   John A. McDermid

8 Use of Ada in safety-critical systems 154
   Ian C. Pyle

9 Fault-tolerant control for safety 187
   Iain H. A. Johnston

10 The problems of an industrial supplier – and how to achieve good quality 205
   Leif Danielsen

11 Design and licensing of safety-related software 227
   Wolfgang D. Ehrenberger

Index 245

Preface

In the economic climate of the 1990s industry throughout the developed world is turning to the use of computer-based technologies to increase production efficiency. Recently this increased usage of computers has become linked to the concerns at the implicit safety aspects of such applications. The debate continues and will do so for some time to come. Nevertheless, the practising engineer, having little time or appetite for the theoretical debate, has to address and appreciate the debate. This book aims to inform just such an engineer of some of the issues he (or she) needs to consider.

In the first chapter Bob Malcolm brings his extensive industrial experience to bear in a survey of the subject; describing the fundamental concepts supported by research directions. In this way the practising engineer should become familiar with the main issues before progressing to the more detailed exploration in the following chapters.

Diane Rowland has a number of years experience as an HSE Factory Inspector so the perspective of the regulatory framework is one of genuine insight. Following from this Dai Davis gives a splendid resumé of the complex legal framework. Both these contributions provide a different perspective which few will be aware of.

Jean-Marie Rata has provided a chapter which is most difficult as the International Standard scene changes almost daily. So it is that by the time the chapter is read there may well be minor changes, though these will not negate the very useful content of this chapter.

Sandro Bologna has provided two excellent chapters which relate to the specification, verification and validation. These subjects are presently of concern and Bologna has many years of experience to communicate in this chapter.

No book on the safety of computer control could be considered complete without addressing the issue of formal methods. John McDermid has written a very useful appraisal of the strengths and weaknesses. Similarly, the book would be incomplete without a mention of Ada. Ian Pyle has thus written an informed perspective on the use of Ada.

Fault tolerance is often cited for systems involving safety but few understand the role it can play. Iain Johnston has therefore provided an overview of the subject.

The problems of procuring a system involving safety in the industrial sector while maintaining quality is well addressed by Leif Danielsen while the concerns and issues addressed by a licensing authority are covered by Wolfgang Ehrenberger.

The structure of the book is a simplified tour through the development life cycle often met by the engineer. After reading the book, I hope the reader is more aware of some of the issues and will be better equipped to seek out the solutions to problems he was not previously aware of. No book can be definitive on safety-related or safety-critical systems at this time – too little is known, too much needs to be researched and each application is unique.

Phil Bennett

Contributors

Phil Bennett The Centre for Software Engineering Ltd, Glanford House, Bellwin Drive, Flixborough, Scunthorpe DN15 8SN

Sandro Bologna ENEA CRE–Casaccia, Via Anguillarese 310, 00060 Santa Maria di Galeria (RM), Italy

Leif Danielsen ABB Automation AB, S-721 67 Västerås, Sweden

Dai Davis Eversheds, Hepworth & Chadwick, Solicitors, Cloth Hall Court, Infirmary Street, Leeds LS1 2JB

Wolfgang D. Ehrenberger Fachbereich Informatik, Fachhochschule, D-6400, Fulda, Germany

Iain H. A. Johnston The Centre for Software Engineering Ltd, Glanford House, Bellwin Drive, Flixborough, Scunthorpe DN15 8SN

John A. McDermid Department of Computer Science, University of York, York YO1 5DD and York Software Engineering Ltd

Bob Malcolm Malcolm Associates Ltd, Savoy Hill House, Savoy Hill, London WC2R 0BR

Ian C. Pyle SD-Scicon UK Ltd, Pembroke House, Pembroke Broadway, Camberley, Surrey GU15 3XD

J. M. Rata Electricité de France, Direction des Etudes et Recherches, Service Information et Mathematiques Appliquées, 1 Avenue de General de Gaulle, F–92141, France

Diane Rowland Department of Law, University of Wales, Aberystwyth, SY23 3DY

1 Software in safety-related systems: basic concepts and concerns
Bob Malcolm

INTRODUCTION

It is easy to think of only the more spectacular types of safety-related system – typically, complex, on-line, real-time applications. There is also a large number of small firms engaged in the production of small but safety-related systems or of components or tools for systems being built by larger suppliers.

The field of safety-related products in which software may be critically involved is large and diverse – often hardly seeming to justify the epithet of 'system'. It includes machinery and vehicle control, medical instrumentation, and off-line modelling, CAD and management systems.

Tradition and trends

Most sectors (though not all) already have traditions of procedure and technical practice to ensure – and assure – the safety of their systems. They have established controls, legislation, supervisory agencies, insurance arrangements and rules for determining liability. Those traditions have, for the most part, proved satisfactory over the years.

However, those existing traditions do not readily accommodate the computer software which is now being introduced. Moreover, in recent times the search for common, 'generic' international standards, and for ways in which software could be accommodated, have begun to pose questions about the rationale which underlies even existing practice. It is not that there is no rationale, but it often neither explicit nor linked clearly to the procedures and techniques which are used.

In parallel with these concerns, there are developments in the marketplace which are putting pressure on existing techniques. A few sectors, such as parts of the avionics industry, have always had the problem of 'continuous control', where it is not possible to separate normal operation from safety through simple monitoring and shutdown. Now new applications of microelectronics in hitherto low-technology application areas, such as active vehicle suspension, are faced with the same high-technology problem.

Many other sectors are faced with commercial pressure for increased availability, so that traditional techniques are not as acceptable as they once were. This is all in addition to the competition to gain market share through enhanced functionality.

Yet computers can actually be *more* reliable than special-to-type hardware.

Computer programs can provide more flexible, sophisticated and responsive functionality. Those who *can* manage the application of computers in safety-related roles stand to gain considerable competitive advantage. Those who cannot will find it increasingly difficult to compete – aside from the risks they run.

Software and systems

While there are indeed potential safety-related problems specific to software, and there are software-specific techniques which may obviate some of those problems, control of the software cannot be considered in isolation from the rest of the system and its situation in the real world. Furthermore, the controls which might be applied to software are often applicable and desirable for programmable elements of a system which are not necessarily viewed as software. The most obvious example is 'firmware', but for other hardware such as VLSI it is hard to distinguish between design with a 'silicon compiler' and programming.

Then again, software can be designed to limit the effects of both hardware failure and unexpected data. Similarly, hardware can be designed to limit the effects of software errors. Therefore the field of consideration should be, at least, 'programmable electronic systems' rather than software alone.

The discussion which follows relates to whole systems and does not distinguish between possible control and protection elements (cf. HSE, 1987). Nevertheless, safety-related systems are, in general, seen as control systems. They control or contribute to the control of something which affects the safety of people, either directly or indirectly. For simplicity, the discussion assumes a system which controls a process, but the arguments, in general, apply to systems as diverse as those which, for example, calculate drug dosage or which model civil engineering structures.

One of the purposes of this discussion is to expose some of the terminological problems. As in all technical disciplines, scientists and engineers use words, drawn from natural language, in special ways. Unfortunately, different groups use them differently, and often in quite contradictory ways. This is especially the case in a new and rapidly developing field such as this.

The first half of this chapter sets out some of the basic concepts associated with the development of software in safety-related systems. Then we move on to the future – to the research which we require, only some of which is taking place.

THE CONCEPTS

Safety, systems and unavoidable uncertainty

Safety is a concept which is not fixed in either time or space. Attitudes to safety, and tolerance of danger, are subjective and variable over time and circumstance. Industries have attempted to address this problem by identification of more objective aspects of safety, with particular definitions of words such as 'hazard' and 'risk'. The intention is that, in any given situation, specifications of safety, whether required or claimed as achieved, should be based on these more objectively defined terms.

Although we are concerned here with the part which software plays in safety-related systems, the software should not be considered in isolation from the systems in which it is embedded, or to which it contributes in some other way. It is the system which is safe or unsafe, not the software. We therefore consider the safety aspects of software in the context of the safety of systems. Further, we mean not just the *design* of systems on paper or computer disk but systems as specified and designed for a real world which we may not understand perfectly and which we may not be able to describe in a universally understood manner, and as built and operated in that same uncertainly known and described real world.

The uncertainty in our knowledge of the real world creates the potential for our specifications to be wrong, including being incomplete. This is apart from any mistakes we may make and uncertainties we may introduce when we describe the requirements in specifications.

This uncertainty of description arises from the need to model the real world, in a specification, in terms of abstractions which are open to subjective interpretation. Therefore even when we think that we understand the requirements of a system, there is inevitably some (even considerable) lack of definition in any requirements specification. This is sometimes described pejoratively as 'ambiguity' in the specification, but, although it may be possible to remove *some* lack of definition, some will inevitably remain. An entirely unambiguous specification is strictly infeasible.

In the face of all this uncertainty let us now introduce, as a reference, the notion of 'ideal operation'. This is what we would like a system to do, whether or not we know what that is, or are able to describe it or are able to specify, design, build and operate the system to do it. It is an entirely notional basis for considering what is required and what can be achieved.

The reason for introducing this notion of 'ideal operation' is that there is a difference between safety-related systems and others. The difference is that even though 'safety' is not a fixed concept, whatever it means for a particular application we want it. That is, we want the safety-related aspects of 'ideal operation' satisfied, regardless of the uncertainties in other aspects of the specification and its interpretation.

It might be argued that the specification is our best understanding of the requirements, and that its errors and ambiguities are not our concern. That may, perhaps, be the legal, contractual, position with *some* products and on *some* bespoke projects, but the engineering challenge is to meet the sub-set of the requirements concerned with safety, in the real world, regardless of the specification. The consequence of all this is that many of the engineering practices of safety-related systems are directed to reduce uncertainty *and cope with residual uncertainty*, while taking account of the needs for timeliness, economy and contractual constraints.

Note that 'regardless of the specification' does not mean that the specification, and its form, should be ignored. The aim of many of these uncertainty-reducing techniques, and of much research, is dedicated to improving the form of the specification, as a way of minimizing downstream problems.

Design, definition and uncertainty

At each stage of design the specification is, in effect, transformed into a more detailed design specification. The end product is some form of build definition, in terms of software language statements and hardware and software components. Sometimes it is said that such a final specification is, in some sense, a concrete representation of the specification. However, as long as the design is still that – a design, as yet unrealized physically – then it is composed of abstractions. These may represent realizable functions, or objects which are intended to perform functions, but they are not those functions.

Therefore at each design transformation the abstractions of the specification are transformed into other abstractions. In terms of the uncertainty in the specification, and its impact on the eventual operation, these abstractions fall into three classes, which are identified for the purpose of this discussion as realizable, definite and indefinite.

Starting with those which represent realizable objects or functions, their uncertainties concern whether they will be correctly realized in construction (will the compiler work?), whether they will perform as expected (what does 'add' mean for a computer representation of real numbers?) or as specified, and whether they will be used as intended. Next come those abstractions which represent universally well-understood concepts, such as logical relationships, which are not yet expressed in a realizable form from the first class. They are 'definite' in that there should not be scope for misinterpretation. They nevertheless suffer the uncertainty of accurate retention through design transformations, and accurate transformation into realizable form, followed, of course, by the uncertainties of the first class above. Finally, though generally first in the chronology of system development, there are those abstractions which represent our best effort to describe something over which there is no guarantee of common understanding of the intended meaning, however 'obvious' it may seem to any particular reader. These indefinite aspects of requirements include the important sub-class of things well understood in the application domain – or in a sub-set of it – but not necessarily by system designers and builders. The uncertainties of this class (in addition to those of the previous two classes) arise from the most difficult question of all – whether there is mutual understanding of these requirement abstractions as they are transformed into realizable form.

The process of design is, then, one of increasing definition, transforming the abstractions of specification until there is a fully realizable representation. Some indefinite elements are made definite, and definite elements made more definite, until they are realizable. At each transformation there is potential for a variety of types of error, each of which gives rise to a different type of uncertainty about the operation of the eventual system. The value of the distinction between these different forms of uncertainty lies in the discrimination it offers when assessing the contribution of different techniques used in safety-related systems development.

Beyond design there are potential errors of construction and operation. It is not enough for a designer to design on the basis that these will not happen. Indeed, it would be irresponsible to make that assumption. Such errors should be taken into account and accommodated by the design. After all, the customer wants a system which performs its ideal operation, at least for the safety-related aspects, regardless – not just on a good day. This is usually achieved by some degree of fault detection, coupled with fault tolerance. It often involves an acceptable reduced functionality – perhaps a fallback capability or fail-safe protection.

There remains still the real world, which may not 'perform as expected'. Though perhaps not strictly within the remit of 'design', there *are* approaches to system development which address this problem. Many of the engineering techniques of safety-related systems are concerned with recognition that we require safety even with our uncertain understanding of the world. For instance, where possible, fail-safe protection of a controlled process will be based not on computation, which requires understanding of the process, but on monitoring of unarguable physical parameters. Prototyping is not always easy or even possible, but where it is, it can contribute as much to understanding of the real world as of the system under development.

Correctness

Unfortunately, this seemingly straightforward word has acquired a number of different usages, where the differences can be very significant. To many engineers, as well as to the public, it means conformance between actual and ideal operation – between what a system actually does in the real world and what we would have liked it to do had we realized what we really wanted.

To some, correctness means conformance of design, or build or perhaps operation, to the specification. For contractual purposes this may avoid some of the uncertainties in our knowledge of the real world. However, given the inevitable uncertainties inherent in the use of abstractions in a specification, this is not such a useful distinction as it would appear, since we must then ask – whose interpretation of the specification?

A third usage is that of mathematicians, who sometimes mean, by 'correctness', that part of this second 'conformance' usage may, in principle, be demonstrable as mathematical or logical consistency between system descriptions – such as that between one level of software specification and a more detailed level of design. (Note 'consistency' – not 'equivalence' as some might claim, except perhaps equivalence over a projection.)

Care must therefore be taken in interpretation of the term 'correctness' in the literature about safety-related systems. In this chapter it has been avoided unless qualified to indicate the particular sense in which it is used.

Completeness

Strictly, this is about incompleteness, and types of incompleteness, rather than completeness. Incompleteness can be considered to be no more than one form of incorrectness, but a distinction might be drawn between errors of *commission* and errors of *omission*. Both are incorrect in the broadest sense, but errors of omission can be considered as incompleteness errors, in which case 'incorrectness' is then sometimes used in a narrower sense for errors of commission.

Discussion of incompleteness, especially with regard to the determinability of the 'correctness' of a system, can be clouded by confusion between different types of incompleteness. What follows is not intended to be a definitive categorization of incompleteness but an indication of the range of types.

First, there may have been a failure to identify all the pertinent factors which must be considered in deciding the response of a system in any situation. Second, the factors which have been considered may not have been properly characterized. The range of possibilities for these factors may be either not sufficiently extensive or not sufficiently finely divided. Third, the responses of a system to the considered factors may be wrong. This last sounds like an error of commission rather than omission. However, if it arises because of a lack of realization that within the responses to a given set of circumstances there should have been further sub-division – recognition of special cases, for example – then it is in some sense an omission, much like the previous case.

Indeed, whatever the cause of incompleteness, a system will nevertheless, whether by default or deliberate design, usually do *something*. Certainly, for on-line systems, even stopping, or failing to respond to an event, counts as 'doing something'. In such cases, it could be said to have been designed to do the wrong thing. Hence a confusion between errors of commission and omission. Is the 'something' which the system does an error of commission? Or does the reason that the correct response was not designed – a lack of identification and characterization of relevant factors – make it an error of omission?

Finally, there is a rather different type of incompleteness – that of indefinition – where a requirement or design is insufficiently definite, so that among the possible interpretations there is scope for some which are incorrect. Purists would argue that errors in this class are, in general, one or other of the other types. Indeed, they would state that all these types of incompleteness are just different ways of looking at and describing the first type, but that is like saying that they are all forms of incompleteness – whch is where we began. The reason for these different descriptions is no more – and no less – than that we think about the errors in different ways.

Certification, conformance and objective tests

Many safety-related systems are developed in an environment where regulatory and licensing authorities require 'certification' of some kind, but there are limitations, both in practice and in theory, to the assurance that such certification can provide. First, the key concept of conformance assessment based on objective testing will be discussed. This concept is essential to certification schemes. Note that 'test' is, in this discussion, used in a wide sense, rather than the more restricted input–output sense, usually implicit in the phrase 'software test', that the right outputs are generated for particular sets of inputs. Testing in this wide sense could, for instance, include visual inspection or checking that people doing the work had the proper authorization. By an 'objective test' we mean one about which all members of the community of interest would have, literally 'in effect', the 'same' interpretation. Referring to the earlier discussion of design and definition, the specification of an objective test must therefore be 'definite', at least with regard to the purposes of the test.

The word 'conformance' has two distinct uses in the field of system development. In a broad sense it is a special case of the general English-language usage, referring to the consistency between two things. However, it also has an added implication of completeness. Therefore if we consider the conformance of a design with its requirement specification, the design must be not just consistent with the requirements, in that it does not explicitly contradict them, it should also explicitly address all the requirements.

'Conformance assessment' is the determination that something or someone satisfies, in this sense, the definite element of an objective test. 'Conformance' is often then used in a narrower sense as shorthand for recognition that a number of such tests has been satisfied.

We must be careful with the term 'certification', since it can be interpreted in very different ways. Though most would agree that it is associated with some kind of pass/fail assessment, there the agreement ends. First, there are those who assume that it is dependent on only objective tests – that is, it is a formal recognition of conformance. Certainly this is usually an ambition of certification schemes; but existing schemes do not necessarily preclude elements of subjective appraisal. Second, there may be requirements for conformance which are not encapsulated in explicit 'certification' requirements, but which have the same type of objective, and similar importance and recognition in particular industries.

By definition, conformance and certification against objective tests cannot address the uncertainties of either the real world or specifications. In other words, 'complete' conformance to all the real-world safety requirements can never be demonstrated. Therefore the prospect of releasing into service only systems which have been 'completely' certified as safe, against objective tests, is not viable. It is also quite simply, if sadly, not possible.

Verification and validation

There are no universally accepted definitions of these terms or of the distinction between them. Nevertheless, a distinction is often made between conformance to a specification and correctness of actual operation in the real world with respect to ideal operation, regardless of the specification.

Working definitions of verification and validation are therefore that verification is concerned with assessment, proof or providing confidence of conformance; and validation with *correct actual operation*. Colloquially, verification then addresses the question 'Are we building the product right?' and validation 'Are we building the right product?'

Again, though, there is terminological confusion. Not only do some software engineers use these words with the meanings reversed, despite the maturity of this distinction (Boehm, 1974), but mathematical logicians have traditionally spoken of the logical validity of an argument independently of the truth or otherwise of the premises. Therefore *some* logicians then differentiate by introducing the notion of 'soundness' to accommodate the real-world premises. Then, to them, a *sound* argument is one which is both logically valid and based on true premises. (Except that still others then say, as in Borowski and Borwein, 1989, '**sound**, *adj.* another word for VALID'!) In fact, verification is generally considered to be concerned with attempting to establish conformance of a representation of design or requirements with an earlier representation, of which the earliest is the original specification.

Given the preceding discussion of specification, design and conformance, then even if conformance is achieved, setting aside the question of ideal operation, a design or a system as built may still not be what was intended. It may be one interpretation of a specification, but it may not be a valid interpretation.

Some verification techniques go beyond strict conformance as discussed previously. They attempt to establish that the later definite or realizable representations *satisfactorily* interpret the earlier indefinite counterparts from which they were derived. Such techniques require human intervention, since they are attempting to determine mutual understanding of abstractions. The techniques are therefore designed to assist human understanding of different representations. They usually provide different 'views', for either analysis or comparison, in order to identify differences of interpretation of the requirements. Such differences of interpretation may imply that one or other is incorrect.

However, in some ways perhaps more importantly for safety-related systems, verification is itself limited, since it starts with the specification rather than the real world. Dealing with our uncertain understanding of the real world is the subject of validation.

Correctness of actual operation compared with ideal operation is, then, addressed by validation. We try to determine that our understanding of the requirements, as embodied in a system or its design, is right. This cannot be 'proven' in the mathematical sense. We can gain only confidence, and not confirmation, that it has been achieved – and will be in future. This confidence can come only from evidence that the system or its operation is consistent with the real-world requirements, i.e. does not contradict them, so far. This is why there are disputes over the role of testing – over whether it is to demonstrate correctness or to find faults. ('Testing' is used here in the narrow sense of exercising a system or part of it.) Even if testing *is* to demonstrate correctness, the *only* way to do that by exercising a system is to fail to find faults.

In limited cases, such as for some very specific conformance tests, it may be possible to exhaustively exercise a system over all of a limited range of conditions. However, in general, the problem of testing is that it is impossible to be exhaustive and difficult to be sure of the coverage and usefulness of the tests which are performed. Nevertheless, however crude, system testing – if not low-level 'module' testing – does have the advantage that the accuracy and sufficiency of our understanding of the controlled process and its environment can be tested. While this may be in a rather hit-or-miss fashion, the other techniques tend to be somewhat introspective.

Indeed, testing is the most common form of validation. Other techniques include prototyping, animation, analysis and walkthrough. The objective is the same in each case – to present a different view of the system from its design representations, to help us to think about it in different ways.

Here we see similarity with the 'beyond conformance' aspect of verification. The multiple views seek to compare interpretations, not of the specification this time, but of the real-world requirements. However, the approach is often similar, and may be one source of the confusion between verification and validation. It is the same confusion that can exist in an interpretation of 'Are we building the right product?' It is possible (though not what was intended!) to read this as 'Are we building the intended product, given the indefinite nature of the specification?' instead of 'Are we building the product which will do the right job in the real world?' Here, the former has been considered to be addressed by verification and the latter by validation.

To summarize validation, there is, in general, no such thing as a correctness proof for the operation of a system, except in the old-fashioned sense of proof as a test – as in 'the proof of the pudding'.

Summary of the story so far

In short, there are *fundamental limitations* to the assurance that can be gained about the operation of practical, entire, safety-related systems. Now we must think about the measures which we might take to improve the situation, and to provide safety nevertheless. These are all in addition to (or refinements of) the essential and traditional approaches to fault avoidance and removal, fault tolerance and fault detection and recovery.

RESEARCH DIRECTIONS

Systems or software?

During the debate in recent years over the way in which to treat software in safety-related systems (IEE, 1989a) it has been said many times that 'Safety is a *systems* issue'. This is entirely accepted. However, it should be remembered that the search for harmonization across industrial sectors had its origins in the search for a common approach to the introduction of *software* into a variety of types of application system. Therefore there are at least four targets for research:

1. How should we produce and manage the production of safety-related software in particular situations and different application domains?
2. Can we find a common approach?
3. What is the rationale for present tradition and practice in a variety of sectors?
4. Can we harmonize them in such a way that a common approach to software can be adopted?

Nevertheless, taken together, these amount to the question with which we began, namely, 'How should we handle software in safety-related systems?'

In addition to the exploration of improvements in specific technologies and techniques, we are looking for understanding and for 'unification' – common criteria and techniques for safety assurance. What is the basis for present practice? Where do industrial sectors differ fundamentally, and why? How common can they be? Can we characterize systems so that they and their appropriate procedures and techniques can all be fitted into a common framework?

Many of the existing practices are based on either explicit or implicit expert judgement. This may be an inevitable element of all safety engineering. If so, how should we control it? Is there anything which can be done to unify qualitative, quantitative and analytic assessment? Are there techniques which will help us reason about these things, both generally and in the context of a particular safety-critical system?

Technologies

Almost invariably, first thoughts on research directions turn to software design techniques and their support tools. These are certainly among the most actively researched technologies, but 'technologies' encompasses many aspects of process, product and their evaluation. The relationship between these different facets of development is also of interest. For instance, techniques for design should be considered for their suitability for assessment and for after-the-event fault diagnosis. Before concentrating on research into software design methods, we will first consider some of the other research themes. This will establish the very broad and rich context within which we should be thinking about software design.

There is now a considerable body of knowledge and technology for the evaluation of system reliability, and it is often possible to obtain accurate estimates and predictions of reliability and know that they are accurate. Unfortunately, these techniques work only for modest reliability levels. In the case of certain safety-critical systems there is a demand for extremely high reliability to be assured against design faults (particularly those arising in the software). Is it possible to give such assurance, and how might supporting evidence be obtained? How does one know when a very high level of reliability has been achieved, or what constitutes a suitable sound basis for forming a judgement that is, in principle, achievable or measurable?

Designers should not be unnecessarily constrained, but do they impose structuring and partitioning constraints on themselves anyway? If so, and if, therefore, it is not strictly necessary to emulate the full flexibility of existing technology, is there scope for simplifying technology to facilitate these other aspects – and perhaps to reduce costs?

Both cost-effectiveness and raw cost are themselves important. Any proposals for the future must take this into account. Is it feasible to put existing technology and practice on a more rigorous footing rather than to develop new? If it is, would it be cheaper and therefore more likely to succeed in the commercial world? Could this avert technological divergence between safety-critical systems development and mainstream development? This would be an interesting prospect for software development, since it offers the prospect of gaining the benefits of mathematical techniques in other ways with other styles of development techniques, such as formalized object-oriented approaches.

Among the important requirements for objective assurance are simplicity, intelligibility and traceability. 'Separation of concerns' is often said to help. This may be seen as one of the benefits of parametric packages and sub-systems – such as the general-purpose programmable process-controller. Also, some sectors are seeing the emergence of 'task programming' of generic applications (or application generators). In each of these cases, reasoning about the assurance of systems is separated between reasoning about the generic package or system; reasoning about the parameterization or programming; and reasoning about the combination. Is it possible to provide a rigorous basis for such separation of concerns?

This may be linked with the question of what is meant by 'objective' in 'objective assurance'. Does it mean mutual agreement based on shared knowledge within domains of expertise? Examination of these issues might provide revealing insights for 'unification'.

Interestingly, the techniques and technology of expert systems might be part of the solution here, rather than, as many seem to think, part of the problem – particularly the problem of 'proof'. Separation of proof of the algorithm generator from proof of the application knowledge on which it operates might be preferable to proof of the algorithm, in which these issues are intertwined. Therefore rather than try to squeeze expert systems development into the mould of mainstream software development, might it be possible to start with the philosophy of separation of concerns, which is implicit in expert systems, and codify and formalize it in some way?

Also, what of the relationship between high-integrity and mere 'quality'? On the one hand, we say that *of course* quality management is good for you. On the other, we have no evidence that there is any correlation between the use of quality management techniques and the quality of delivered products. So how *can* we add knowledge about quality management into the construction of a safety argument in any reliable and quantifiable way? Can we, indeed, add *any* process knowledge into the argument, and if so, how?

Although it is possible that some specific technological developments will contribute to safety, it is important to consider their impact on human factors in the broad and on the whole system, rather than in isolation, with regard to just local 'improvement'. We must take care to avoid 'displacement', whereby the problem is pushed elsewhere – and perhaps made worse overall.

Human factors

This subject is much wider than ergonomics and consideration of the human–computer interface. It encompasses all aspects of human involvement in systems from conception to operation and beyond. If a Failure Modes and Effects Analysis were to be performed for this whole 'system' rather than just the system under development, then many of the failure modes which would have to be included would be those of humans, whether operators, maintainers, designers or software programmers. The effect of leaving them out of the calculations is to treat them as perfect whereas, ultimately, humans are *always* the weakest links in the chain.

In all cases, it is not sufficient simply to identify a problem. In addition to understanding the problem better, we would like guidance on what to do about it, such as recommendations on appropriate forms of design language and management structure, preferably supported, yet again, by an explanation in terms of contribution to a safety argument. We need to address the perception and tolerability of risk, the role and validity of expert judgement and the contribution of human reliability (in management and design as well as in operation).

In addition, despite having broadened the field of human factors beyond just the human–computer interface, there is still a wealth of potential HCI research which might be addressed. In doing so we must remember that although the human – the H of HCI – is usually described as the operator, in many systems this may be too simplistic. The implication of a technically trained operator will often be wrong. In vehicles the operator is the driver; in medical systems there is the patient as well as the doctor and the nurse. In these circumstances unpredictability is not an aberration but the norm.

We need to address display and control ergonomics; the role of perceptual and cognitive processes in interface design; operator performance monitoring and on-line support, including expert system support. There are many others. The limiting factor seems to be our ability to conceive of ways of tackling the enormous range of problems and potential solutions.

Unification

Unification is distinct from harmonization, which may be little more than agreement on common words and procedures. That is an important step in the right direction, but unification does more. It is an attempt to provide an objectively sound basis for reasoning about the safety of particular systems, including reasoning about very diverse contributions, of very different natures, to safety.

We would like unification to enable coherent practices within sectors, with integration of a range of procedures and techniques applied to a range of technologies; a common rationale to underpin practices in different sectors; and common standards across sectors. A guiding principle is to consider how the results of any research might assist in making a 'safety argument' such as some industries require, and as has been recommended for all safety-related systems (IEE, 1989a) (sometimes called a 'safety case' or 'safety justification'). A safety argument might be either supported or supplanted by a quantified safety analysis – such as Probabilistic Risk Analysis. We must then ask how such techniques might help integrate objective elements of an argument (e.g. mathematical proof; proven automated transformation) with subjective elements (e.g. preferences in specification languages and management organization). Then, how can such arguments be incorporated into generic standards (in a unifying role, rather than for prescription about a particular part of development or assurance)?

Reference has already been made to the lack of an explicit rationale for much of the existing practice in safety-critical systems development. However, many of the techniques used embody sound engineering principles and rules of thumb. Can these be identified, perhaps formalized, and their value, in terms of contribution to a safety argument or to a quantitative assessment, be exposed?

Unification should, in turn, provide a sound underpinning for harmonization, as well as for particular safety arguments. For instance, it would be desirable to develop objective criteria for before-the-event selection of technologies to be used on a development and for after-the-event assessment of their effectiveness. Note that support of before-the-event selection will require statistical measures over the ranges of application of the technologies, rather than just particular measures in a given situation. An additional aim is an objective assessment of the benefits and costs of risk reduction. A safety argument might then be more than a safe/unsafe argument: it might include the calculation of trade-offs. Even attempting to enable such trade-offs could yield a characterization of various techniques in terms of the extent to which they support or facilitate them.

A solution to the problem of unified assurance will require contributions from the so-called 'soft' sciences, as well as the 'hard' sciences and technologies, particularly the disciplines which attempt to bridge the two in a real-world context. Operational research techniques, for instance, may well have a role. Particular contributions might come from subjects such as generalized hazard analysis, reasoning under uncertainty, informal argument (from philosophical logic), measurement theory, decision theory and decision making in the presence of uncertainty, quantified risk analysis, quantified dependability analysis and links between these and objective metrics, quantification of subjective judgement, judgemental and approximate quantification of, for instance, human communications effectiveness and performance capability. Is there a general rule that the list of contenders to help solve any problem is in inverse proportion to the obviousness of any answers?

Software design

Now let us return to the much-debated topic of software design. The emphasis here is on design notation, particularly about its role in 'proof', and the role of notation in structuring our reasoning. It is also about the reason different notations are appropriate in different situations, with a view to eventually understanding better what representations, and what associated methods, would be appropriate for what purposes.

Note that most 'methods' are notations rather than methods. They leave open the question of how one maps from the real world, or an earlier representation, to the concepts represented in the notation.

A note of caution: the word 'representation' has a special meaning in the context of expert systems, usually referring to the representation of *knowledge*. There is indeed a considerable literature devoted to discussion of the most appropriate representation of knowledge in different domains and for different purposes (e.g. Jackson, 1984). This is *not* the sense in which it is used here. We are concerned with the representation of *intent* and the representation of *intent* and the representation of *design* and with what we require *of* such representations.

From intent to realization

First, a quick overview of the steps of system development, beginning with *an intent*. The intent is the 'ideal operation' discussed earlier in this chapter. It is what we would like the system to do, whether or not we know what that is.

We then have a *conceptualization* of that intent – perhaps a cognitive model of the world and the system within it. It is this which we try to describe in a specification. Moreover, we hope that that description will convey to the system developer our conceptualization. Note that it would be even better if it conveyed our intent – even if, and perhaps especially if, our intent is not completely known even to ourselves as problem owners. Thereafter there will be a process of transformation into other representations more suitable for design and construction – the increasing 'definition' discussed earlier.

Now we might argue that, if at some stage there is a representation for which there could, at least in theory, be formal semantics, then all is well, since we could then reason at that level about the system and its requirements, and further aspects of design could be theoretically perfect – perhaps mechanizable. We might further argue that *all* processes which offer that facility are in some sense isomorphic – that they are just different ways of saying the same things and achieving the same effects.

Therefore are all such 'sound' development processes are as good as each other? No. The goodness of different approaches will depend on:

1. The form of representation at the highest levels of description, as a vehicle for thinking about one's own needs and then communicating them to another, or to a machine;
2. The nature of the transformation process and its intermediate representations;
3. The projections, or 'alternative views' which are available to facilitate reasoning about the system from different angles.

Furthermore, these issues will depend, in turn, on the type of system and the domain and environment in which it is operating.

Bridge that gap

A brain surgeon, specifying his requirements for a robotic support system, might, say, offer a description of those requirements in terms of transistor states in the final computer system, or even electron states. Perhaps, he would not go so far – perhaps a Turing tape for the computer system? That would be precise, but it would hardly be the best representation to facilitate reasoning about whether the system would do what the surgeon intended.

Alternatively, he could just talk about what he wanted. The listening system developer might understand some of it and build *something*. The system *might* include some of the things which the surgeon wanted but did not ask for, as long as the developer thought to ask about them. It would be unlikely to embody the requirements which neither had thought about. This perhaps typifies many software systems today.

We need an approach which is more realistic than the first of these and more satisfactory than the second. The question is then, 'How can we best bridge that gap between intent and realization?'

Minimizing change ramification

In addition to bridging the gap during initial specification and design, we would like to keep the bridge open during subsequent changes. An alternative metaphor, though, might be to say that we want to minimize traffic on the bridge, *despite* subsequent changes.

A representation which is executable clearly requires less error-prone transformation by human designers than one which needs intermediate stages of design and verification. The intermediate error-prone stages are avoided not only during initial development but also during all subsequent stages. A representation which is modular requires less transformation than one which is monolithic. A representation which requires complete re-verification and re-validation after a minor change to the requirement is simply not practicable.

We need a form of modularization which localizes the effects of change, minimizing propagation of changes, and thereby minimizing consequent additional rework. It seems likely that such a modularization will also facilitate reasoning about validity in the first place.

Structured design

Through the 1970s and early 1980s the panacea was thought to be third-generation languages coupled with top-down structured programming and structured design methodologies. It was certainly an improvement over meandering code derived from spaghetti-like flow charts, but it turned out to present two major problems still with us today.

First, the customer was asked to approve thick volumes of high-level design specifications – the top of the design tree – and then, so we said, there would be mere 'refinement' and implementation. Unfortunately, we later discovered that labelled boxes do not necessarily mean a lot. Customers found that they were not happy with the delivered systems – the developers' realization of the boxes – and yet they had 'signed off' these abstractions. This has proved a rich source of angst, anger and acrimony. In some ways, by thinking that we had solved the problem with what we thought was a common communication medium – the interestingly shaped boxes – we made matters worse by fooling ourselves and our customers, storing up trouble for the future.

The second problem is that the 'refinement' is a mixture of requirement refinement and design refinement. Important aspects of functionality turned out to be buried deep down in a hierarchy of code. Understanding what it all did was supposed to be easy, but it was not. Understanding of where and how to make changes was supposed to be easy, but it was not.

Mathematical logic? – aka 'formalism'

As with other 'methods', 'formal methods' are, for the most part, notations rather than methods. This is not to deny the value of the notations, or the value of the disciplines which their use necessitates, nor the value of the analyses which they facilitate.

However, we must beware a false sense of security of formal notations through their apparent, but not actual, precision. Using the terminology from earlier sections, they usually provide a definite framework within which there can still be considerable lack of definition in the objects and their relationships. They have been likened to the assembly languages of specification – well-defined operators, leaving open the meaning of the operands and whether the operation of the operators on the operands achieves the desired effects. The definite framework is a distinct advance, but no panacea.

There are at least three different types or aspects of formal methods, each of which may be supported by software tools. First, there is the use of a notation, ranging from diagrammatic aids, based upon simple categorization of types of object and their relationships, to highly mathematical formalisms, such as predicate calculus. Then there are consistency or verification techniques, which usually require that the design be expressed in a formal notation so that it can be manipulated. These tend to deal with simple syntactic, structural properties of the system. 'Proof' techniques fall into this category. Sometimes they are confusingly referred to by mathematicians as correctness proofs (see earlier discussion of 'correctness'). In our terminology they are proofs of conformance with an earlier specification, perhaps of a program module or of the whole system. It is also possible to 'prove' certain properties of the specification itself, such as some aspects of self-consistency. Finally, there are the program analysis techniques. These tend to be based on analysis by suites of tools. On the one hand, they may verify that a program has certain required properties; on the other, they may present the program from a different angle – hence providing some limited support for validation.

Therefore formal techniques are concerned with expression of design in a formal notation which allows some kind of manipulation of a mathematical nature, in order to assist verification. This is a considerable step forward, and it is a development which should be encouraged, but it should be set in the context that, as already discussed, verification is itself limited in what it can achieve by our understanding of the requirement and our ability to express that understanding clearly, precisely and consistently throughout the design process.

In Sommerville (1989) we are given an example of the use of the formal notation 'Z' and shown how it can be used to describe the operation of a hopper. After representing the normal operation of adding to the contents of the hopper, we are then shown how to represent the potential overfilling of the hopper. Too often we are told that it is the precise mathematical notation and the use of mathematical logic which allows us to represent these things and to reason about them. Yet it is only because the description used the words 'container', 'hopper', 'capacity', etc. that we can begin to think about, ask questions about, and elaborate upon such details. In other words, it is because of the connotation in our heads, not the 'mathematically precise' denotation on paper, that we are prompted to reason about the important aspects of the specification. Certainly, a logical form of the paper description might trigger us to think about some aspects we had not thought about before, in much the same way that a flow chart (or a Nassi–Schneiderman chart of yore) would remind us to think about some aspects of completeness. So it is with the famous 'lift' example, beloved of software design methodologists. It would not make nearly as much sense if words like 'lift', 'floor', 'up' and 'down' were not used – even if the same logical effect were to be achieved. We do not have this luxury when dealing with new or less well-understood domains.

Yet it is precisely questions such as the potential overfilling of containers with which we are concerned in safety-critical systems. There is a growing body of case histories (e.g. IEE, 1989b) to suggest that most system safety failures arise from unforeseen events and conditions in the real world – and in the application domain rather than the computational one.

Bigger conceptual lumps

We started by wanting to bridge the gap between application and computational domains. At the same time, we wish to minimize the traffic on the bridge. We try to achieve the latter through 'separation of concerns'. The intention is threefold:

1. To minimize the complexity of reasoning and re-reasoning, as discussed above. In fact, we do not really want merely to *ease* the process. We would rather *avoid* it – by 'knowing' that we had done the right thing;
2. To ensure that individuals are operating, as far as possible, entirely within the scope of their own competence, uncluttered by worries about things outside their own field;
3. To enable individuals to partition even their own thinking in time, minimizing muddling interactions between partitions.

The classical way to do all this is to use bigger 'conceptual lumps'. In software engineering, we used to think, as in top-down structured design, that any old lumps would do. We talked glibly of the need for abstractions, but we have since found that any old abstractions will not do (see 'Structured Design' above). For anything other than perhaps for the third of the objectives above, they need to be *abstractions with shared semantics.* (Compare the earlier discussion of *objective* assurance.)

As in other domains, we bridge the gap with higher-level standard components, standard architectural structures and standard interfaces between them. They might be specific to an application domain – such as application-specific languages and reference architectures. They might be generic to a class of application domains – such as expert system inference engines. Or they might be entirely generic – like the spreadsheet or word processor.

In all cases, they provide a more powerful virtual machine, building a bridgehead from the computational domain to the application domain, and minimizing the building work for particular applications (Malcolm, 1988, 1990). By a combination of separation of concerns, and greater re-use and more 'objective' assurance through greater 'genericity' of both application concepts and computational components, we will both simplify and minimize the reasoning required to create confidence in our systems.

REFERENCES

Boehm, B. W. (1974), *Guidelines for Verifying and Validating Software Requirements and Design Specifications*, TRW, Redondo Beach, CA

Borowski, E. J. and Borwein, J. M. (1989), *Dictionary of Mathematics*, Collins, London

HSE (1987), *Programmable Electronic Systems in Safety-related Applications*, HMSO, London

IEE (1989a), *Software in Safety-related Systems*, October

IEE (1989b), *Proceedings of 1st International Conference on 'Computers and Safety'*, November

Jackson, P. (1984), 'Review of knowledge representation methods', *IEE Proceedings*, **134**, No. 4, July

Malcolm, R. (1988), 'The future of software engineering', *Proceedings of 1988 DTI-IED Conference*, Swansea

Malcolm, R. (1990), 'The future of software engineering – revisited', *The BCS Computer Bulletin*, December

Sommerville, I. (1989), *Software Engineering*, 3rd edition, Addison-Wesley, Reading, MA

2 Regulatory issues
Diane Rowland

INTRODUCTION

The versatility and cost-effectiveness of computer control has led to its widespread adoption in all areas of industry, including those in which safety is of paramount concern. Although the use of such systems brings many advantages, the consequences of failure may involve both loss of life and environmental damage. Failure of these systems may occur for a number of reasons, but the possibility of failure due to defects in the software has created problems relating to safety which have not previously been encountered.

A necessary objective of manufacturers and designers of safety-critical systems must be that both users and others who may be incidentally affected may be satisfied that an adequate safety margin has been provided. It is commonly assumed that one way in which this can be ensured is by introducing some form of regulation. However, the reasonableness of this assumption depends not only on a solution to the technical problems of ensuring software safety but also on addressing a number of legal and moral issues raised by regulation, both in general and with specific reference to hazardous activities. This chapter will examine and assess various methods available for regulation and then discuss whether they are appropriate for application to software and system safety.

METHODS OF ENSURING SAFETY

It is a sad fact that health and safety issues only appear in newspaper headlines following a disaster. When subsequent inquiries reveal a catalogue of events which demonstrate a scant regard for safety, the inevitable impression gained is that safety is only accorded minor importance. Although reaction to disaster is usually swift, and safety improvements may be speedily implemented, discussion of safety issues in the aftermath of a disaster has the result of turning safety into an emotive topic.

The ultimate aim both for the rational discussion of the issues involved and for the prevention of accidents should be to ensure that safety is made an objective at the first possible opportunity, i.e. at the design stage. This means not only that all foreseeable eventualities can be considered but also prevents safety issues from being marginalized, as safety mechanisms can be included as an integral part of the design process rather than as an afterthought. Nevertheless, nothing can be made inherently safe, and so any assessment of the safety of an object or process will depend on balancing a number of factors. Some accidents are completely predictable, but many occur because of the juxtaposition of a number of events which, in themselves, seem unlikely, and it appears an even more remote possibility that they will act in coordination. Also, unfortunately for manufacturers and engineers, factors governing perceptions of safety are not all technical: sociological and psychological factors may also play a part and cannot be discounted.

That there may be a public outcry following a disaster has perhaps less to do with the fact that those involved have had their safety compromised as with the fact that the individuals concerned were not in control of their own fate. We are all accustomed to taking risks. Even though, statistically, crossing the road is a more dangerous activity than being a passenger in a fly-by-wire aircraft, it may not be perceived as such because the individual no longer feels in control. This element of control is removed when safety is apparently entrusted to machines. It then becomes the responsibility of other people such as designers and manufacturers to make the decisions which affect our safety; society needs to be able to put its faith in the integrity of their designs.

As with all safety issues, a balancing of risk with consequences is necessary, but this may be heavily influenced by public and political perceptions of the safety level that is required, and may not be a straightforward relationship. Even in cases where there is general agreement on safety as an objective, there may be no consensus on the best way to achieve this in practice.

A good example of the effect of public perceptions of safety is found in a consideration of the nuclear industry. It is well known that a nuclear accident can have severe consequences both initially and in the long term. This leads to pressure groups who campaign against the industry believing that even the high safety levels which are built in are insufficient in view of the catastrophic events which can occur in the case of failure, however unlikely this may appear on paper. No one believes risk can be completely eliminated but the question of how much residual risk can be tolerated is extremely subjective. It cannot be assumed that the levels which are acceptable to society are those that would be agreed by informed opinion within the industry. It can thus be argued that regulatory frameworks also need to take these factors into account in exactly the same way that the technical issues are considered.

As society has become increasingly dependent on technology, the potential for widespread disaster and devastation becomes ever greater. If there is any doubt about this we only have to consider the events leading to the disasters at Seveso, Bhopal and Chernobyl. In a pre-technological era the only possible parallels could have been with the effects of a major earthquake or a volcanic eruption, and it is doubtful whether even catastrophes of this magnitude would result in the long-term effects which some man-made disasters are capable of producing. In earlier times, journeys such as sea voyages were not embarked upon lightly but with the full knowledge that death, if not inevitable, was a very real possibility. We no longer have such concerns but expect a high standard of safety; as technology has brought an increased potential for disaster so it has created the expectation of protection from such events. When calamity does strike, although arguably the major objective should be to prevent a recurrence, there is an inevitable need and desire to apportion blame. It is at this stage that there is likely to be public outrage if design faults have compromised safety. Society therefore has very high expectations of the safety levels which can and should be achieved. This not only creates pressures to produce safer products but is also one of the major reasons for introducing regulation.

As technology advances, proportionally fewer people hold the requisite knowledge to ensure that safety receives proper consideration. Those with such knowledge are likely to be the designers of the product itself. However, they may not be in the best position to assess objectively the hazards introduced by the system. Designers tend to be interested primarily with what the system can and is intended to do; safety considerations are usually concerned with what the system must not do. The latter is unlikely to be so well defined and it takes a different type of expertise to envisage all possible eventualities against which precautions need to be taken.

In addition, there is the problem of familiarity: those intimately involved with the design may not be so appreciative of the risk as the informed outsider. This is the classical argument in favour of third-party assessment. To use a simple illustration, ladders are widely used both at home and at work, and everyone is familiar with them. Yet, probably because of this very familiarity, they are a frequent cause of both domestic and industrial accidents, despite being the subject of a number of standards and codes of practice. Ladders are so common that they are often not perceived as a source of danger, and it is often the outsider who is best placed to detect misuse: the onlooker may see that the user is over-reaching, for instance, and is in danger of a fall. The user, although perhaps initially careful, no longer has a realization of the danger, as he has 'got away with it' so many times on previous occasions. Many readers will recognize an analogous situation in the development of software.

For many systems, producing a safe design will be as reliant on safety awareness as on the technical expertise of the design team; often an awareness of the possible problems will be more than half-way to solving them. The problem is usually more difficult for computer-controlled systems. The complexity of such systems means that it may not be possible to identify all possible failure modes. Neither is exhaustive testing in all possible conditions and environments feasible, even in the unlikely event that they could be accurately predicted. This distinguishes the safety problems of computer-controlled systems from those of other systems where failure modes and testing methods and procedures may be well understood.

In addition, the sociological and psychological factors outlined above play a large part in determining what the public expects from such systems. Users of safety-critical systems need (and expect to have) extreme confidence in the reliability and integrity of such systems. Such confidence may be damaged irrevocably by only one malfunction if it affects the safety of the system. Because of this, it is inevitable that some sort of external regulation of these activities should have been proposed and implemented. The aeronautical industry has developed its own guidelines for the certification of software in aircraft, and IEC standards on both software and system safety are currently being developed. In addition, a number of systems may attract the application of general legislation such as that relating to product liability or health and safety at work. This may be particularly important in reassuring the public and for increasing awareness of the problems in the industry itself, but, if the appropriate technology to produce assurance of safety has not been developed, there is an obvious limit to what regulation can achieve.

PURPOSE AND PRINCIPLES OF REGULATION

Since the nineteenth century, when technology first began to have an effect on the lives of ordinary people both at home and at work, it has been perceived that a degree of paternalism could be justified to protect society from the consequences of technological failure. Regulation of hazardous activities is thus not a new topic, and for many applications there will be an existing framework of legislation and other guidelines such as standards and codes of practice which determine and establish the appropriate safety level. Regulation usually consists of defining the level of safety, quality, etc. to be achieved and providing for sanctions in the event of failure to reach this specified level. However, it may be that the existing methods are neither effective nor appropriate in dealing with the problems raised in trying to ascertain or establish the safety of a computer-controlled system, and this will be considered further at the end of this chapter. It is usually the practice not just to rely on one method, and effective regulation will frequently consist of a mixture of those available. Different countries may achieve similar results by use of different regulatory processes; which of them is chosen may be more a matter of policy and politics than an assessment of which method may produce the best results. It is important, however, to be aware of what can and cannot be achieved by each type of regulatory measure.

Although there is usually ample justification for the regulation of potentially hazardous activities, many types of regulation are also criticized on the basis of paternalism; that the regulatory bodies are making decisions for individuals with the obvious inference that they cannot be trusted to make such decisions for themselves. Regulation may also be seen as an interference with freedom of contract and economic rights. While there may be substance to these criticisms for certain types of regulated activity, safety is one topic in which a degree of paternalism is often accepted, and even welcomed, as technology becomes increasingly complex and inaccessible to all but the specialist, and those outside the field are no longer in any position to evaluate the attributes of a particular system.

A further criticism of regulation is based on economics: the requirements of compliance with standards or other rules may have the effect of increasing the cost of the product. This may apply rather less to safety-critical systems because the value of life is widely considered as a fundamental, which is not perhaps amenable to calculations that balance costs with benefits. Even so, it is unlikely that economic considerations will have no influence at all, and there will be a point at which additional benefits become disproportionately expensive.

The ultimate objective of the regulation of potentially hazardous activities is the protection of those who may be harmed if a hazard becomes uncontrolled, and of society as a whole from physical and environmental disaster. However, regulation may also provide the subsidiary function of giving a degree of protection to the system designers, who may be able to escape liability if they can show adherence to specified procedures. Regulation is most effective when voluntary, where those concerned recognize and accept the necessity for such measures. Nonetheless, the provision of suitable sanctions is a necessary requisite of any successful regulatory scheme, and an obvious corollary of this is that there must be an effective enforcement system for such sanctions.

Regulatory measures may conveniently be divided into two types; direct and indirect. Direct regulation is usually industry-specific, and includes, for example, certification and licensing requirements for both products and personnel. This may mean that a product cannot go on the market unless it meets certain standards or has been created by a designer with suitable qualifications. Clearly, if this is to be effective and meaningful, standards and qualifications must be amenable to definition. Direct regulation includes both government constraints and measures introduced by the industry itself or by professional organizations in that particular sector.

Indirect regulation includes wider legislative measures in the field of health and safety. These may be concerned with the workplace, the environment or consumer safety. Whereas direct regulation is usually primarily concerned with detailing very specific ways in which the ultimate objective is to be achieved, indirect regulation usually specifies the end but not the means. In addition to legislative measures, indirect regulation can be effected by the possibility of civil liability arising in the case of system failure. Some codes of practice may also act in a regulatory capacity.

For all types of regulation one of the fundamental problems which must be addressed at an early stage is the formulation of a suitable definition of safety. Clearly, no system will be inherently safe in the sense that it creates no risks at all; the problem will be to decide what risks can be tolerated, and then to ascertain that these are, in fact, the only risks that are present. It is therefore necessary to distinguish the measurement of risk from the determination of the acceptability of that risk. The former may involve calculations of probability, but, in any event, should be an objective assessment. On the other hand, a decision as to the acceptability of that risk will inevitably involve a subjective and social judgement. This may vary between societies, and with time. Advancing technology brings benefits to industry, society and the consumer in terms of increased efficiency of production and the availability of new and novel products. It also creates expectations of quality and safety and increases intolerance to faults and defects.

DIRECT REGULATION

In the past, direct regulation has usually been based on the premise that if specified precautions were taken in design, manufacture and operation then the risks associated with a particular activity under consideration could be reduced to an acceptable level. This approach can work well for systems for which it is possible to quantify the hazard level with a reasonable degree of precision, and then to match this figure to the achieved safety level using hazard analysis and risk assessment. Software is usually not amenable to such analysis, and this can cause difficulties in utilizing this type of approach. A modification of the usual method may thus be needed for regulation of such areas.

Standards

The use of both general and more detailed technical standards has been traditional for regulating hazardous activities. Responsibility for the formulation of such standards is usually given to some national or international organization; examples include the British Standards Institute and the International Electrotechnical Commission. Standards by themselves will not have the force of law unless also incorporated into some legislative measure, but adherence to their requirements can provide persuasive evidence to counter any allegation of negligence.

Standards may be produced in response to social and political as well as technological factors: concern may be expressed, perhaps through the media, about some activity perceived to be actually or potentially hazardous (standards are also produced that have no safety implications, but we shall restrict our discussion to areas where safety is an issue). This may, in turn, lead to political pressure for the production of a standard. Alternatively, professional or trade associations representing the industry itself may provide the impetus for setting a standard for the particular activity. This varied input leads to a wide range of types of standard, from detailed technical documents to those giving broader-based rules which may be applicable in many areas.

For whatever reason a standard is desirable, production of a suitable document will not be a speedy matter. In relation to the specific area with which it is concerned, a standard needs to be comprehensive and sufficiently detailed so that compliance with its requirements will eliminate, as far as possible, the problems which led to its production. However, these objectives may be thwarted by the very process of producing the standard; much of the necessary and available information is held by the industry itself, and it is usual practice for representatives of the manufacturers together with other interested parties such as government and consumer groups to be a part of the standard-setting process. This highlights the necessity for cooperation, and also means that the end-product will represent a consensus view which may therefore be a compromise rather than a definitive safety standard.

Different attitudes may be found to such negotiations: it is essentially a closed process in the UK, but there is much more public accountability in the USA (Ramsay, 1989), although this does not appear to affect the results materially. Further complications may be found in Europe, where the removal of barriers to trade is such a central tenet of the Treaty of Rome that this may take precedence over safety issues.

Breyer (1982, Chapter 5) discusses a number of difficulties likely to be encountered in creating a completely new standard. Accurate information is essential, but from where should it be obtained? If it is supplied by industry, there may be suggestions of bias, but pressure groups may be equally biased against industry. The use of independent experts is frequently advocated, which, in practice, often means academics. This may be successful, but often they will not have sufficiently detailed knowledge of the industry, and if they do, it may be because they are sponsored by industry and so are not truly independent. It would be possible for the regulatory agency to develop the requisite expertise itself, but this would be a waste of resources and would lead to an increase in the time scale for producing a standard.

A further question to be answered is, what type of standard is appropriate to deal with the problem? Should it be general or more specific? Performance standards are those that govern what the product should or should not do. Their advantage is to permit flexibility in design methods as long as the end-product is assured, so that design development is not stifled but allowed to progress. However, design standards are more usual, as they are easier to enforce, but they may have the effect of freezing existing technology, thereby inhibiting research and development of a better and safer product. One interesting issue is whether standards should force technological development by requiring industry to meet a standard for which the technology has not yet been developed.

The relative importance of all the above points may need to be modified in the light of economic factors such as the cost of testing and enforcement. Standards cannot be effective unless they can be enforced, and this presupposes the existence of an appropriate regulatory agency backed up by effective sanctions.

Certification and licensing

Another method of direct regulation is by certification or licensing. These possess many similarities and will be considered together. Either products or personnel may be certified or licensed. Although often used interchangeably, they do have different meanings, and it should be ascertained which is intended; in particular, the word 'certification' is often used when 'licensing' is what is really occurring. Certification means that there must be a demonstration that either the product or the practitioner conforms to some specified standard. However, there is no bar to either marketing of uncertified goods or to uncertified persons practising. This preserves some element of choice to the procurer; either to seek the assurance of using a certified product or practitioner or to select the uncertified option which is likely to be more favourably priced.

Licensing is, in a sense, a more severe form of certification. In this case the product cannot go on the market at all or the practitioner operate unless the product is licensed or the practitioner is in possession of the requisite licence. Examples of this approach are found in a variety of occupations, ranging from medicine to taxi driving. In a free-market economy this can be seen as a restrictive practice which needs ample justification if it is to be countenanced. The usual justification for licensing measures is that of the public interest, but a frequent criticism is that, rather than protecting the public, licensing has the effect of protecting professional interests by raising entry barriers to the profession and encouraging correspondingly high prices for services.

It has been argued (Friedman, 1962) that because licensing protects professional interests and interferes with freedom of contract and personal freedoms, it can never be justified except perhaps in so far as the activities may affect third parties. Friedman's view is that as the actual procurer will be in a contractual relationship with the provider, any necessary redress can be pursued in that way. This seems to carry non-interventionism too far when hazardous activities are under consideration. Friedman's example was of the medical profession, a traditional area in which licensing is imposed. He believed that in this case the only possible justification for licensing was if it could stop the spread of an epidemic. Where only the individual was affected by malpractice then that could be remedied on a personal basis and could be safeguarded against by selecting a competent practitioner.

Although Friedman was propounding these theories some 30 years ago, they are particularly relevant at the present time when a *laissez-faire* attitude to economic activity is in vogue, with a consequent emphasis on free-market competition and non-interventionism. His argument may hold some credence where the activity is one which does not impinge on health or safety, but where safety is a major issue this seems a little too simplistic, assuming, as it does, that the procurer is bound to be in a position to assess the competence of the practitioner. Proponents of licensing (and also of other forms of regulation: see e.g. Breyer) for safety-critical systems argue that it is impossible for consumers and procurers to be in possession of sufficient information to assess either the risk or whether it is under control. Licensing is thus seen as a mechanism for supplying information that cannot be obtained in the market and ensuring that the user is provided with the requisite safety level.

The fact that the pressure for licensing frequently comes from those within a profession need not necessarily indicate motives of self-interest; they are likely to be in a better position to appreciate the dangers of unlicensed practitioners or products. Nevertheless, motives for introducing licensing must always be carefully analysed to ensure that it is not merely a disguised method of protecting professional interests. There are thus a number of arguments against licensing, and it seems reasonable to reserve it for activities in which the consequences of failure will have a major impact on the environment or the health and safety of those involved.

An advantage of licensing is that it is anticipatory: if correctly carried out it tackles the problem at source and will also minimize the risk to third parties. In addition, it can be used to economize on enforcement costs. As mentioned earlier, no regulation can be effective without enforcement, and licensing creates the possibility of potentially powerful sanctions by removal of the licence. A disadvantage, certainly as far as licensing of practitioners is concerned, is that it assumes that there is a high correlation between the required qualifications for granting a licence and the end to be achieved. Although this may seem intuitively reasonable, it is *only* an assumption, and to ensure that it *is* reasonable there must be a careful consideration of the parameters necessary for the receipt of a licence.

Licensing may be introduced by government measures or by professional associations already operating in the area. In general, professional organizations are probably in the best position to assess the competence of prospective applicants, but account should be taken of the passage of time. Where technology is changing rapidly, expertise must be shown to be maintained if the licence is to retain its credibility. It may be that qualifications which are usually taken as a measure of professional competence are not necessarily indicative of competence to produce safety-related systems. It is by no means clear what criteria can be used to assess such competence. It is of little practical use, for instance, to require that development of safety-related software and systems be conducted only by personnel experienced in that subject when there is no route by which they can gain the requisite experience. This may indicate that various levels of licensing may be appropriate, perhaps related to the safety level of the system under development or the degree and type of participation in the development team.

A variation is licensing of the product rather than the practitioner, i.e. the product cannot be marketed unless it conforms to a predetermined standard. (This should not be confused with the familiar licence to use software.) This has the advantage that it then becomes unnecessary to assess whether the developer's qualifications are adequate or appropriate; the question is purely whether the product meets the appropriate standard. The problem of safety assurance is then transferred back to the adequacy of the standard used.

Many of the criticisms levelled at licensing, such as creation of technical monopolies and restriction of freedom of contract, cannot be used to the same extent to attack certification. In this case, the existence of uncertified practitioners or products is not outlawed, and the system should be self-regulating to the extent that abuse of the privilege of certification is likely to lead to increased price differentials which may reach a level at which they are no longer tolerated. This cannot occur, of course, in a licensing regime which leaves the market open to exploitation by the technical monopoly.

However, although it may be accepted that licensing is only used where a degree of paternalism is tolerable to protect the user against the possibility of hazard, this cannot be applied to certification because of the existence of uncertified products. Can certification ever be justified? To answer this question it is necessary to ascertain what certification can achieve.

From the point of view of assurance of safety, the problems of licensing and certification are similar: establishing appropriate criteria on which to base the certification requirement. However, where uncertified products are sold, or an uncertified practitioner chosen, it is for the consumers or the procurers to satisfy themselves that what is being supplied meets the necessary requirements. This assumes that it is possible that an uncertified product could be as safe (or reliable or whatever criterion for which certification has been introduced) or perhaps, more accurately, that the degree of risk is such that failure to come up to standard could be tolerated. Is this ever the case? If the degree of risk is large enough to warrant some sort of intervention then surely the appropriate regulatory mechanism is licensing? If the degree of risk does not warrant any such intervention then how can certification be justified?

Codes of practice

Codes of practice can perform a useful regulatory function because they can incorporate flexibility that is often more difficult to achieve in a detailed standard or in legislation. The codes are often voluntary, devised and administered by trade associations, and are thus an important method of self-regulation. Although not legally binding, a code of practice may produce legally binding effects if it is incorporated into the terms of a contract, and failure to comply may be presented as evidence of negligence. Otherwise, if it is to be effective, there must still be sanctions for non-conformity, and this can create a problem in a voluntarily adopted code with no legislative back-up. Although, in theory, a range of sanctions may be available, with the ultimate possibility of expulsion from the association, in practice this may be difficult to enforce on the recalcitrant. Where a code of practice is administered by a trade association then, clearly, there is no possibility of enforcement against non-members. Enforcement against members may also be difficult: if legislation on the subject is unlikely then acceptance of a restrictive code may also be unlikely (European Consumer Law Group, 1983). This may be especially true when there is opposition to introduction of the code or disagreement in its content at the negotiation stage, but is a factor which needs to be borne in mind when considering any type of voluntary (i.e. non-legislative) regulation.

As with all methods of regulation, if a code is to be effective it must be carefully constructed, kept up to date and its operation monitored. This is where codes enjoy advantages over legislation, since their flexibility is compatible with a rapid updating to keep pace with technological change. Industry may also be more inclined to accept a negotiated code of practice, which they feel more adequately represents their views, than a legislative measure, even though there is bound to be a significant input from industry in formulating detailed technical legislation.

Many codes are industry- or process-specific, but there are examples of codes of practice with more widespread application. Some British standards are in the form of codes of practice (for example, BS 5304: Code of Practice for the safeguarding of machinery). It is possible that codes of practice may be used as a method of information gathering when a government department is deciding whether legislation is required on a particular topic. However, this may produce a negative result; if the code is successful at regulating the perceived problem, then legislation would appear to be unnecessary because codes of practice are cheaper to effect and implement than is legislation. However, if there are difficulties in enforcement as discussed earlier, then legislation may need to be considered, although it should not automatically be assumed that this will be the most appropriate course of action; other forms of regulation may prove to be more suitable.

REGULATION BY LAW

Regulation by law is often viewed as a measure of last resort, only to be introduced when all other methods have failed. There is a popular belief that a problem insoluble by any other method will magically be made to disappear by passing a law against it! In reality, as we shall see, legal regulation suffers from a number of the same disadvantages as other forms of regulation. One advantage which legal regulation is assumed to have over some other types is that of enforceability. While this is true in theory, practical problems may be encountered which make enforcement difficult. These may be technical; the way in which the measure is formulated may allow for a degree of subjectivity in interpretation, thus impeding the enforcement of the objective, or there may be other problems such as undermanning in the agencies with responsibility for enforcement. Unless there is a severe deterrent such as the penalties likely to be incurred, law often suffers from the disadvantage that it is reactive rather than preventative. The legal machinery only grinds into action after a breach has been perpetrated so that the problem is transformed into provision of appropriate remedies rather than prevention.

Law can be sub-divided into a number of categories, e.g. criminal law deals with the regulation of society whereas civil law is concerned with the regulation of relations between individuals, including artificial legal persons such as companies. Perhaps one of the most useful distinctions for the purposes of examining the regulatory effects in this area is to consider those of statute, on the one hand, and common law (i.e. case law decided by the courts), on the other. Many statutes dealing with safety issues are couched in general terms, leaving a certain degree of flexibility for individuals to decide for themselves how to comply. However, for regulation of complex technical problems, detailed secondary legislation is often introduced explaining how compliance should be effected. This may be contained in instructions within the legislative measure itself, by reference to a relevant standard or by requiring a licence to be obtained from a particular body. Where the legislation itself contains the details necessary for compliance, then similar problems will be encountered as with standard setting, but this will be compounded by the fact that the time scale is inevitably lengthened by the procedures involved in the legislative process, and this process will need to be repeated every time amendments prove necessary.

There is also often a piecemeal approach as problems are identified which have proved insoluble by other means and measures are passed in an attempt to deal with them. The result of this is that legislation will inevitably lag behind the technology it is attempting to regulate. This can create serious consequences in areas such as computer control, where the technology is advancing very rapidly.

Legislation may create criminal offences or give a civil right of action enabling an individual to obtain a remedy for any wrong suffered. Broadly speaking, criminal offences can be classified as one of two types; 'traditional' criminal offences against persons or property, for which it is usually necessary to show some sort of intent, knowledge, etc. (*mens rea*, to use lawyers' jargon) regarding the particular act, and strict liability or regulatory offences for which no intent is needed nor indeed any knowledge that the particular activity is a crime.

Provisions creating regulatory offences have proliferated in the twentieth century as a convenient way of regulating an increasingly technological society, and are now a common method of legal regulation for safety problems, whether at work or relating to product liability (for a general discussion of regulatory offences see, for example, Ramsay, 1989, Chapter 6). The convenience is for those responsible for enforcement; there is no need to embark on the difficult problem of proving *mens rea*; only the facts need be established. The advantage of the criminal law as a means of regulation is that it enables some sort of moral censure to be applied to the accused which is intended to convey society's displeasure at the particular activity in question. The use of strict liability offences is also one way in which incorporated bodies such as companies can be made liable for their activities, since, as there is no need for proof of *mens rea*, courts do not have to struggle with the controversial question of whether a company can possess the necessary mental element to commit a crime. Unfortunately, although regulatory offences do form a part of the criminal law they are rarely considered by the parties involved as being as serious a legal contravention as 'real' criminal offences. This is not helped by the fact that fines for regulatory offences have frequently been low, which has not created a deterrent effect. There are signs that this is beginning to change, perhaps as the result of publicity, and a number of larger fines have been imposed on companies in the UK for breaches of the health and safety provisions in recent years. If this trend continues then the deterrent effect of these measures may increase.

Strict liability may also apply in relation to some civil claims for damages. For example, in the UK, the Consumer Protection Act introduces a strict liability regime for claims for damages due to injury resulting from defective products provided the requisite criteria are met. As there is no need to prove negligence in such cases, this may be more effective as a regulatory mechanism than the criminal regulatory offence, epecially as damages for personal injury are often well in excess of a typical fine for a breach of other safety regulations.

In addition to statutory regulation as discussed above, the common law may also produce a regulatory effect. Thus, for example, in the case of breach of contract or of personal injury due to negligence, the individual may be able to obtain a remedy, usually in the form of monetary compensation, for the damage suffered as a result. Although, theoretically (Epstein, 1982), legislative and administrative measures should be more effective, since such compensation may be quite high, it can be a considerable deterrent to think that if the product does not conform to adequate standards of safety, etc. the manufacturer may be open to a number of claims for damages. The primary purpose of such actions is to provide redress, and a consequent disadvantage of the system as a regulatory mechanism is that it is reactive and only comes into operation after the damage has been done. It is also reliant on the injured party actually taking the initiative and starting an action; there can be no deterrent effect produced by the possibility of large compensation if no one is prepared to submit to the hassle of a long expensive lawsuit. This is likely to be partially alleviated where liability is strict with no need to prove negligence, and it is submitted that actions for compensation for injury caused by product failure, for whatever reason, should fall into this category. In addition, the deterrent effect of being liable for large sums in compensation may be alleviated by the existence of product liability insurance.

Common law rules relating to breach of contract or negligence are primarily designed to provide a remedy after the event. Where injury or death are the possible outcomes of negligence or breach of contract, then a more important objective in terms of regulation is the prevention of injury. This is unlikely to be achieved by the common law acting alone, but it can provide a useful adjunct to the other regulatory provisions. Common law rules are also dependent on judicial interpretation; a definition of the legal status of software, in particular whether its nature is tangible or intangible, is the subject of heated legal debate. The outcome of this debate is unlikely to be the concern of designers and manufacturers, persons seeking compensation nor even of society at large. An example is whether software might be classified as goods or services, for instance. It is possible that contradictory results may be produced, and a number of writers have suggested that whether or not software can be considered as goods will ultimately depend on the form of the software package in question (see, for example, Clarke, 1989). This is not the result which would be expected by the man on the Clapham omnibus, especially as it will affect the liability incurred by the failure of different types of software.

Another way in which the common law can affect the regulatory process is in the development of liability for professional negligence. Although it suffers from the usual disadvantages of common law discussed above, it has also some advantages. In particular, it provides a method of external regulation of a profession or an industry which can thus avoid the problem of the creation of technical monopolies which may be encountered with other schemes for regulation, especially where these are voluntarily administered. There is a long history of actions involving professionals or craftsmen who have been held liable for not exhibiting the required degree of care and skill (see Veljanovski and Whelan, 1983). A further advantage is that the standard of skill which must be displayed to avoid liability can change with time, enabling it to reflect the current professional standards. The existence of such personal liability may provide a powerful regulatory effect which could be further developed and interpreted by the courts; in particular, there is at the moment no method of distinguishing between misjudgement and malpractice.

A further effect of the law on the regulatory process is found in the operation of administrative law. This controls the activities of administrative bodies. If there is an agency which has responsibility for the issue of licences or the setting of standards then administrative law provides a mechanism for ensuring that the agency does not use these powers either arbitrarily or capriciously. Thus if a licence is refused there may be scope for the applicant to challenge the decision of the administrative body by way of judicial review. The court can then examine the acts of the agency to ensure that they have acted reasonably, without bias, etc. Although the court cannot substitute its own view for that of the regulatory body, it can quash its decision and remit the matter for reconsideration. This prevents the regulatory bodies from having completely unfettered powers, but any hearing for judicial review of the decision not to issue a licence, for instance, must necessarily consider the effect on all interested parties and is therefore likely to be a lengthy procedure.

SOME ASPECTS OF REGULATION OF SOFTWARE SAFETY

There are a number of reasons why regulation of the safety of computer-controlled systems is imperative. For safety-critical systems, the arguments against regulation based on paternalism are largely thought to be irrelevant. Regulation is expected in the interests of society and is also a means of ensuring that responsibility for ensuring safety falls on those in the best position to achieve it. This is most likely to be those who produce the systems; despite free-market principles, the user or procurer may not have the expertise to assess the software adequately and should therefore be ready to accept the perhaps restricted choice available as a consequence of the imposition of standards or of a licensing requirement. Although the ultimate responsibility for safety is then on the producer, this may be welcomed, since, if it can be demonstrated that all the necessary regulatory provisions have been complied with, this will provide valuable evidence against negligence in the event of a subsequent system failure.

Unfortunately, appropriate regulation is not just a matter of selecting and implementing one of the regulatory mechanisms. The reader will probably have realized that the nature of software makes the actual process of regulation difficult. One of the primary objectives of safety regulation is to prevent dangerous states from arising, and effective regulation will require an asessment of the safety level required, followed by a matching of that level to the level actually achieved by the design.

Particular difficulties are encountered in assessing the integrity of a system containing software. For safety-critical systems, the probability of failure must be very low, which raises questions of whether it is possible to achieve such low levels and also, perhaps more importantly for assurance of safety, whether it is possible to know such levels have been reached. This will restrict what regulation can achieve in this area and may make enforcement difficult. However, the potentially catastrophic effects of failure have acted as a spur to regulation and there is continuing activity to surmount the problems. These attempts at regulation demonstrate a number of the general points outlined above and also illustrate problems peculiar to software.

In its attempt to create an international standard for safety-related systems the IEC is intending to use standards to ensure software safety. These standards have been in gestation for some time, demonstrating the protracted nature of consensual negotiations. However, a more fundamental problem is to formulate the precise details of the standard, given the difficulty in defining certain parameters (such as the probability of failure) for software. This need not be a reason to suggest that standards are an inappropriate way forward, since their attempted formulation may provide a stimulus to accelerate the development of the necessary metrics. Until this occurs, it does seem to indicate that any enforceable standard for software safety must necessarily be a design standard; a performance standard would create extreme difficulties both in assessing compliance and in enforcement. In addition, as the available technology is advancing there is the very real possibility that any standard produced may be obsolete as soon as it is published, creating a need for expeditious ways in which it can be updated. Of interest is the fact that although there are powerful arguments in favour of third-party testing for safety assessment, the draft IEC standard does not make this mandatory, although it is recommended at the higher integrity levels. Despite the problems, standards on software safety do provide one valuable way forward in this difficult area, both in terms of stimulating research and of raising awareness of the difficulties.

An example of this is the UK DEF STAN 00 55, which attempted to stimulate the industry by requiring the use of formal specification methods in all safety-critical applications. Although this was not backed up by any legislative measure, there was the strong economic sanction of not obtaining defence contracts, which is often equally as effective in securing compliance. The outcry with which this standard was greeted by many practitioners shows the problems in introducing a strict requirement.

Other regulatory mechanisms are also in use in some sectors. An example is the certification and licensing requirement for software systems in the aeronautics industry. The technical distinction has been drawn between certification and licensing, but these words are often used interchangeably. It is often said that software for use in aircraft must be certified (against Eurocae ED-12A in Europe or RTCA DO-178A in the USA). In so far as software cannot be used for this application unless it conforms to these documents, this is more correctly a licensing requirement. For the reasons outlined earlier, it is important to be aware of which sense is intended. Where there is a requirement that software must be licensed ('certified' in common parlance) before use in a specific application, it is particularly important that this should not stultify the technology and that there should be a constant effort to update the requirements imposed by the licence, consistent with safety assurance.

The problem with legislation and legal regulation is that there are, as yet, few provisions which relate specifically to software. The result is that the wording of existing measures has to be manipulated to fit systems containing software. This has not been very successful, and has created a great degree of uncertainty, which undermines the regulatory effect. In particular, where a statute creates a criminal offence it is desirable that it should also give notice of what action must be taken to avoid liability. This will not be the case if it is not possible to ascertain how software fits into the existing legal framework.

Generally, it seems that the difficulties surrounding legal regulation will not be resolved until it is made clear by the legislature whether any particular provision is applicable to software. The attitude taken to the nature of software in future provisions may help to clarify the position in the common law, where there has been extensive debate in many jurisdictions as to whether provision of software constitutes goods or services, for example. Although these uncertainties dilute any regulatory effect, legal measures remain the only way by which a victim of the failure of a computer-controlled system can obtain any redress. It thus appears that, at the moment, legal regulation is not the most appropriate primary regulatory mechanism, although it will always be important for determining liability, if any. This situation may change if new legal measures are introduced which are aimed more specifically at systems containing software.

As the preceding discussion has shown, effective regulation of the safety of computer-controlled systems is not an easy matter, and the reader will doubtless be able to think of other difficulties. No one method will achieve the desired result, and an appropriate combination of those outlined here needs to be instigated through the consultative process that is already established.

REFERENCES

Breyer, S. G. (1982), *Regulation and its Reform*, Harvard University Press, Cambridge, MA

Breyer, S. G. and Stewart, R. B. (1985), *Administrative Law and Regulatory Policy (Problems, Text and Cases)*, 2nd edition, Little, Brown, Boston, MA

Clarke, R. (1989–1990), 'Who is liable for software errors?' *Computer Law and Security Review*, 28

Epstein, R. (1982), 'Social consequences of common law rules', *Harvard Law Review*, **95**, 1717–1751

European Consumer Law Group (1983), 'Non-legislative means of consumer protection', *Journal of Consumer Protection*, **6**, 211–212

Ramsay, I. (1989), *Consumer Protection (Text and Materials)*, Weidenfeld and Nicholson, London

Veljanovski, C. and Whelan, C. (1983), 'Professional negligence and the quality of legal services – an economic perspective', *Modern Law Review*, **46**, 700–718

Wilson, G. K. (1984), 'Social regulation and explanations of regulatory failure', *Political Studies*, **32**, 203–225

3 Legal liability
Dai Davis

INTRODUCTION

Background

As with all complex creations of man, computer control systems are prone to containing errors. This is particularly so because of their underlying complexity. The widespread use of computer control systems in safety-critical applications means that, in today's society, it is not difficult to find examples of potential areas in which a catastrophe may occur. For example, all modern chemical production plants have computer control systems. If those computer control facilities fail, catastrophic consequences are all too easy to envisage.

These matters need to be set against a background of increased environmental awareness. Therefore it may only be a matter of time before the public's realization of the inherent dangers within safety-critical control systems increases. To a certain extent, the dangers are already perceived. This increased perception is manifested in the additional legal burdens placed on manufacturers and suppliers of safety-critical control systems, including computer control systems. Those legal aspects are discussed below.

It is not necessary to consider the computer control system in a chemical production facility to find an example of a safety-critical computer system. Even the all-pervasive motor vehicle today contains complex computer control systems. For instance, the anti-lock braking system to be found in many modern vehicles is dependent upon a microprocessor control unit for its operation. A failure in the hardware or software which constitutes this control unit could easily result in a disaster (Figure 3.1).

Other common household electrical goods such as washing machines, tumble driers and dish washers contain microprocessor control units. Although less likely to cause a catastrophe on the same scale as a malfunctioning chemical plant, errors in this unit could lead, for example, to the motor in the washing machine over-running and causing damage to the clothes being washed. In a more extreme situation a defect in the unit could cause the washing machine motor to operate beyond its tolerance level. Any violent destruction of the motor could cause damage to the washing machine and its surroundings.

All these situations could give rise to potential legal liability on the part of the manufacturers and suppliers of the defective articles. Such liability may also fall upon manufacturers and suppliers of any defective components, including manufacturers of hardware, authors of software and suppliers of computer control units.

This chapter summarizes the legal basis of the liability imposed on the

36 Safety Aspects of Computer Control

Figure 3.1 *Modern vehicles have sophisticated computer-controlled anti-lock braking systems*

manufacturers of the hardware and on the authors of the software, as well as the legal responsibility of other persons involved in the supply chain of a complete product and of the components of that product. As with all commentaries of this nature, the chapter can necessarily only provide a broad outline of the legal background. Before undertaking any particular transaction, specific guidance should be sought.

Detailed example

It is often easier to picture the various legal liabilities which can arise by reference to an example. A frequent example that will be referred to in this chapter is that of a motor vehicle which contains an anti-lock braking system. Let us suppose that this system is controlled by a microprocessor control unit. The microprocessor device will itself consist of both hardware and software. Clearly, a defect in these could cause the brakes to fail to operate in the manner in which they are intended and therefore cause an accident. The persons who may be involved in the supply of the microprocessor control unit are shown in Table 3.1.

Legal liability 37

Table 3.1 Example of a supply chain for a microprocessor controlled, anti-lock braking system fitted in a motor vehicle.

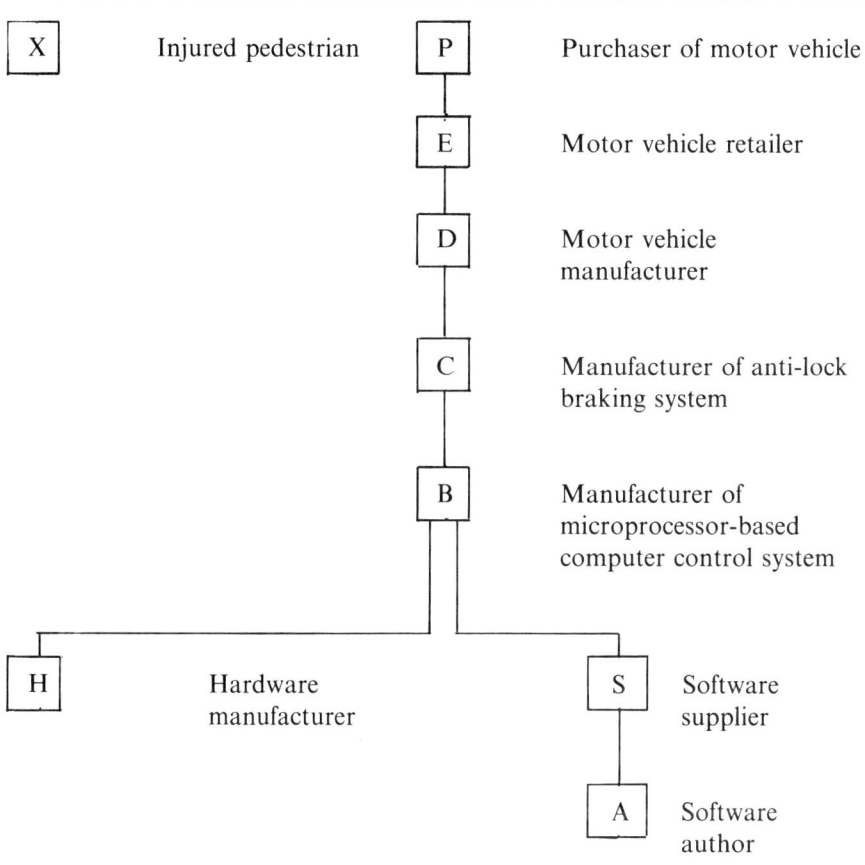

The links indicate the contractual relationships between the parties.

In this example it is assumed that there is a microprocessor manufacturer, B, who supplies a computer control unit. B has sub-contracted the manufacture of the microprocessor chip itself to H, and B has also sub-contracted the provision of the software to a software house, S. The software house has, in turn, sub-contracted the writing of the software to a consultant, A, who is the author of the software. The manufacturer of the microprocessor control unit, B, supplies the unit to C, who is the manufacturer and supplier of the complete braking system.

The braking system manufacturer, C, may purchase the various components of the system (the microprocessor control unit, the brakes themselves, the brake housings from different sources) and then combine them. C supplies a complete braking system to the motor vehicle manufacturer, D. The vehicle is then sold to a retailer, E, who, in turn, supplies the vehicle to the ultimate purchaser, P.

Table 3.1 also illustrates an injured pedestrian, X. X could also be an innocent passenger in the motor vehicle who is injured when the anti-lock braking system fails. Although loss and injury could be suffered by the purchaser, P, in the more general case the party suffering the loss and injury, X, will not be part of the supply chain, as depicted in Table 3.1. In practice, the supply chain may be shorter or longer. This will not, however, affect the contents of this chapter, which will apply by analogy, whatever the actual supply chain. The example depicted in Table 3.1 will be referred to throughout this chapter by way of explanation.

Types of legal liability

There are two basic types of legal liability: criminal and civil.

Criminal liability

If a criminal act is performed then the state is, for the most part, the prosecutor. For the more serious offences (such as theft) imprisonment can follow if an offender is judged guilty of committing the offence: for the less serious ones the maximum penalty may only be a fine. In contrast, where the 'wrong' is not a criminal offence, the only sanction is that an injured party may bring legal proceedings against the party at fault for compensation for the loss or injury he or she has suffered.

In many instances a particular act or omission may give rise to both a civil and a criminal case. For instance, it is an offence to fail to maintain electrical systems so as to prevent danger arising in a factory. This offence will only be committed if the factory owner fails to fulfil the duty so far as is reasonably practicable (The Electricity at Work Regulations 1989). A factory owner who commits this offence will also be liable to compensate an employee who is injured as a consequence of the breach of duty.

This chapter does not deal in any detail with criminal liability. In general, this requires a higher degree of 'fault' than civil liability. Therefore, where persons act to reduce their civil liability they usually also avoid the possibility of a criminal action being brought against them.

Particular mention needs, however, to be made of the general criminal liability imposed by Section 6 of the Health and Safety at Work Act 1974. This Section requires that a person who designs, manufactures, imports or supplies an article for use at work must ensure that, so far as it is reasonably practicable, the article is designed to be safe when it is properly used. There are further provisions contained in Section 6 which require that testing and examination must be carried out in order to ensure that the obligation to produce safe articles is complied with. Similarly, there is an obligation upon the manufacturer to provide adequate information to ensure that the article can be used in a safe manner. In the case of a breach of this provision the maximum penalty which can be imposed is two years' imprisonment, together with an unlimited fine.

The law imposes many other criminal liabilities in specific circumstances and sometimes in particular industries. For example, goods supplied for use in coal mines must meet the safety standards required by the Mines and Quarries Acts.

Civil liability

The other type of liability which concerns manufacturers and suppliers of goods is imposed by the civil law. This may provide a remedy for an injured individual or corporate entity who takes proceedings against the wrongdoer. The usual remedy which is sought against the wrongdoer is that of damages. In the context of the safety of control systems, civil liability is most important, given the large damages claim that could arise if the system is unsafe. In particular, where disastrous consequences flow from a defect in hardware or software, a large liability for damages under the civil law may accrue.

There are three areas of potential liability under the civil law, and each of these areas is dealt with separately below:

1. Liability under contract law;
2. Liability under the law of negligence;
3. Liability under the new product liability legislation.

LIABILITY UNDER CONTRACT LAW

Implied terms

In a contract for the sale of goods the law imposes certain obligations on the seller. Sometimes all the seller's obligations are expressed in writing in a formal contract. Often, additional obligations are implied by law. This will be the case where the contract is only partly reduced to writing or where there is no written contract at all.

For example, in a contract to sell computer control systems to the manufacturer of a complete braking system (as in the contract between B and C in the example depicted in Table 3.1), the law implies certain obligations. Among the obligations which are most important from the point of view of computer safety are that the goods (1) will comply with their description; (2) are of merchantable quality; and (3) are fit for the purpose. Each of these is dealt with in detail below.

First, there is an obligation that the goods will comply with any previous description which has been given, or with any sample of the goods. Section 13(1) of the Sale of Goods Act 1979 states that: 'Where there is a contract for the sale of goods by description, there is an implied condition that the goods will correspond with the description.' Therefore if the computer control system has been specified in writing, this imposes upon the manufacturer, B, an obligation that the microprocessor device will comply with that specification. For example, the manufacturer of the computer control system, B, may have indicated to the braking system manufacturer, C, that the computer control system is capable of processing a given volume of data within a certain period of time. This may be a simple statement of the number of floating-point operations per second or it may be embodied in a more complex description. In either case, the statement or description would become an obligation implied under the contract.

Second, there is an obligation that the goods are of merchantable quality. Section 14(2) of the Sale of Goods Act 1979 states that:

'Where the seller sells goods in the course of a business, there is an implied condition that the goods supplied under the contract are of merchantable quality, except that there is no such condition –
(i) as regards defects specifically drawn to the buyer's attention before the contract is made; or
(ii) if the buyer examines the goods before the contract is made, as regards defects which that examination ought to reveal.

The obligation that the goods are of merchantable quality will be satisfied if the goods 'are as fit for the purpose or purposes for which goods of that kind are commonly bought as is reasonable to expect having regard to any description applied to them, the price (if relevant) and all other relevant circumstances' (Section 14(6) of the Sale of Goods Act 1979).

The concept of 'merchantable quality' is therefore composite, depending upon a number of different elements such as description, purpose, condition and price. In particular, where goods are sold cheaply the circumstances may often point to a lower standard of merchantable quality than would otherwise be the case.

Finally, there is an obligation that if the goods are, to the knowledge of the seller, to be used for a specific purpose by the buyer then the goods will be fit for that specific purpose. Section 13(3) of the Sale of Goods Act 1979 states that:

Where the seller sells goods in the course of a business and the buyer, expressly or by implication, makes known ... to the seller ... any particular purpose for which the goods are being bought, there is an implied condition that the goods supplied under the contract are reasonably fit for that purpose, whether or not that is a purpose for which such goods are commonly supplied, except where the circumstances show that the buyer does not rely, or that it is unreasonable for him to rely, on the skill or judgment of the seller.

In the context of an anti-lock braking system an obligation that the braking system is fit for a specific purpose could arise where the brakes are being supplied for a large earth-moving vehicle. In those circumstances, the braking system may have to be built more rigorously than for a domestic motor car. Accordingly, it would be necessary for the manufacturer of the anti-lock braking system to build the system to a higher standard than for a car. For example, the brake devices may need to be built out of more rugged material to ensure that they are fit for the specific use required in an earth-moving vehicle. This would, for instance, extend to protecting the microprocessor chip from damage due to excessive vibration and shock.

In the context of computer software the obligation that the software be fit for a specific purpose is of particular application. For instance, software operating in a safety-critical environment, such as within a chemical plant, must be written in a more careful manner, and with a greater emphasis on verification and validation, than games-oriented software.

All these implied terms are to be found in the Sale of Goods Act 1979. It has not yet been decided in a court that the Sale of Goods Act applies where the only supply is that of software. However, it is almost certain that where the supply involves both software and hardware, as, for example, in the supply of a microprocessor control unit containing embedded software, the Sale of Goods Act 1979 will apply. In any event, even if the supply was of pure services (as, for example, supply of the service of the consultant A who is employed to write the software), then some implied terms would apply. In a case involving the supply of services, the Supply of Goods and Services Act 1982 imposes other similar implied obligations upon the supplier. For example, Section 13 of the Supply of Goods and Services Act 1982 requires the services to be provided with reasonable care and skill.

Express terms

Frequently, the express terms of a contract will be recorded in writing. In a computer supply contract express terms often relate to safety-critical attributes which the hardware and software must possess. For example, it may be expressly stated in a contract for the supply of a microprocessor control unit which is to be included in a motor vehicle braking system that the computer will be able to respond within a specified time period to a signal, indicating that the brakes have jammed. Similarly, in a contract for the provision of a complete control system for a chemical factory, specific safety requirements will often be required to be embedded within the computer control system.

In a different context, the supplier of a computerized accounts system to a bank or building society will be required to enter into specific performance guarantees, usually expressed in terms of the response time which the system will have. The financial institution will not want its tellers or customers kept waiting unduly while the computerized accounts system performs any given transaction!

A breach of these express obligations will give rise to a potential legal action, which may be brought by the party supplied with the computer system. Often, express terms of a contract do not create a problem since, merely, by reducing the problem to writing, the parties' minds are addressed to the issues involved. Those issues are therefore the ones which are least likely to become a practical problem!

Action under the law of contract

So far as contractual liability is concerned, the most important practical limitation is that, in order for contractual liability to arise, there needs to be a contract! Table 3.1 shows the many parties which may typically be involved if a safety-critical computer system fails. The table also indicates the contractual relationships between the parties in the particular example shown.

In our example a pedestrian, X, may be injured when the anti-lock braking system fails. The injury may arise because of an error in the software driving the microprocessor control unit within the anti-lock braking system. The pedestrian, X, has no contract with any of the manufacturers or suppliers – A, S, H, B, C, D or E – and cannot therefore make a contractual claim against any of those persons.

If the pedestrian is the only person who suffers loss or injury then no contractual claim could be made.

However, where the motor vehicle itself is damaged then the purchaser of the vehicle, P, may wish to bring a claim for damages. P may have a contractual right of action against the retail supplier of the motor vehicle, E. The purchaser would need to show that there was a breach of contract. There may, for instance, be a breach of the implied term that the motor vehicle is to be of a merchantable quality. The vehicle would not be of merchantable quality if the brakes had failed to operate.

A more complex scenario may arise where the purchaser, P, alleges that there is a defect in the software which resulted in the anti-lock function of the brakes not operating within the anticipated time period. In this context, the relevant time period is likely to be milliseconds. Here, a claim may be brought by the purchaser, P, against the retail supplier of the motor vehicle, E, perhaps alleging breach of the implied terms that the vehicle would comply with its description, the description in question being the anti-lock nature of the brakes.

From the point of view of an injured party, the remedy in contract law is severely limited, since it only provides a legal remedy against those persons with whom the injured party has a contractual relationship. As this example shows, the injured party may not have a contractual relationship with anyone.

Extent of contractual liability.

The law states that a civil claim must be brought within a specified time limit. In the case of a claim arising out of an alleged breach of contract, the legal action must be commenced within six years from the date on which the alleged breach took place. As with most rules, there are exceptions, but a full discussion is outside the scope of this chapter.

Where the aggrieved party can show that there has been a breach of contract, the court will award monetary damages in order to put the aggrieved party into the position he or she would have been in if the contract had been properly performed. By way of illustration, suppose that a contract has been entered into the owner of a chemical plant with a computer company for the provision of a complete computer control system. The computer company breaches the contract because the software controlling the plant proves to be defective. We can assume that there has been a breach of contract, since the computer company has failed to ensure that the computer control system (and the software in particular) is 'fit for the purpose'. What damages can the chamical plant owner claim?

The chemical company can claim compensation for all of its loss which is *caused* by the breach of contract. Some of this loss will be of a more direct nature than other loss. If the software has caused one of the pressure vessels to become contaminated with a chemical, the contents of the pressure vessel may have to be discarded. The value of these contents and the cost of cleaning the contaminated pressure vessel will be direct loss.

However, the chemical company may also claim for loss of a more indirect nature, such as the loss of profits which it suffers during the decontamination process. The loss may arise because the chemical company cannot use the pressure vessel to produce chemicals while it is being cleaned. The software fault may prevent the computer control system being used at all. As a result, the chemical company may have to use a manual control system for several weeks until the computer control system is rectified. There may be a loss of profits during this intervening period since the chemical manufacturer may find that the manual system is less efficient than the computer system. This loss of profits can also be included in the claim for damages brought by the chemical company.

Given the extent of the potential loss which may be suffered by the owner of the chemical factory, it is not surprising that the supplier of the computer system may wish to try to limit his liability. This can be done in the contract which exists between the supplier of the computer system and the owner of the chemical factory. However, not all limitations of liability are valid in law. Although this field is complex and not easily summarized, the law will enforce reasonable limitations included in a contract entered into between businesses. In order to prove what limitations of liability were agreed, all the limitations, together with the main terms of the contract, should be recorded in writing. Attempts by suppliers of computer systems to exclude all liability for loss of profits are common.

LIABILITY UNDER THE LAW OF NEGLIGENCE

Circumstances of action

In order for liability to be established under the law of negligence a person who has been injured must prove three elements:

1. That a duty of care was owed to him by the person causing the injury;
2. That the duty of care was breached and caused the injury; and
3. That the damage which arose from the breach of duty was of a type reasonably foreseeable as a consequence of the breach of duty.

This summary is extracted from the more detailed definition of an action of negligence given in the case of *Donoghue* v. *Stevenson* (1932). Here, the duty of care which must be followed was expressed in the following manner:

> You must take reasonable care to avoid acts or omissions which you can reasonably foresee would be likely to injure your neighbour. Who, then, in law is my neighbour? The answer seems to be – persons who are so closely and directly affected by my act that I ought reasonably to have them in contemplation as being so affected when I am directing my mind to the acts or omissions which are called in question.

It was also stated in this case that

> a manufacturer of products which he sells in such a form as to show that he intends them to reach the ultimate consumer in the form in which they left him

with no reasonable possibility of intermediate examination, and with the knowledge that the absence of reasonable care will result in an injury to the consumer's life or property, owes a duty to the consumer to take reasonable care.

In the context of computer control systems, manufacturers owe a duty of care to all persons to ensure that the systems they produce are safe and do not give rise to injury. This is certainly true for the computer control systems which have previously been discussed in this chapter, such as chemical control systems and motor vehicles, as well as washing machines, etc. If any of the computer control systems in these devices fail, then it could be reasonably foreseen that, as a result, persons would be injured. Therefore, there is a duty of care placed upon manufacturers of computer control systems which applies primarily to manufacturers. Where a retailer is merely selling on the product he has purchased, he would not normally be expected to check the safety of the product himself.

The duty imposed is to take reasonable care to avoid injury to end-users. The difficulty faced by a person who has been injured (X in the example given in Table 3.1) is that the manufacturer of the defective product (the defendant in the legal action) can raise a number of defences. Those that may be available include:

1. That the defendant took all reasonable care while making the product to ensure that the defect was not present; and/or
2. That the product should have been tested by the user before its use, and that had it been tested the defect would have been identified and the accident avoided; and/or
3. That the product was not initially dangerous but became dangerous because of the action of some intervening person.

Practical problems

From a practical point of view, a person bringing an action under the law of negligence may have difficulty in establishing that the manufacturer has fallen short of the standard required of him, and has not taken reasonable care in manufacturing the product. In the context of software the concept of 'reasonable care' gives rise to particular difficulties.

One can never be absolutely certain that computer software is accurate. Although verification and validation procedures can (and should) be followed, it is never possible (except in a minority of cases, which are not really significant from a commercial point of view) to establish, beyond doubt, that a computer program is absolutely accurate. What, then, should a manufacturer do? What is clear is that a manufacturer should take note of those standards which do exist (such as BS 5750 and, in certain contexts, Nato Defence Standard AQAP 13). Manufacturers must keep abreast of technology, and follow established verification and validation procedures wherever possible. If a manufacturer can show that he has taken reasonable care, then he will be able successfully to defend an action in negligence against him.

From the consumer's point of view an action of negligence is more powerful than an action in contract, since no contract needs to be established. In the context of the example outlined in Table 3.1 this means that the injured pedestrian, X, can bring an action against any of the persons, E, D, C, B, H, S or A, provided that he or she can establish that the particular defendant has failed to take reasonable care. Where a component is defective, he can bring an action against the component manufacturer (in Table 3.1, any of C, B, H, S or A). He may also be able to bring an action against the manufacturer of the complete product, D, if he can show that the manufacturer of the complete product failed to take reasonable care.

It may, however, be that the injured party has difficulty in establishing which of the various manufacturers failed to take reasonable care. In general, there is a liability on the manufacturer of a complete product to ensure that the complete product functions in a safe manner. Accordingly, the injured party is most likely to take an action against the manufacturer of the complete product. However, the injured party is by no means precluded from taking an action in negligence against any of the other persons involved in the supply chain, where he can show that those other persons failed in their duty to ensure that the product was safe.

An injured party may face great practical difficulty in discovering and locating who to sue, particularly if some of the manufacturers are foreign companies. Problems can also arise if the injured party is unsure of the exact fault in the product, or if some of the potential defendants are no longer in business. Even if the injured party is aware of the nature of the fault he still needs to show that a defendant has breached the duty of reasonable care. Not all faults will give rise to liability under the law of negligence.

Extent of liability for negligence

In the case of a legal action such as that envisaged in this chapter, namely where death or personal injury has arisen because of negligence, a claim must be brought by the injured party within a limitation period of three years. These three years generally commence on the date when the action of negligence took place, although there are exceptions.

Where an injured party can show negligence, the law will award compensation in order to put the injured party back into the position as if the negligence has not taken place. The damages which can be claimed in negligence are not as extensive as those available for a breach of contract. In particular, a claim can invariably not be brought for what is often termed 'pure economic loss'. Such loss may typically be the loss of profits suffered by a business affected by the negligent act or omission.

As depicted in Table 3.1, consider a pedestrian, X, who is injured when a motor vehicle collides as a result of defective software in the anti-lock braking system. If, as a result, the individual has time off work or if he is self-employed he suffers a loss of income, this is not 'pure economic loss' but direct loss which the individual can claim under the law of negligence. As a result of the defect in the anti-lock braking system the motor vehicle manufacturer, D, may feel compelled to recall many similar vehicles to rectify the fault. A person whose vehicle is recalled may not be able to sue the manufacturer of the anti-lock braking system, C, for the cost of a hire car which that person requires while the fault in his vehicle is being rectified. This type of loss is regarded as 'pure economic loss'. It should be noted that the person whose vehicle is recalled may still have a contractual remedy against the motor vehicle retailer, E, and be able to claim the cost of the hire car from the retailer.

Where liability under the law of negligence is established it is not possible to exclude that liability by a contractual provision, at least in most practical circumstances. This is because there is usually no contract between the injured party who is claiming damages under the law of negligence and the person who is at fault. As in Table 3.1, the injured pedestrian, X, has no contract or prior relationships with any of the other parties and will therefore be unimpeded in his claim for damages in negligence against the party at fault.

Even where there is a contract between the injured party and the party at fault, liability under the law of negligence for death or personal injury cannot be excluded (Section 2 of the Unfair Contract Terms Act, 1977).

PRODUCT LIABILITY

Background

A third area which is of relevance is that relating to the law of product liability. Product liability legislation in the UK results from a Directive of the European Community date 25 July 1985. As its name suggests, a Directive directs member states to enact local legislation. In this instance, the Directive requires the member states to enact legislation on the subject of 'liability for defective products'.

Local legislation was enacted in the UK and it is to be found in Part 1 of the Consumer Protection Act 1987. The provisions of the Act apply in respect of products first supplied on or after 1 March 1988. As a result of the European origin of the legislation, most of the comments made here are applicable in respect not only of products supplied in the UK but also of those supplied in other member states. (The member states of the European Community are Belgium, Denmark, France, Germany, Greece, Italy, Ireland, Luxembourg, the Netherlands, Portugal, Spain and the UK.)

There are certain important exceptions to the harmonization of European law in this area. The most important is that in some member states (but not in the UK) an overall limit has been placed upon the product liability of a manufacturer where the liability arises out of the same defect in identical products (this limit is currently £50 million).

Essentially, the Act provides that certain persons are liable to compensate an injured party who suffers damage caused by a defect in a product. An analysis of the legislation can take place by examining each of five elements, namely, the damage, the causation, the defect, the product and the persons liable.

Analysis of product liability legislation

The damage

Only damage of a specific type may form the basis of an action under the Consumer Protection Act 1987. The damage may be death, personal injury or damage to property. However, only property which is of a type ordinarily intended for private use may be the subject of a claim under the Act.

Therefore if a chemical plant were to explode because of a faulty computer control mechanism (Figure 3.2) the damage to any surrounding office buildings could not be the subject of a claim under the Consumer Protection Act 1987. This is because office buildings are not ordinarily intended for private use. However, if the homes or possessions of nearby individuals were also damaged, liability to pay compensation would arise for the damage to those houses and possessions under the Consumer Protection Act 1987.

The Consumer Protection Act 1987 also exclude an action for a claim for damage to the product itself. Therefore where it is alleged that a motor vehicle is, for instance, defective because the anti-lock braking system contains a defect, no claim can be brought by the owner of the motor vehicle in respect of damage to the motor vehicle itself. A further limitation is also imposed, namely, that in order to bring a claim the damage must exceed the sum of £275.

Figure 3.2 *Factories may be dependent upon computer control systems which are safety-critical*

Causation

The law of causation is complex. However, it can be adequately summed up for these purposes by stating that a person injured and bringing an action under the Consumer Protection Act 1987 would be required to show that, as a result of the defect being contained in the product, it was reasonably foreseeable that an injury of the type suffered would occur. In the context of the safety-critical systems which have been discussed in this chapter, the test of reasonable foreseeability would easily be satisfied. An injured party would easily be able to persuade a court that a safety-critical product such as the microprocessor control unit embedded in an anti-lock braking system, the control system of a chemical plant or, indeed, the software embedded in the microprocessor of a washing machine must be safe, and that if it is not safe, that it is reasonably foreseeable that persons will be injured and property damaged as a result.

The defect

For the purposes of the Consumer Protection Act 1987 a 'defect' is defined in terms of safety. A defect in a product will exist if the safety of the product is not such as persons are generally entitled to expect. For these purposes, safety includes safety not only in terms of avoiding death or personal injury but also in the sense of avoiding damage to a person's property.

In determining whether the required level of safety has been achieved all the circumstances need to be taken into account. These include the manner in which the product is being marketed; whether there were any warnings on the product; whether the product was put to a reasonable or unreasonable use; and the time at which the product was supplied.

Several conclusions can be drawn from the concept of a 'defect' under the Consumer Protection Act 1987:

1. The purpose for which the product is designed will be of relevance. Therefore, if a defect arises because the product is abused this points to there not being a defect for the purposes of the legislation. For example, a manufacturer of an anti-lock braking system may show that he supplied a braking system suitable for use in domestic motor vehicles, as he was requested. In fact, the braking system may be used in a commercial dumping truck. If the manufacturer can show that it was not reasonable to use the braking system in this manner, and that, as a result, the defect arose, he will be able to escape liability under the legislation. This will not be of much assistance to software manufacturers but it may be useful to those of hardware, where hardware is used in an environment for which it is not suited.
2. The warnings which are put on a product are relevant. If a product is only safe when used in a particular way, and adequate instructions are given on the product as to how it is to be used, this may provide a defence for the product manufacturer. This may be relevant for the control system of a chemical production plant. In such a system safety over-rides may be included. For example, it may be that these in-built over-rides are required

for maintenance purposes. By operating the over-rides the control system can be used in an 'unsafe' manner. If this is the case, full instructions and warnings should be embedded within the system (often within the software) to indicate to the operator that what he or she is doing is potentially dangerous.
3. The question of whether or not the product is safe is to be answered at the time of supply of the product. The mere fact that subsequent products are safer does not mean that an earlier product contains a defect for the purposes of the Consumer Protection Act 1987.

The product

From the point of view of a software supplier, the most critical question relating to the Consumer Protection Act 1987 is whether or not software is a 'product' for the purposes of the legislation. The statute provides that a product is still a product even though it is comprised within another article. For example, the anti-lock braking system is still a 'product' even when it is embodied within another product, namely, a motor vehicle. It is possible, therefore, for both the motor vehicle manufacturer and the manufacturer of the component anti-lock braking sytstem to be liable under the legislation for a defective anti-lock braking system.

The Consumer Protection Act 1987 defines a product as 'any goods or electricity'. It is almost certain that the supply of a computer product which incorporates both hardware and software is a supply of goods (for an example see *Mackenzie Pattern and Company* v. *British Olivetti Limited*). The question as to whether or not a supply purely of software is a supply of 'goods' has not yet been judicially decided. However, the author believes that a supply of software will be a supply of goods under the legislation. This is particularly so where the software being supplied is not bespoke.

In many instances, however, the question may not be crucial, since software will be supplied in conjunction with hardware. In such circumstances it is almost certain that a supply of goods has been made, and therefore a product will be supplied for the purposes of the legislation. Even the software author, A, in the example envisaged by Table 3.1 may be making a supply of goods if he sends the software to the software company, S, on a floppy disk or other physical medium.

Persons liable

The persons who are liable under the legislation are the producers of the product. For these purposes, a producer can mean a manufacturer or else, where the goods are not actually manufactured, a person who carries out an industrial or other process to the product. Since a produced comprised within another article is still a product for the purposes of the legislation, a number of persons may each be liable under the legislation in respect of the same defect.

Referring to the example in Table 3.1, if the hardware device which is a part of the anti-locking braking system of the motor vehicle is defective, the following parties will be liable: the manufacturer of the entire motor vehicle, D; the manufacturer of the anti-lock braking system, C; the manufacturer of the complete computer control unit (which comprises both the hardware and the software), B; and the manufacturer of the hardware, H. Each of these persons is liable to compensate in full an injured party where the defect in the hardware causes the damage.

There are also further persons who may be liable under the legislation as 'producers'. Where goods are imported into the European Community, the importer is a producer for the purposes of the Act. If an own-brand retailer puts his name upon the product he is also liable as a producer. This would apply, for example, in the case of a washing machine where a high-street retailer sells the washing machine under his own brand name rather than under the actual manufacturer's trade mark. Furthermore, in certain circumstances, where a retailer of the product refuses or fails to supply details of the actual manufacturer to an injured person, then the retailer may be liable as a producer under the legislation.

Defences

Although the Act provides a total of six defences, most of them are not of practical or commercial significance. Two defences which are of interest from a practical point of view and are dealt with below are the state-of-the-art defence (also commonly described as the development risk defence) and a defence relating to compliance with instructions.

Development risk defence

This defence depends upon the state of scientific and technical knowledge at the time when the producer supplied the product. It applies if a producer can show that a 'typical' producer could not have been expected to have discovered the defect in the product because of the state of scientific and technical knowledge. The test is applied to the time period during which the product was under the control of the producer claiming the defence. In fact, the Act does not mention a typical producer but rather a 'producer of products of the same description'. The exact scope of the defence is somewhat uncertain.

It is not clear whether the intention was to create a defence based upon what a reasonable producer would do, or whether the legislation is stricter and is intended to require a producer to take all steps which even the most prudent producer would have taken. The latter higher standard, namely that the defence only applies if the scientific and technical knowledge was not such as would allow the defect to have been discovered is the defence that is allowed in the Directive. As a consequence, the UK government may be required by the European Community to amend the Consumer Protection Act 1987, to indicate clearly that the test is stricter than one based on a concept of 'reasonableness'.

From a practical point of view, manufacturers and suppliers of computer hardware and software must take notice of (and comply with) those standards which do exist in the computer industry. Similarly, manufacturers should ensure that adequate verification and validation procedures in the production of software are followed. They should also take note of any other procedures generally followed by cautious manufacturers. Only then will this defence be available to them.

Compliance with instructions

This defence is most easily explained by an example. Referring to the scenario detailed in Table 3.1, let us suppose that the manufacturer of the motor vehicle, D, gave instructions to the manufacturer of the anti-lock braking system, C. Where a defect arises in the anti-lock braking system and that defect is wholly attributable to the compliance by the manufacturer of the anti-lock braking system, C, with those instructions, then C will have a defence. This defence has the following limitations:

1. It is only available to the manufacturer of a component;
2. The component manufacturer must receive instructions from the producer of a product in which his component is comprised;
3. The component manufacturer must have actually complied with those instructions; and
4. The component manufacturer must be able to show that the defect is wholly attributable to his compliance with those instructions.

From a practical point of view it is unlikely that the defence will operate in many circumstances. This is because, in most situations, manufacturers of complete products will not be giving instructions which are so detailed as to enable a component manufacturer to take advantage of the defence. In practice, the instructions which are received will not be sufficient as to enable the defence to be relied upon by a component manufacturer. This is particularly so given that, in order for the defence to apply, the defect has to be *wholly* attributable to compliance with instructions.

It may, however, be that a software author who is writing software in accordance with a specification supplied to him will be able to take advantage of this defence. To do so, the software author will need to show that his complying with the specification gave rise to the particular defect.

A further example of a situation where this defence could apply is where B, the manufacturer of the microprocessor control unit embodied within the anti-lock braking system, is told by C, the manufacturer of the anti-lock braking system, that a certain signal strength will be sent to the microprocessor control from the receptors in the wheels. This will clearly be of crucial importance in the event that one or more of the wheels lock. If this instruction proved to be erroneous because the signal strength was much weaker than that which the braking system manufacturer, C, had indicated, the manufacturer of the component microprocessor, B, may be able to claim that this was the cause of the defect, and therefore he, the component manufacturer, is not liable under the Consumer Protection Act 1987. This would not affect the liability of either C, the manufacturer of the anti-lock braking system, or D, the manufacturer of the complete vehicle, both of whom would remain liable under the legislation.

Extent of liability

The Consumer Protection Act 1987 requires that two limitation periods be satisfied in order for a claim to be brought under the Act. The first is an overall ten-year period within which any claim under the Act must be brought. For any given defendant in an action the ten-year period commences on the date of supply by that defendant. Since the date of supply may be different for potential defendants, the limitation period under the Consumer Protection Act 1987 will expire on different dates for each of those potential defendants.

In the example depicted in Table 3.1 it could be that the supply made by the manufacturer of the microprocessor computer control system, B, is made 6 months after the supply of the software to him by the software supplier. Ten years later, in a case brought under the product liability legislation and arising out of defective software, there will be a 6-month period during which a claim may be brought against B, the manufacturer of the complete computer control system but not against S, the software supplier.

Second, as well as satisfying this ten-year limitation period there is a 3-year period which a claimant must satisfy. Where a claim is brought for death or personal injury, the claim must be brought within 3 years. This period will generally commence upon the date the injury occurred.

The damage for which compensation may be claimed in an action under the product liability legislation has been discussed earlier in this chapter. Any attempt to exclude liability under the product liability legislation is not effective, although it is possible to obtain an indemnity, as discussed below.

CONCLUSIONS

Given that a manufacturer or supplier will be liable for damages for a breach of contract, for a negligent action or omission or as the producer of a defective product, what steps should he take? This concluding section sets out some of the practical steps which a manufacturer should consider.

Practical steps

Compliance with standards

Manufacturers and suppliers of both hardware and software should look to those external standards which are available in determining the safety of their products. Although the concept of formal computer safety standards is relatively new, a court will not regard that as an excuse for not following those standards which do exist.

Identification of risks

Manufacturers and suppliers should then consider their remaining potential liability under both criminal and civil law for the goods which they produce or distribute. This process will probably require consultation with legal advisors. It is, however, important to determine what residual risks remain, and the extent to which it may be practical to take steps to reduce that residual risk.

Insurance

Manufacturers and suppliers should consider insuring against their residual risk, which will involve a risk analysis of their products and the areas in which they trade. Although it may be difficult to obtain insurance in certain fields, particularly in the area of software production, efforts should be made to obtain what cover is available on an economic basis.

Trading structures

In respect of certain high-risk activities, the legal structures and entities which an organization uses to trade may be capable of giving it some protection. One of the benefits of trading as a limited company is that advantage can then be taken of the protection given to limited liability companies. Other steps of a similar nature can sometimes be taken to limit liability by establishing the most beneficial corporate structure for the business concerned.

Obtaining of an indemnity

It may be possible to obtain an indemnity from another party involved in the production or supply of the products. The obtaining of an indemnity is particularly important for product liability given the various people against whom action may be taken under the legislation. For example, using the scenario depicted in Table 3.1 it may be possible for the manufacturer of the entire motor vehicle, D, to obtain an indemnity from the manufacturer of the anti-lock braking system, C, in respect of claims brought against D for defects in the anti-lock braking system. In such circumstances the manufacturer of the anti-lock braking system, C, can be obliged under the terms of this contract with D to indemnify D for the consequences of such defects.

Such indemnities are relatively common in many industries. Of course, for various practical and commercial reasons, it may not always be possible to obtain an indemnity. Indeed, the effect of such indemnities is often to pass the buck (i.e. the liability) down the line, in this example perhaps to the software author, A, or hardware manufacturer H. It would then be especially important for those persons to obtain adequate insurance.

Testing of products

Manufacturers should review their testing facilities. They should consider testing all products themselves and also ensure, through the contracts which they have with their component manufacturers, that those component manufacturers rigorously test the components they are supplying. Indeed, it is quite likely that any testing requirements will be linked in a contract to the indemnity, which is to be obtained from the component manufacturer. The indemnity may exclude defects which should have been identified by tests carried out by the manufacturer of the complete product but include those which should have been identified in tests by the component manufacturer.

Maintenance of records

Careful records should be kept. This is so that a manufacturer can determine which defective product gives rise to a particular claim. For example, it may be that the manufacturer of the complete anti-lock braking system receives supplies of microprocessor control units from a number of different sources. Accordingly, he will need to be able to prove, for any particular anti-lock braking system in which it is alleged that there has been a hardware fault, which company supplied the microprocessor control unit in question. This is particularly so if the manufacturer of the anti-lock braking system has been prudent enough to obtain indemnities from all his various component suppliers.

Under the product liability legislation a claim could be brought ten years after the date of the supply. Therefore, records will need to be preserved for, at the very least, this period of time, and preferably longer.

The future

There are many proposals, mainly stemming from the European Community, which are likely to affect the question of liability for producers of hardware and software. One example is a proposal for a Directive on general product safety. The European Community is also active in establishing harmonized laws and standards for certain specific product areas. Where those product areas include articles which incorporate computer hardware or software, there will be implications for the manufacturers and suppliers of computer components.

In the space available, it is not practical to mention all the current proposals which may affect computer manufacturers and suppliers in this way. Indeed, it is probably not desirable either, given the propensity or change in proposals emanating from the European Community.

One firm proposal, which is now embodied in a Directive and therefore deserves particular attention, relates to further safety requirements for machinery. The member states are required to enact legislation before 31 December 1992 to comply with the provisions of this Directive, although there are some transitional provisions. It is expressly stated in the Directive that control systems must be designed in a safe and reliable way to 'prevent a dangerous situation arising'. The Directive also provides that errors in logic must not lead to dangerous situations.

Despite the ambiguity of what constitutes a 'dangerous situation', it seems highly probable that this obligation will be extremely difficult (if not impossible) to fulfil. There are probably no commercially useful computer systems which can be proved to be free of all errors of logic!

There are other requirements in the Directive concerning computer software. For example, there is an unqualified statement that 'interactive software between the operator and a command or control system of a machine must be user-friendly', but the concept of user-friendliness is not defined. Clearly, this is something which will need to be taken into account in future by manufacturers of computer control systems.

ACKNOWLEDGEMENTS

The author wishes to express his thanks for the assistance provided by his colleagues at Hepworth & Chadwick in the preparation of this chapter. The law is stated as at 6 August 1991.

REFERENCES

Consumer Protection Act 1987 (1987, c. 43), especially Part 1

Directive of the European Community of 25 July 1985 (85/374/EEC) entitled *On the approximation of the laws, regulations and administrative provisions of the Member States concerning liability for defective products* (OJ No. L 210, p. 29)

Directive of the European Community of 14 June 1989 (89/392/EEC) entitled *On the approximation of the Member States relating to machinery* (OJ No. L 183, p. 9) as amended by COM (90) 462 (OJ No. C 268)

Donoghue v. *Stevenson*, House of Lords (1932, AC 562)

The Electricity at Work Regulations 1989 (SI 89/635)

Health and Safety at Work etc. Act 1974 (1984, c. 37)

Mackenzie Patten and Company v. *British Olivetti Limited* (unreported 1984 QBD)

Proposal (dated 27 April 1989) for a Directive of the European Community concerning general product safety (OJ No. C 193, p. 1) as amended by COM (90) 259 (OJ No. C 156)

Sale of Goods Act 1979 (1979, c. 54), especially Sections 13 and 14

Supply of Goods and Services Act 1982 (1982, c. 29)

Unfair Contract Terms Act 1977 (1977, c. 50)

4 Standardization efforts worldwide
J. M. Rata

WHY STANDARDS ARE NEEDED

Software has become increasingly complex, and large programs are developed by teams involving many people. Standards are therefore necessary to establish common approaches, to facilitate the verification and validation processes as well as maintenance, and to allow the efficient use of common support environments. Software standardization encompasses languages, methods, documentation, test plans and error reporting. Standardization is both a technical and a commercial necessity and pursues the following goals:

1. To give a common language to different commercial and technical partners;
2. To assure the user of a given product that it conforms to certain quality criteria, or has been developed according to methods the efficiency of which is well established;
3. Eventually to constitute a legal reference basis when disputes arise or in cases of failures.

On the last point, new directives from the European Community on responsibility for product defects urge developers to abide by quality standards.

Users are becoming increasingly demanding in matters of product quality. Standardization of quality-related procedures allows segregation of problems and facilitates quality implementation. Nevertheless, it must be kept in mind that conformance to standards is not enough to achieve quality: developers must continue to listen to users in order to satisfy their real requirements.

Standardization may also be oriented towards setting up regulations, especially in matters of system safety. Finally, it allows harmonization of practices among different countries, and so reduces commercial barriers.

HISTORY OF SOFTWARE STANDARDS

Before the Industrial Revolution, quality appearance was the sole responsibility of the craftsmen. The appearance of standards allowed acceptance criteria for sub-assemblies to be identified, which segregated tasks and improved productivity while a given level of quality could be guaranteed. As far as software is concerned, the current state of software engineering methods and quality assurance can be described as 'post-craftmanship'.

In the software quality domain, the first standards appeared as early as 1974 in the American military establishment, with MIL-S-52779, which required the establishment of a software quality assurance programme and strongly influenced later quality standards. The motivation of military personnel for establishing standards for software quality assurance can be found in the exponential increase in embedded software design and maintenance costs, as well as in the quality of products.

In the civil domain, FAA-STD-018 was published by the Federal Aviation Administration in 1977 and the IEEE produced its first draft standard for quality assurance in 1980 (ANSI-IEEE 730: IEEE Trial-use standard for software quality assurance plans), which was revised in 1981 and 1984.

For safety-related systems one of the first software standards developed was IEC Publication 880: Software for computers in the safety systems of nuclear power stations, published in 1986. In 1987, the European Space Agency published ESA PSS-05-0: ESA Software Engineering Standards. These standards cover the whole software life cycle, and, to some extent, deal with problems at the system level.

INTERNATIONAL STANDARDS ORGANIZATIONS

Standards can be established internally in organizations, but the trend is now to adopt international ones. These are developed through official international standards organizations, which include ISO and IEC, and specific organizations such as CCITT. Standards in these organizations are mostly produced by reaching a consensus among participating countries, in which users and manufacturers should be represented. The standardization process is always a long one: many years are spent in developing drafts, and obtaining this consensus. To obviate this, a procedure has been set up in which standards developed by other bodies with a sufficiently international participation can be submitted without change to ISO or IEC. This consensus-based approach is most suitable when dealing with product standardization. For pre-market stages of development, functional prototypes do not exist, and a different, more theoretical, approach has to be followed, such as that used for developing OSI standards. The IEEE is promoting such an approach (for example, with Futurebus). Figure 4.1 shows the principal standard-setting organizations and their relationships, and brief descriptions of these are given below.

ISO

The International Standardization Organization (ISO) was established in 1947, following a conference of representatives from 25 national standards organizations held in London in October 1946. It now includes 90 national committees, and its aim is to promote the development of standards and associated activities worldwide, with a view to facilitating exchange of goods and services and to implement a common understanding in intellectual, scientific, technical and

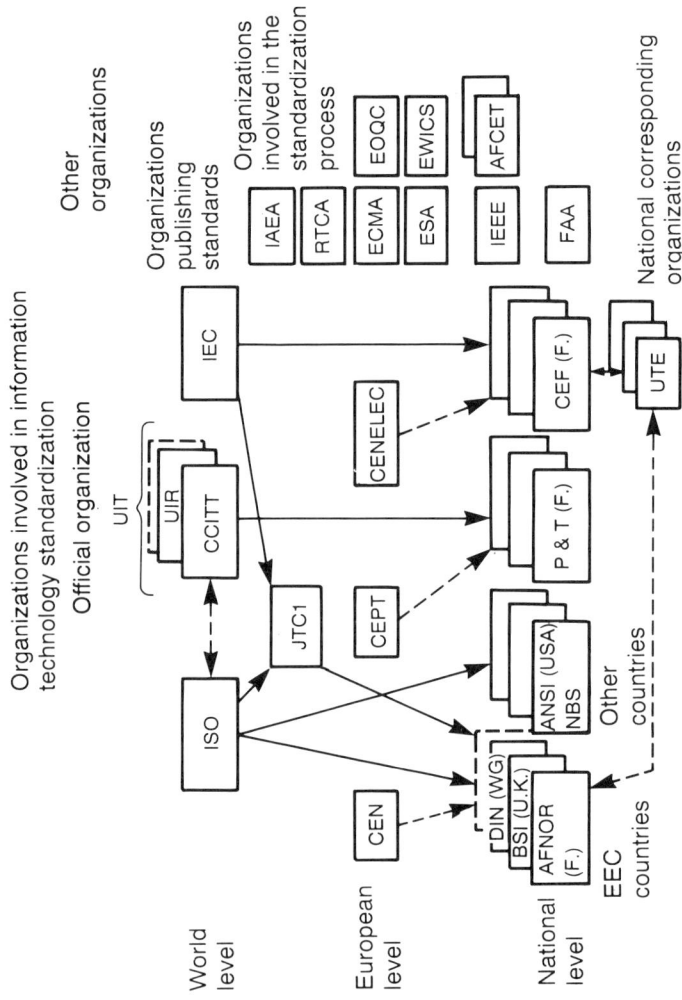

Figure 4.1 *Relationship between standards organizations*

economical domains. ISO Technical Committee 176 is responsible for generic quality assurance problems. The address of the ISO Central Office is:

1 rue de Varembé, PO Box 56, 1211 Geneva 20, Switzerland
Telephone: (41) 22 34 12 40
Telefax: (41) 22 33 34 30
Telex: 23887 iso ch

IEC

The International Electrotechnical Commission (IEC) was established in 1906, following the recommendations of the International Congress on Electricity held in St Louis (USA) in 1904. It now includes 42 national committees, and its standards are being used by more than 100 countries. Its work is mainly in the electrical and electronics domains, and, recently, information technology, as a result of industrial applications of computerized systems in process control. It includes system dependability (safety, reliability, availability, maintainability) in industry. IEC Technical Committee 45 (Nuclear instrumentation) published in 1983 one of the first standards on software for nuclear protection systems. In order to deal with safety problems arising from the use of computers in non-nuclear applications, Subcommittee 65A (System considerations) from Technical Committee 65 (Industrial process measurements and control), has set up two working groups, WG 9 ('Safe software') and WG 10 ('Functional safety of programmable electronic systems'). The address of the IEC Central Office is:

3 rue de Varembé, PO Box 131, 1211 Geneva 20, Switzerland
Telephone: (41) 22 34 01 50
Telefax: (41) 22 33 38 43
Telex: 28872 ceiec ch

ISO and IEC have established an official agreement stating the relationship between both organizations, in order to better complement each other. In the information technology domain a joint ISO/IEC technical committee (JTC1) was established in 1987, which comprises the main committees from each organization involved.

CEN/CENELEC

These organizations have been established by the Commission of the European Communities. CEN (Comité Européen de Normalisation) and CENELEC (Comité Européen de Normalisation Electrotechnique) are aiming at the harmonization of standards inside the European Community. They include national standards organizations from the twelve member countries of the Community, as well as from the European Free Trade Association (EFTA), which includes Austria, Finland, Iceland, Norway, Sweden and Switzerland. These international organizations have corresponding bodies at the national level, such as BSI in the UK, AFNOR and CEF in France, DIN in Germany and ANSI and NBS in the USA. Other organizations work in specific domains.

CCITT

The Comité Consultatif International Télégraphique et Téléphonique (CCITT) is part of the International Telecommunications Union (ITU) and its committees are involved in specific communication software problems, especially for quality assurance and reliability.

CEPT

The European Conference of Post and Telecommunications (CEPT) prepares recommendations for national administrations as well as technical specifications for telecommunications equipment used in Europe.

ESA

The European Space Agency (ESA) establishes its own standards for software used in space applications, through its Board for Software Standardization and Control. Standard ESA PSS-05-0 Issue 1 (January 1987) includes two parts, aimed respectively at the product and at the development process associated with its quality control.

RTCA and FAA

The Radio Technical Commission for Aeronautics (RTCA) is involved with problems linked to avionics, and also publishes quality assurance standards. It issued RTCA/DO-178A: Software considerations in airborne systems and equipment certification in March 1985. In the USA the Federal Aviation Administration (FAA) has also published FAA-STD018: Computer Software Quality Program Requirements.

IAEA

The International Atomic Energy Agency (IAEA) is concerned with safety aspects in the nuclear field, and published a standard in 1987: Quality assurance for computer software. Other organizations are pre-standards.

IEEE

The Institution of Electrical and Electronic Engineers (IEEE) is established in the USA and includes more than 250 000 members worldwide. Its Computer Society is important as it is actively drafting standards, which are then submitted at the US national level to ANSI, and forwarded at the international level to IEC and ISO, or ISO/IEC JTCI.

ECMA

The European Computer Manufacturers Association (ECMA) is composed of computer manufacturers, mainly from Europe, and produces standards or participates in their development.

EOQC

The European Organization for Quality Control (EOQC) was established in the 1960s and set up a Software Committee in 1983. It aims to produce a common set of reference documents on software quality based mainly on IEEE standards.

EWICS

The European Workshop on Industrial Computer Systems (EWICS) aims to promote the usage of computers in the industry. Its Technical Committee 7, Reliability, safety and security, produces pre-standards which are then used as references by international standards organizations, mainly the IEC. It is supported occasionally by the European Commission of the European Communities.

STANDARDIZATION WORK REALIZED THROUGH ISO OR IEC

Standards which are not specific to software but relevant to system safety will now be described.

Safety aspects of computer-based systems in the nuclear field: IEC SC45A WG3

This Technical Committee deals with nuclear instrumentation and carried out early work on standards for software in safety systems, due to the emerging use of programmable equipment (mainly microprocessor based) in nuclear protection systems. Software was chosen because of the lack of software standards at the time, and also due to its complex nature. WG3 was given the task of developing such a standard.

This working group produced IEC Publication 880: *Software for computers in the safety systems of nuclear power stations* in 1986, after many years of work, due to the lack of standards upon which to draw at the time. It was also felt necessary to include in this document parts which were more relevant to hardware systems than to software, as there was no companion document on these aspects. Special recommendations are:

1. Established criteria as far as they affect software, taking into account the high degree of interdependency between hardware and software;
2. A general approach to software development to ensure the production of the highly reliable software required:
3. A general approach to software verification and computer system validation;
4. Procedures for software maintenance, modification and configuration control.

Since the publication of this standard, this working group has been involved in the preparation of a companion document, addressing the system and hardware aspects which were not covered in the standard. The draft was proposed to be published at a meeting of SC45A in York in October 1988 and is now available as IEC Publication 987: *Programmed digital computer important to safety for nuclear power stations*. This gives requirements specific to digital systems hardware, especially for redundancy, independence and structural distribution. At its meeting in York, the working group decided to propose an updating of Publication 880, in the form of a supplement, in order to take into account the technological evolution of software engineering practice. This will include requirements for:

Software incorporated into the safety system software
Software used for the development of safety system software
Automatic analysis tools for software code
Computer-aided engineering tools for code, data and logic preparation
Functional diversity against common-mode failure
Acceptance criteria for programming languages
Mathematical formal specification methods and software prototyping
Software for hardware self-supervision
Software drivers
Communications software

Prerequisites for the use of pre-existing software will be included, as well as criteria for the evaluation of development, test and acceptance documentation for the product and its operating experience. Conformance criteria for the requirements of Publication 880 will also be developed and hardware/software integration and maintenance complemented for points not already covered in Publication 880. Security aspects and their implications on safety will also be included. Other IEC SCC45A Working Groups are involved in matters related to safety i.e.:

WG 6: Emergency electric power systems
WG 7: Safety classification

Reliability and maintainability standardization aspects: IEC TC56

This committee is involved in reliability and maintainability in a generic way. It has been working mainly on equipment, but is now also involved with computer-based systems and software aspects. It has produced a dictionary of terms relevant to its field in collaboration with TC1, which will constitute Chapter 191 (Reliability, maintainability and quality of service) of the International Electrotechnical Vocabulary (IEV). It includes the following working groups:

SWG1 Human aspects of reliability (set up in June 1988 in Tokyo)
WG1   Terms and definitions
WG2   Data collection
WG3   Equipment reliability verification
WG4   Verification and evaluation procedures
WG5   Formal design review
WG6   Maintainability
WG7   Component reliability
WG8   Reliability and maintainability management
WG9   Analysis techniques for system reliability
WG10 Software aspects

This committee has been very prolific, and many standards have been produced which should be familiar to people involved in reliability and safety assessment. This committee has published a series of standards:

IEC Publication 50(191) June 1988: Chapter 191 of the IEV: *Reliability, maintainability and quality of service*

IEC Publication 271, 271A, B and C:
List of basic terms, definitions and related mathematics for reliability

IEC Publication 300 (2nd edition 1984): *Reliability and maintainability management*. This publication is already under revision to ensure compliance with ISO proposed standards 9000 and 9004.

IEC Publication 319: *Presentation of reliability data on electronic components (or parts)*

IEC Publication 362: *Guide for the collection of reliability, availability and maintainability data from field performance of electronic items*

IEC Publication 409: *Guide for the inclusion of reliability clauses into specification for components (or parts) for electronic equipment*

IEC Publication 410: *Sampling plans and procedures for inspection by attributes*

IEC Publication 419: *Guide for the inclusion of lot-by-lot and periodic inspection procedures in specifications for electronic components (or parts)*

IEC Publication 605: *Equipment reliability testing*
  605–1 Part 1   *General requirements*
  605–3 Part 2   *Equipment for stationary use in weather protected locations – High degree of simulation*
  605–3 Part 3   *Preferred test conditions*
  605–4 Part 4   *Procedures for determining point estimates and confidence limits for equipment reliability determination tests*
  605–5 Part 5   *Compliance test plans for success ratio*
  605–6 Part 6   *Test for the validity of a constant rate failure assumption*
  605–7 Part 7   *Compliance test plans for failure rate and mean time between failures assuming constant failure rate*

some of which are under revision

IEC Publication 706: *Guide on maintainability of equipment*
  706–1 Part 1, Sections 1,2 and 3   *Introduction, requirements and reliability programme*
  706–3 Part 3, Section 6 and 7   *Verification and collection, analysis and presentation of data*

IEC Publication 812: *Analysis techniques for system reliability – Procedure for failure mode and effects analysis (FMEA).*

IEC Publication 863: *Presentation of reliability, maintainability and availability predictions*

A number of drafts have been approved for publication:

56(C.O.)106   Publication 605–2: *Equipment reliability testing – Part 2 – Guidance for the design of test cycles*
56(C.O.)109   *Guide on maintainability of equipment*
56(C.O.)120   Publication 605–3: *Equipment reliability testing – Part 3 – Preferred test conditions – Test cycle 5: Equipment installed inside ground vehicles*
56(C.O.)122   *Reliability improvement and growth programmes*
56(C.O.)127   Supplement to Publication 605–7: *Procedure for design of time terminated test plans*

Many standards drafts are in the balloting process:

56(C.O.)121   *Fault tree analysis*
56(C.O.)133   *Amendment to FTA*
56(C.O.)137   *Reliability block diagram methods* and a new draft:
56(Sec.)207   *Reliability block diagram methods*
56(C.O.)137   *General considerations for reliability/availability analysis methodology*

Other drafts have been submitted:

56(Sec.)214   *Parts count reliability prediction*
56(Sec.)232   *Markov analysis techniques*
56(C.O.)132   *Maintenance and maintenance support planning*

Among the various subjects under consideration, SWG1 will work on reliability of human elements and WG9 will develop a standard for Markov processes.

A proposal, *Risk assessment requirements and guidelines*, has been made by the Canadian National Committee, according to a decision at the TC56 meeting in October 1986 in Paris. Some National Committee members have nevertheless felt that safety is a very important subject and outside the scope of TC56, and IEC SC65A/WG10 would be more appropriate to deal with this aspect. A close link has been established between TC56 and SC65A in this matter, and work already in progress in TC56 on risk analysis has been a good starting point for cooperation.

In the domain of information technology, TC56/WG10 will continue to deal with software aspects:

56(Sec.)224 *Software reliability management*
56(Sec.)236 *Software dependability testing*

The following works has been assigned to IEC TC56 WG10 in Tokyo:

Software analysis requirements
Software reliability and maintainability management
Software test methods
Software reliability growth
Software failure mechanisms

Industrial-process measurement and control: IEC TC65

This committee is involved in the preparation of standards for system and elements used for industrial-process measurement and control. It includes the following sub-committees and working groups:

TC65: Industrial-process measurement and control
    WG1   Terms and definitions
    WG2   Service conditions
    WG3   Safety for industrial-process measurement and control instruments
    WG4   Electromagnetic interferences
    WG5   Graphical symbols and identifying letters for industrial-process measurement and control functions and instrumentation
SC65A: System considerations
    WG4   Interface characteristics
    WG6   Programmable control systems for discontinuous industrial processes
    WG8   Evaluation of system properties
    WG9   Safe software
    WG10 Functional safety of programmable electronic systems (PES)
SC65B: Elements of systems
    WG5   Temperature sensors
    WG6   Methods of testing and evaluation of performance of system elements
    WG8   Dimensions of panel- and rack-mounted industrial-process measurement and control instruments

WG9   Final control elements
WG10 Process stream analytical equipment
SC65C: Digital data communications for measurement and control systems
WG1   Message data format for information transferred on process and control data highways
WG3   Programmable measuring apparatus
WG6   Industrial-process computer inter-subsystem communications

Among the publications issued by this committee, the following are relevant to safety and reliability evaluations:

IEC Publication 801: *Electromagnetic compatibility for industrial-process measurement and control equipment.*
   801–1 Part 1: *General introduction*
   801–2 Part 2: *Electrostatic discharge requirements*
   801–3 Part 3: *Radiated electromagnetic field requirements*
   801–4 Part 4: *Electrical fast transient requirements*
IEC Publication 902: *Industrial-process measurement and control – Terms and definitions*

SC65A WG6 has developed a series of drafts concerning programmable controllers, which have been submitted to the ballot process. It is currently working on:

Evaluation of system properties (WG8):
   Part 1 General considerations and methodologies
Evaluation of the integrity of system functions:
   Part 2 Assessment methodology
   Part 3 Assessment of system functionality
   Part 4 Assessment of system performance
   Part 5 Assessment of system dependability
   Part 6 Assessment of system operability
   Part 7 Assessment of system safety
   Part 8 Assessment of system support

Part 5 should be related to TC56 work on reliability, and Part 7 to SC65A/WG9 and WG10 in order to avoid inconsistencies.

IEC SC65A/WG9 (Safe software) delivered a draft document in October 1991: *Software for computers in the application of industrial safety-related systems.* This will be applicable to reliable software required for computers used in high-integrity industrial systems. It provides requirements for each stage of software generation for the purpose of achieving highly reliable software.

SC65A/WG10 (Functional safety of programmable electronic systems – Generic aspects) also delivered a draft standard in April 1992: *Functional safety of programmable electronic systems: Generic aspects.* This working group resulted from an *ad hoc* group set up in December 1986 by ACOS, the Advisory Committee on Safety for the IEC. The work was transferred to SC65A in July 1987. It takes into account a German pre-standard DIN V 19 251: *Proposal for a guide of fundamental safety aspects to be considered for measurement and control protective equipment.* The terms of reference for WG10 are as follows: Task: To prepare an IEC publication which provides guidelines on programmable electronic systems (PESs) having safety functions. It must be noted that WG9 and WG10 are working closely together.

The Austrian National Committee proposed at the Stockholm meeting in September 1988 to work on the *Documentation of programmable electronic systems* and a special working group has been consequently set up to

1. Survey existing publications and work in progress on the documentation of programmable electronic systems; and
2. Make specific recommendations for future work.

It was decided that current work in WG9 and WG10 would cover this domain.

Quality management and quality assurance: ISO TC176

This technical committee has a working group:

WG1 Measuring and test equipment

and also includes the following sub-committees:

SC1 Quality assurance – terminology
SC2 Quality systems

SC2 has the following working groups:

SC2/WG2   System guidelines
SC2/WG4   System integration
SC2/WG5   Software quality assurance
SC2/WG6   Quality assurance for services
SC2/WG7   Quality audit

The following standards have been published:

ISO 9000: *Guide for the selection of Quality Assurance measures in the customer–supplier relationships types-models*
ISO 9001: *Quality systems – Model for quality assurance in design/development, production, installation and servicing*
ISO 9002: *Quality systems – Model for quality assurance in production and installation*
ISO 9003: *Quality systems – Model for quality assurance in final inspection and test*
ISO 9004: *Quality management and quality system elements – Guidelines*

as well as a quality vocabulary:

ISO 8402: *Quality vocabulary*

Drafts which can also be taken into account are:

ISO/TC176/SC2/WG5 (January 1988): *Quality system – Model for quality*

assurance of software in specification, design/development, test and maintenance.
DP 9001/2 (September 1989): *Guidelines for the application of ISO 9001 to software.*

Other ISO committees of interest are:

ISO TC46 Information and documentation
    SC3   Terminology of information and documentation
    SC4   Computer applications in information and documentation
    SC9   Presentation, identification and description of documents
ISO TC69 Applications of statistical methods
    SC1   Terminology and symbols
    SC2   Interpretation of statistical data
    SC3   Application of statistical methods in
    SC4   Statistical quality control
    SC5   Acceptance sampling
    SC6   Measurement methods and results

Information technology: ISO/IEC JTCI

This joint ISO-IEC Technical Committee was set up in 1987, and gathers committees from both organizations which deal with information technology. Sub-committees which may be relevant to safety, reliability, quality assurance are:

SC1   Vocabulary
SC6   Telecommunications and information exchange between systems
SC7   Software development and system documentation
SC13   Interconnection of equipment
SC14   Representation of data elements
SC20   Data cryptographic techniques
SC21   Information retrieval, transfer and management for open systems interconnection (OSI)
SC22   Languages
SC25   Information technology equipment (ex TC83 from IEC)
SC26   Microprocessor systems (ex SC47B from IEC)
ISO/IEC JTC1/SC7: Software development and system documentation
   WG1   Symbols, charts and diagrams
   WG3   Program design

This sub-committee prepared a DP (9126) for Project 7.13.01:
Evaluation of software product – software quality characteristics and guidelines for their use, which has been revised and submitted for a third ballot (standard expected in June 1990). It also developed ISO 6592: *Information processing – guidelines for the documentation of computer-based application systems*, which will be complemented by a current project, *Guidelines for the management of software documentation*. The sub-committee also has other current projects:

Project 97.7.10:   *Documentation of consumer software packages*

Project 97.7.12:   *Structured programming design rules*
Project 97.7.14:   *Criteria for evaluation of programming methods*
Project 7.13.02:   *Evaluation of software product – software quality subcharacteristics*
Project 7.13.03:   *Evaluation of software product – software quality measurement and rating*
Project 7.18.01.01: *Guidelines for software development methods – overall structure*
Project 7.18.01.02: *Guidelines for software development methods – methodology classes*

Another project is on hold, depending on the outcome of project 7.18.01.01:

Project 7.14   *Criteria for the evaluation of software development methods*

A draft has also been prepared, (N–123): *Conceptual classification of software development methods, and a guideline for practical use.*

It seems that problems have arisen between TC176 and JTC1/SC7/WG3 on account of software quality. The latter is of the opinion that software quality is within the scope of JTC1/SC7 (Software development and systems documentation) and outside that of TC176. Terminology problems arise also between TC56 and SC65A concerning the definitions and concepts of faults, errors and failures. Borders are sometimes unclear between the domains of work of standards committees, and communications and information exchange between groups dealing with similar domains could be improved.

Other committees which may be related to safety

IEC TC44: Electrical equipment of industrial machines

Scope: To prepare international standards primarily relating to the application of electrical and electronics equipment and systems to industrial machines (including a group of machiners working together in a coordinated manner excluding higher-level systems aspects) not portable by hand while working. The equipment covered begins at the point of connection of the supply to the machine's electrical equipment. It includes equipment or parts of equipment which operate with a nominal voltage not exceeding 1000 V d.c. between lines and nominal frequencies not exceeding 200 Hz. For higher voltages and frequencies greater than 200 Hz special requirements may apply.

IEC TC74: Safety of information technology equipment including electrical business equipment and telecommunications equipment

Scope: To prepare standards for the safety of information technology equipment including electrical business and telecommunications equipment. Consideration of safety includes, for example, heat, fire and radiation; acoustic shock; and electrical, mechanical and chemical hazards.

IEC TC77: Electromagnetic compatibility between electrical equipment including networks

Scope: To prepare standards concerning electromagnetic compatibility of electrical and/or electronic equipment and with electrical power networks.

Security aspects may also be relevant to the domain of safety and reliability, through breaches in the system integrity. ISO TC184 (Industrial automation) is proposing a new standard on industrial automation safety, which will also include software aspects. The following ISO committees are involved in the security domain: TC68, JTC1 SC6, SC17, SC18, SC20 and SC21. A new committee will be set up to deal with these security aspects.

OTHER STANDARDS PREPARED OUTSIDE ISO AND IEC

United States National Standards published by the IEEE

Terminology

ANSI/IEEE Std 610.2:	Glossary of computer applications terminology
ANSI/IEEE Std 729	IEEE standard glossary of software engineering terminology (under revision –P.610.12)

Software quality assurance

ANSI/IEEE Std 730	IEEE standard for software quality assurance plans
ANSI/IEEE Std 828:	IEEE standard for software configuration management plans (revision planned)
ANSI/IEEE Std 829:	IEEE standard for software test documentation (revision planned)
ANSI/IEEE Std 830	IEEE guide to software requirements specification (revision planned)
ANSI/IEEE Std 983:	IEEE guide for software quality assurance planning
ANSI/IEEE Std 1008:	IEEE standard for software unit testing
ANSI/IEEE Std 1012:	IEEE standard for software certification and validation plans
ANSI/IEEE Std 1016.1:	IEEE recommended practice for software design description
ANSI/IEEE Std 1042:	Guide to software configuration management

IEEE Standards and projects

IEEE Std 982.1:	Standard dictionary of measures to produce reliable software
IEEE Std 982.2:	Guide for the use of IEEE standard dictionary of measures to produce reliable software.

IEEE Std 1028   Standard for software reviews and audits
IEEE Std 1058.1   Standard for software project management plans
IEEE Std 1063   Standard for software user documentation

The IEEE has also accepted the following projects:

P 610.12   Glossary of software engineering terminology
P 730.2   Guide for software quality assurance planning (revision of ANSI/
           IEEE Std 983)
P 982   Standard for software reliability measurement
P 1016.2   Guide to software design descriptions
P 1044   Standard for classification of software errors, faults and failures
P 1045   Standard for software productivity metrics
P 1058.2   Guide for software projects management plans
P 1059   Guide for software verification and validation
P 1061   Standard for software quality metrics methodology
P 1062   Recommended practice for third party software acquisition
P 1045   Standard for user documentation
P 1074   Standard for the software life cycle process
P 1076   Standard for system design description language
P 1077   Recommended practice for design management
P 1078   Standard for information model description language
P 1209   Recommended practice for the evaluation of CASE tools
P 1219   Standard for software maintenance
P 1220   Standard for system engineering management
P 1228   Standard for software safety plans
P 1233   Standard for system requirements specification

Other United States national standards documents

In addition to the above ANSI/IEEE documents there are the following standards.

NBS (National Bureau of Standards)

FIPS PUB 38:   Guidelines for documentation of computer programs and
               automated data systems
FIPS PUB 64:   Guidelines for documentation of computer programs and
               automated data systems for the initiation phase
FIPS PUB 101: Guideline for lifecycle validation, verification and testing of
               computer software
FIPS PUB 105: Guidelines for software documentation management
FIPS PUB 106: Guideline on software maintenance

NBS SP500-87: Management guide for software documentation
NBS SP500-88: Software development tools (guide)
NBS SP500-93: Software validation, verification and testing techniques and
               tool reference (guide)

NBS SP500-98: Planning for software validation, verification and testing (guide)

US military standards

MIL-HDBK-224: Evaluation of a contractor's software quality assurance program
MIL-STD-483: Configuration management practices for systems, equipment, munitions and computer programs
MIL-STD-490: Specification practices
MIL-STD-1521A: Technical reviews and audits of systems, equipment and computer programs
MIL-STD-2167: Military standard defence systems software development
MIL-STD-2168: Military standard software quality evaluation
MIL-STD-SQAM: Software quality assessment and measurement
DOD-STD-SDS: System software development
USAF (SD/AQ) Management guide for independent verification and validation (IV and V)

FAA

FAA-STD-018: Computer software quality program requirements

ESA standards:

ESA BSSC 1A: ESA software engineering standards (1984)
ESA BSSC 1: Software configuration management (1985)
ESA BSSC 1B: ESA software configuration management standards

RTCA standard

RTCA/DO-178A: Software considerations in airborne systems and equipment certification.

British standards

BS 5515: Code of Practice for documentation of computer-based systems
BS 5887: Code of Practice for testing of computer-based systems
BS 6224: Design structure diagram for use in program design and other logic applications (guide)
BS 6238: Performance monitoring of computer-based systems (guide)
BS-6488: Code of Practice for configuration management of computer-based systems
BS-6650: Code of Practice for the control of the operation of a computer

British defence standards

DEF-STAN 00–16/1: Guide to the achievement of quality in software
DEF-STAN 00–41: Practices and procedures for reliability and maintainability, Parts 1–5
DEF-STAN 00–55: Requirements for the procurement of safety critical software in defence equipment
DEF-STAN 00–56: Requirements for the analysis of safety critical hazards
DEF-STAN 05–21: Guide to contractor assessment. Computer QA systems, Book 4
DEF-STAN 05–57/2: Configuration management policy and procedures for defence material

Federal Republic of Germany standards (all in German)

DIN-66 230: Information processing: software documentation with fixed structure
DIN-66 231: Information processing: documentation of software development
DIN-66 232: Information processing: data documentation
DIN-66 285: Application software: principles of testing

French standards (all in French)

X 50–120: corresponds to ISO 8402
X 50–121: corresponds to ISO 9000
X 50–122: corresponds to ISO 9004
X 50–131: corresponds to ISO 9001
X 50–132: corresponds to ISO 9002
X 50–133: corresponds to ISO 9003

The following should be added to the above ISO standards:

X 50–102: Questionnaire for quality evaluation of a contractor
X 50–111: Guide for selecting quality assurance dispositions in customer–manufacturer relations
X 50–113: Quality management – guide to the drawing up of quality manuals
X 50–114: Quality manual – questionnaire guide to the drawing up of quality manuals
X 50–136: Quality management – guide for evaluation of costs resulting from non-quality
X 50–151: Guide to the drawing up of functional requirements documents

Danish standards

ECR-154: Standards and regulations for software approval and certification (ElektronikCentralen)
ECR-182: Handbook of standards and certification requirements for software (ElektronikCentralen)

Canadian standards

The following Canadian standards are relevant to critical applications:

CAN/CSA-Q.396.1.1.-89 Quality assurance program for the development of software used in critical applications
CAN/CSA-Q.396.1.2.-89 Quality assurance program for previously developed software used in critical applications

CONCLUSIONS

There are numerous standards on quality and its specific application to software, and some on system dependability have been developed during the last decade. Their use may sometimes appear restrictive and full of constraints, and some are often tempted not to apply them when they are not mandatory.

In any case, costs incurred by a poor-quality product are often out of proportion to those of implementing correct procedures. Lack of confidence by users must also be taken into account. In increasingly competitive markets the implementation of quality plans and the adoption of standards can be a question of survival for many firms.

In the past, standards have been used as a tool for protectionism by many countries, impeding exchange of goods and services. The approach followed by the Commission of the European Communities is to remove such barriers through the adoption of common European standards, which then become mandatory in each participating country. This is considered to work well for industry, but it is anticipated that there will be problems, at least for a while in the defence domains, where economic incentives are not so powerful as in industry.

It is also to be stressed that standards should evolve with feedback from their use in the field, as well as taking account of technological progress. Measurements of the efficiency of standards should always be made to evaluate them. Standards should then be submitted for revision (say, every five years or so) in order to maintain their validity on a planned basis.

Finally potential users are too often unaware of relevant standards, and some means of information dissemination is needed.

REFERENCES

Humphrey, W.S. (1989), *Managing the Software Process*, SEI Series in Software Engineering, Addison-Wesley, Reading, MA

Redmill, F.J. (1988a), *Dependability of Critical Computer Systems 1*, Elsevier Applied Science, New York

Redmill, F.J. (1988b), *Dependability of Critical Computer Systems 2*, Elsevier Applied Science, New York

Schulmeyer, G.G. and MacManus, J.L. (eds) (1987), *Handbook of Software Quality Assurance*, Van Nostrand Reinhold, New York

Tausworthe, R.C. (1978), *Standardized Development of Computer Software*, Part II, Jet Propulsion Laboratory, California Institute of Technology, Standards Pasadena, CA

5 Real-time software requirements specification and animation using extended Petri nets: theory and application
Sandro Bologna

WHY WE NEED A REQUIREMENTS SPECIFICATION MODEL

Real-time software is a special class of software with some unique characteristics, the most important of which is that often the inputs are not fixed in time or foreseeable; the timing is determined by the real world and not by the programmer. This implies that we cannot anticipate *a priori* all possible conditions with which the software may have to deal. Another important characteristic is that normally such systems are distributed among different processors, each controlling different real-world processes which potentially interact. Synchronization of different processors and/or different software processes on the same processor is a difficult problem; conceptual tools make the modelling of real-time process intercommunication easier to analyse and to implement. Real-time systems normally also have rigorous time constraints that introduce one more dimension into the problem of verification of these systems; to verify the correctness of the functional aspects is not sufficient (Quirk, 1985; IEEE, 1986).

Testing real-time software presents special problems. It is impossible to predict all the possible input situations or sequences of input events when external interrupts are a feature of the system. Furthermore, even if such tests were possible, the interpretation of the output results may be difficult. For these reasons, analytic techniques are essential to verify the correctness of real-time software. A number of conceptual and technological tools exist to model and analyse 'conventional' software, but only very few of them are applicable in this area and we continue to speak of the 'lost real-time world' (Glass, 1980).

The traditional view of requirements specification is that it produces a document in natural language which acts as an interface between a customer and a supplier. Although some interaction may precede the production of the document, it is largely taken as the 'signing on' point for the software producer. The customer issues a specification so that suppliers can provide what he or she wants. As such, the customer sees the document largely as a description of the system he would like to have. The supplier views the specification document as a list of ingredients to be put together in order to solve the customer's problem. This prescriptive view is affected not only by the difficulties of a descriptive document but also by information which, intentionally or not, pre-empts or limits the freedom of the supplier. Within this customer–description–supplier prescription framework the specification is seen as a formal separation between the parties. To the customer, it represents the minimum acceptable while to the supplier, it is the maximum required.

Recently, more rigorous treatments of specification treat it as a model of the system. Freed from the design constraints, such a model should predict the system performance which will be observed if the system is subsequently designed to meet this specification. Providing that the underlying semantics of the model are sufficiently tightly established, such a specification provides an unambiguous statement of the requirement. This is invaluable for future validation and verification of the system. By constructing a semantic model of the main critical functions, pointing out the time aspects, it is possible to verify the consistency of the requirements stated and to analyse the system behaviour, under certain conditions, for estimating the response time and to prevent system failures such as deadlocks.

Petri nets, in all their different versions and extensions, seem to be receiving much attention and several papers can be found in the literature on the use of Petri nets for real-time systems modelling and associated tools. Petri nets are now used for requirements specification and analysis in a variety of applications (Peterson, 1981; Bruno and Marchetto, 1986). Among their strengths they are easy to use and modify, and easy to comprehend without a strong mathematical background.

One of the characteristics of real-time software is that it has to work correctly within a specific time period. The variable time is not part of the original definitions of Petri nets. As a consequence, the use of Petri nets for real-time applications requires an extension of the original definition by the introduction of the variable time; these are usually called timed Peri nets. They are derived from the classical definition of Petri nets, by specifying, for each transition, a minimum firing time t_{min} and a maximum firing time t_{max} (Ghezzi et al., 1989).

PETRI NETS MODEL

According to the original definition, a Petri net is composed of the following:
1. A finite set of places, graphically depicted as circles;
2. A finite set of transitions, graphically depicted as bars;
3. A finite set of directed edges, graphically depicted as arrows connecting a place to a transition or vice versa.

Figure 5.1 is an example of Petri net.

A place is called an input place if it represents a pre-condition of a transition and is tied to the transition by a directed edge. It is called an output place if it represents a post-condition of a transition and is tied to the transition by a directed edge. By analogy, input and output transitions are defined as for the places.

In the Petri net graph a marking is a set of tokens depicted as dots which reside in the place. One or more tokens in a place mean that the represented condition holds. The set of tokens in the places of the net define its state? The occurrence of

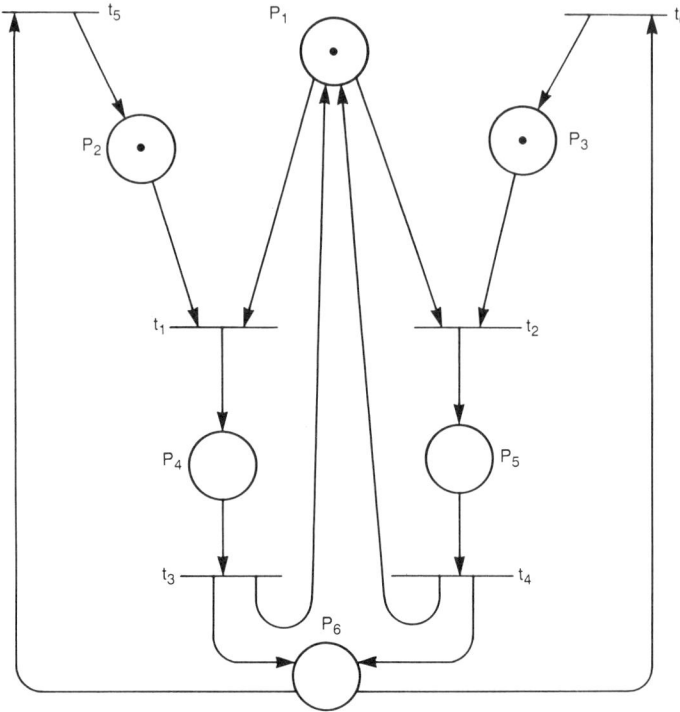

Figure 5.1

an event in a Petri net graph means that all input places of a transition must contain at least one token (i.e. all input conditions hold) and from each input place one token will be removed and to each output place one token will be added (i.e. all output conditions will become 'true'). The occurrence of an event is called a firing of a transition. In the case of Figure 5.1, both the transitions t_1 and t_2 can fire. If the transition t_1 fires first we have the state depicted in Figure 5.2, whereas if the transition t_2 fires first we have the state depicted in Figure 5.3. It should be noted that the firing of t_1 prevents the condition of firing t_2 and vice versa. In such cases the two transitions are said to be conflicting. Instead, in a situation like that depicted in Figure 5.4, both the transitions t_1 and t_3 can fire without preventing each other from doing so. In such cases the two transitions are said to be concurrent. In the first case the events modelled by the two transitions are mutually exclusive. In the second case the events may occur in any order, leading to the same result.

An important property of Petri nets is that there exists no inherent measure of time as the nets deal with cause–consequence relations only, and firings take 'zero time'. Petri nets do have non-deterministic properties. Whenever the input conditions of several events hold in a particular state, the Petri net will not give any information on which event will occur next; in this case, the sequence of firing is not determined. Thus, the sequence of firings is not totally ordered but is a partial order. In addition, describing the algorithmic aspects of the process is not

Real-time software requirements 79

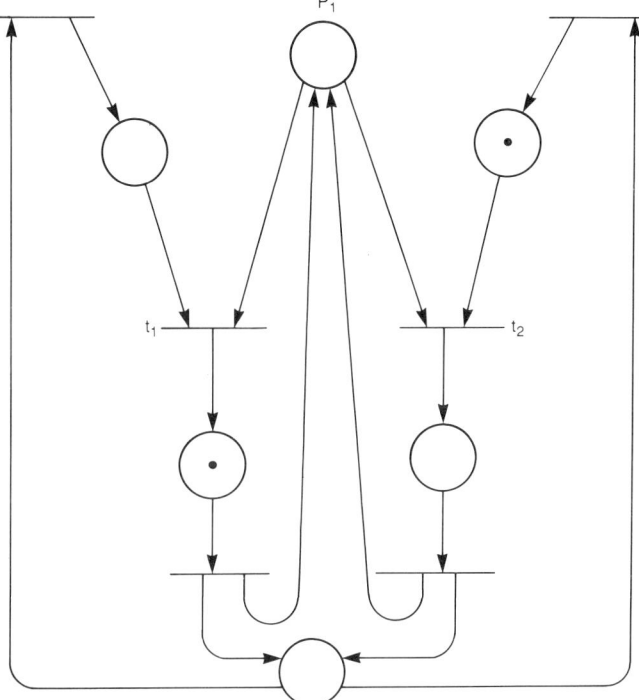

Figure 5.2

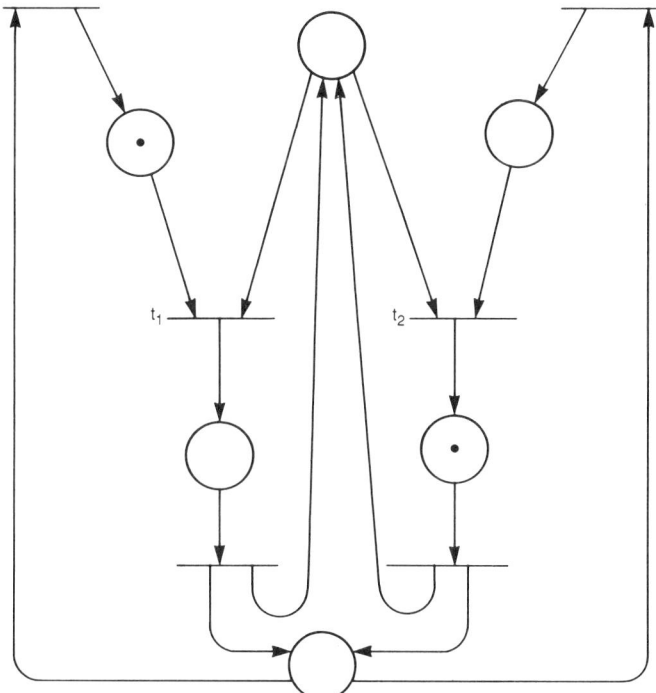

Figure 5.3

80 Safety Aspects of Computer Control

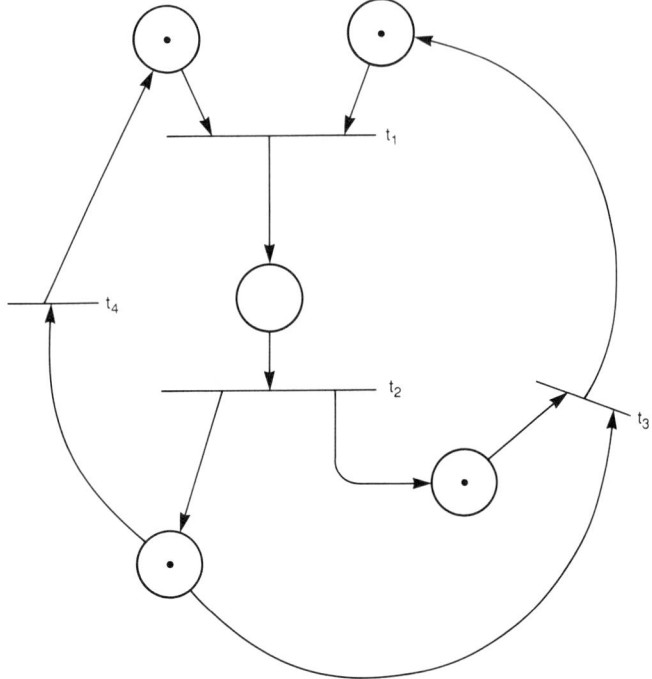

Figure 5.4

allowed. For example, it is not possible to describe the following requirement by a Petri net:

If a value read from a channel is even, then the message must be sent in channel 1, otherwise in channel 2.

EXTENDED PETRI NETS MODEL

The original definition of Petri nets suffers several limitations to be applicable to real-time systems. Among these the two majors limitations are:

1. The variable time is not part of the original definition of Petri nets;
2. Describing the algorithmic aspects of a process is not allowed by the original definition of Petri nets. This represents a serious constraint when synchronization among processes depends on the value produced during a computation.

In the extended Petri nets (EPN) (Bologna *et al.*, 1988) the following new features have been introduced:

1. An environment is defined for each token;

2. There are three types of places:
    (a) Static place; this cannot contain more than one token;
    (b) Bag place; this is a default case and it can contain more than one token, but the token movement is non-deterministic;
    (c) FIFO place; this is a bag place, but the token movement follows the first-in-first-out logic.
3. For each transition it is possible to define a predicate and a function. The predicate imposes on the token environments a condition which must be satisfied for transition firing. An *n*-tuple of tokens is said to be ready when it satisfies the transition predicate. The firing of a transition eliminates this *n*-tuple from input places and puts one token on each output place. The new environment of the tokens are computed applying the associated function.
4. For each transition a minimum and maximum firing time are defined. When the transition is enabled, it must fire in an instant between t_{min} and t_{max}; the two values t_{min} and t_{max} can be either a constant or a function of token environments.

THE SPECIFICATION LANGUAGE

Specifying a system by the EPN model means:

1. Defining a graphic structure of the net;
2. Defining the token's environment, predicates, functions and possibly t_{min} and t_{max} associated with each transition.

To implement the latter point it has been necessary to define a formal specification language to be used in parallel with the graphic notation already introduced to represent the original Petri nets. This language is based on the following syntax description.

Token environment definition

The syntax to define an environment is:

⟨environment⟩ ::= "{"["⟨"token_name", "string_value"⟩"]"⟨list_of_pair⟩"}"
⟨pair⟩ ::= "⟨"⟨name⟩", "⟨value⟩"⟩"

The fields *name* and *value* can be computed by means of a function associated with the transition or can be constant. In this case the syntax is:

⟨name⟩ ::= ⟨identifier⟩
⟨value⟩ ::= ⟨integer_constant⟩ | ⟨array_constant⟩ | ⟨record_constant⟩
⟨array_constant⟩ ::= "["⟨list_of_values⟩"]"
⟨record_constant⟩ ::= "⟨"⟨list_of_values⟩"⟩"

It is also possible to associate with a place a token without an environment. This type of token is called 'pure' because it is comparable to the tokens of the classical definition of Petri nets. This can be useful in the early phase of system development, when the model is not fully specified.

Places definition

In the EPN there are three types of places: static, bag and FIFO. The syntax to define places is:

⟨place_type⟩ ::= ⟨static_place⟩ | ⟨bag_place⟩ | ⟨queue_place⟩
⟨static_place⟩ ::= ⟨place_identifier⟩ static ":"⟨token_type⟩":"⟨initial_value⟩
⟨initial_value⟩ ::= ⟨list_of_values⟩
⟨bag_places⟩ ::= ⟨place_identifier⟩ bag [of ⟨token_type⟩]
⟨queue_place⟩ ::= ⟨place_identifier⟩ queue [of ⟨token_type⟩]

Predicate definition

The syntax of predicate definition is similar to the Pascal logic expression:

⟨predicate⟩ ::= ⟨boolean_expression⟩

where ⟨*boolean_expression*⟩ can be constructed by the usual operators logical, arithmetic, relational and the traditional use of parentheses. If a transition is defined without an associated predicate, it is assumed that the predicate has the constant value true and that each n-tuple of tokens is ready.

Functions definition

The definition of a function associated with a transition implies the definition of a function for each output place of the transition. The syntax is:

⟨function_definition⟩ ::=
[auxiliary_function_definition]⟨list_of_place_function_definitions⟩
Each ⟨*place_function_definition*⟩ is constituted by a pairs list ⟨*identification, value*⟩ with the syntax:

⟨place_function_definition⟩ ::=
"{"[⟨token_name_definition⟩;] [⟨list_of_pair_definition]"}"
⟨token_name_definition⟩ ::= "⟨"token_name", "⟨string_expression⟩"⟩"

where ⟨*string_expression*⟩ is an expression that produces a result of the string type.

Place invariants definition

For a place it is possible to define a predicate. Since it must be true for each token associated with the place, it can be defined as an invariant. For example, if a token environment is constituted by a buffer it is possible to make the condition that the buffer must not be full in a specified place. The invariant definition can be used as a comment, but also it can be employed in the process of symbolic execution. The syntax of the invariant definition is the same as the predicate transition:

$\langle place\_invariant \rangle ::= \langle boolean\_expression \rangle$

Time constraints definition

The syntax to define time constraints is:

$\langle time\_constraints \rangle ::= \langle t\_min \rangle "," \langle t\_max \rangle$

where *t_min* and *t_max* are integer values.

EXTENDED PETRI NETS ENVIRONMENT

An environment based on the EPN conceptual model has been implemented. Before starting to list the main features of the environment we will mention some of the requirements that a modern software specification and analysis environment should satisfy.

It must support the definition of software requirement specification in a simple and natural manner. A system requiring an effort to introduce a conceptual idea in an appropriate notation representing it loses much of its utility. For this reason, great importance is put on the user interface of the system, and it is now universally recognized that there is a utility to using graphical and pictorial notations. In addition, it is useful to have available a notation specific to the field of application.

It must support, when desirable, a formal and rigorous definition of the system requirement specifications. For many so-called 'real-time safety-critical applications' informal or semi-formal notations are not sufficient to describe the desired behaviour of the system with the required rigour. From here the requirement is that the environment should support formal notation.

It must include appropriate analysis tools. It is not sufficient to support only the definition of the software requirements specification, it is also necessary that the environment includes tools for the dynamic analysis of the model.

It must support the preparation of the specifications in an incremental way. The activity of software requirements specification is very complex and cannot be expected to be done at once, especially at the very beginning of the development phase. From the conceptual point of view it is normal to perform it in an iterative and incremental way. For this reason, it is important that the environment supports this natural way.

It must support the description of asynchronous activities in a natural way. Many of the systems commercially available and publicized as oriented to the specification of real-time systems are based on models of type synchronous (i.e.

the finite state automata). We believe that such models lead to an unnatural specification and environments based on asynchronous models should be preferred.

It must explicitly support the time concept. This is a requirement of primary importance for the specification of real-time critical software, for the simple reason that the correct behaviour of the system is not only a function of the correct definition and implementation of the algorithm but also of the time given to the different actions required.

Bearing in mind the requirements mentioned above, an environment based on the EPN conceptual model has been implemented. The environment includes two tools at present: the net editor and the prototyper.

Net editor

The net editor is a tool that allows the construction, modification, storage and retrieval from a library, and printing of extended Petri nets as described earlier. Net editing is performed by selecting appropriate commands from a menu through the use of a mouse and placing the objects on the screen by that mouse. Textual editing is done by the use of masks. The net editor, as with other parts of the environment, is an application of MS-Windows from the programming point of view.

Net animation

Specifications can be animated, i.e. they can be executed by a component of the environment called a prototyper. By animating the net it is possible to test formal specifications against the desired behaviour. This is the main tool for analysing specifications, since the ambiguity prevents most useful properties from being checked algorithmically. As an example, there is no way to prove algorithmically whether a certain state of the net is reachable or not. However, one can have 'satisfactory' evidence of the truth of the statement by animating the net.

There are several modes of execution of EPNs: batch versus interactive, numeric versus symbolic. In batch mode a net is executed under certain user-provided directives. In interactive mode a net is executed step by step, each step being the firing of a single transition, chosen under the user's control.

By numeric execution we denote the conventional processing by which the actual values of variables are manipulated. In contrast, symbolic execution means that variables can hold symbolic values represented by symbolic expression. The interest of symbolic execution is that a symbolic run represents a set of numeric runs on actual data.

As for the editor component of the environment, interaction with the prototyper is accomplished via a user-friendly interface using pop-up menus, dialog boxes, push-buttons, etc.

In an interactive session, results of the animation are shown in two windows. One displays the 'token game', i.e. the evolution of the marking of the net. The other contains a textual description of the environment. Upon request, predicates and function associated with transitions may be visualized.

Menus and commands

The menu of commands are of type 'pop-up'. The first line of the screen presents the different categories of executable commands. By selecting one using of mouse it is possible to see on the vertical line a list of options applicable for the selected command. The desired option can be selected by the mouse.

AN EXAMPLE OF MODELLING WITH EXTENDED PETRI NETS

The following example shows how systems may be modelled and analysed by the use of extended Petri nets and the associated environment.

Figure 5.5 models the behaviour of a weapons system: it can be decided to shoot at a target once the target has been framed and the pointing system is ready

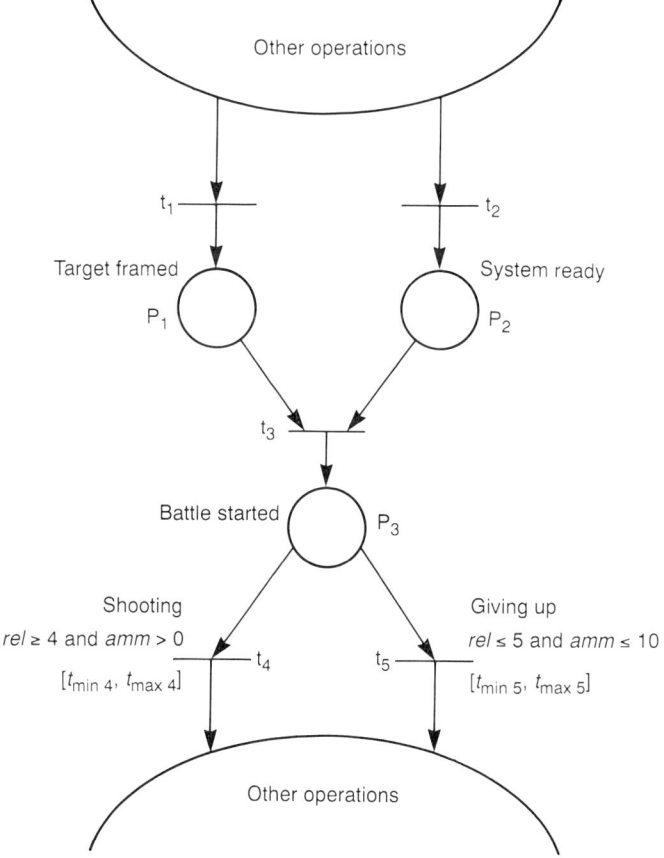

Figure 5.5

to operate. In Figure 5.5 some transitions and places are labelled by comments for easy referencing. Transition t_1 models the framing of a target. Its firing produces an environment in place p_1, representing the target framed. The environment produced contains information on the framed target. For instance, it has information on the relevance of the target, stored as the value of an integer variable *rel*. The cloud that is input to transitions t_1 and t_2 represents a portion of net whose internal details are deliberately left unspecified. Depending on the structure of such a sub-net, transition t_1 might fire several times before transition t_3 fires, thus modelling the framing of a number of different targets. For simplicity, we assume here that a target, once framed, is available to be hit at any subsequent time. Transition t_2 represents the end of a set of actions, represented informally by the cloud. An environment in place p_2 represents the fact that the pointing system is ready for operations. The environment produced contains information on the availability of ammunition, stored as the value of a variable *amm*. We assume that transition t_2 does not fire two or more consecutive times before transition t_3 fires; i.e. the net is such that, at most, one environment will always be contained in place p_2, which represents the fact that only one pointing system exists.

Transition t_3 models the engagement of a battle. The environment it removes from place p_1 upon firing represents the choice of a target among those previously framed. The environment it produces in place p_3 contains variables *rel* and *amm*, whose values are given by the values of the corresponding variables in the removed environments. The battle can either be concluded by a shot (transition t_4 fires) or not (transition t_5 fires). In both cases, the battle leads into a configuration not modelled here. We represent this by edges leading into a cloud which includes 'other operations'.

The firing of transitions depends not only on the presence of environments in their input places but also on particular timing characteristics and conditions associated with the transitions. The time intervals $[0, \infty]$ associated with transitions t_1 and t_2 simply state that the firing time of the transition can be any positive real, which reflects the fact that a target can be identified at any time and the pointing system can become ready at any time.

Finally, transitions t_4 and t_5 may fire within the time intervals $[t_{min4}, t_{max4}]$ and $[t_{min5}, t_{max5}]$, respectively (we assume that these time intervals overlap). They can fire conditioned on the relevance of the target and the availability of ammunition. In particular, t_4 can fire only if the target is relevant enough (associated predicate: $rel \leq 4$ and $amm > 0$). Transition t_5 can fire only if the target is not relevant and there is a shortage of ammunition (associated predicate: $rel \leq 5$ and $amm \leq 10$). Note that there may be situations where both transitions t_4 and t_5 are concurrently enabled, since the predicates are not mutually exclusive. Thus, a non-deterministic choice has to be made.

CONCLUSIONS

The development of embedded real-time systems is an area characterized by two major factors – high complexity and hard real-time constraints. The benefits of using executable, formal models to simulate the behaviour of a future system are well known. The use of Petri nets as a means of formally representing the software requirements specification has the benefit of offering the basis for extensive animation of the requirements. Petri nets can be used for proving specific properties of the system before implementation.

A prototype based on the EPN conceptual model has been implemented to demonstrate the feasibility of the approach. Future work is needed to deal with the problem of complexity of real-life systems. This problem, together with time aspects and also problems in connection with distributed software development, is addressed in the IPTES project inside the ESPRIT II Programme of the CEC, where the use of Petri nets is hidden from the user and used as an internal execution model of the description made by SA/RT – VDM.

ACKNOWLEDGEMENTS

Part of the work presented here has been developed within the framework of a Research Contract given from ENEA to ARG. The author wishes to thank C. Ghezzi, D. Mandrioli, S. Morasca, M. Pezze, F. Pisacane and A. Tursilli for their contributions.

REFERENCES

Bologna, S., Pisacane, F., Ghezzi, C. and Mandrioli, D. (1988), 'An environment for requirements specification and analysis of real-time software based on timed Petri nets', *Proceedings IFAC SAFECOMP '88*, 9–11 November, Pergamon Press, New York

Bruno, G. and Marchetto, G. (1986), 'Process-translatable Petri nets for the rapid prototyping of process control systems', *IEEE Transactions on Software Engineering*, **SE-12**, No. 2, February

Ghezzi, C., Mandrioli, D., Morasca, S. and Pezze, M. (1989), 'A general way to put time in Petri nets', *Proceedings Fifth International Workshop on Software Specification and Design*, 19–20 May, IEEE Computer Society Press, New York

Glass, R. (1980), 'Real-time: the "lost world of software debugging and testing",' *Communication of ACM*, **23**, No. 5

IEEE (1986), *Transactions on Software Engineering*, Special Issue on Reliability and Safety in Real-time Process Control, **SE-12**, No. 9, September

Peterson, J. (1981), *Petri Net Theory and the Modelling of Systems*, Prentice-Hall, Englewood Cliffs, NJ

Quirk, W.J. (ed.) (1985), *Verification and Validation of Real-time Software*, Springer-Verlag, New York

6 Independent software verification and validation in practice: methodological and managerial aspects
Sandro Bologna

WHAT IS IT?

Independent verification and validation (IV&V) is a technical activity performed by a team independent of the developer, aimed to increase the reliability of the product and to provide visibility into the quality of the development process. The objectives of an IV&V are to:
1. Improve project visibility;
2. Improve system reliability and operability;
3. Insure that the system properly performs all intended functions, and does not perform unintended ones;
4. Reduce life-cycle cost by exposing errors as early as possible.

In order to achieve high reliability, a primary goal of verification is to detect software development errors which occur throughout the life cycle and to ensure that each software product meets the objectives specified in the specification for such a product. Verification is a confidence-raising process. It implies increasing confidence in the belief that the software will operate as intended.

WHEN IT IS DONE?

Because of the cost, an IV&V activity should be initiated only if it is required from the application or by contract, or when it is economically justified in terms of potential life-cycle benefits. A fault in requirements costs many times more to correct if it is not discovered until test and integration.

Verification emerged in the aerospace and nuclear industries from the need for reliable software in systems where an error would cause mission failure and result in time and financial loss, if not in loss of human lives. Verification is now widely applied to computer programs performing functions such as chemical process control, medical monitoring systems, on-line railway systems control, missile tracking, and in any other system where the risk is extremely high.

HOW IT IS DONE?

The IV&V process in its most cost-effective form is carried out in parallel with the software development cycle, using a time-phased sequence of steps and techniques (Redmill, 1988). Independent verification and validation should be tailored to the unique needs of the project and the overall system requirements. A software verification plan is required for a specific project to agree the verification policy to be adopted for the project (Buckland and Reifer, 1982). There is no single approach that can be universally applied to all projects. Human judgement is needed to adapt the concepts and methods to the specifics of the job in a manner that is cost effective.

The software verification plan is a living document throughout the period of system development. It should be updated to reflect details as they become available during each development phase. Verification results in a systematic procedure of review, analysis and testing which are employed throughout the software development life cycle, beginning with the software planning phase through to the end of software use. Planning is the key to establishing an effective and appropriate verification activity. The plan represents an agreement between all parties specifying how the particular verification tasks should be accomplished. The verification process must be tailored to satisfy the needs of a specific project. The purpose of the verification plan is to identify and describe the verification strategies and activities to be performed and the techniques and tools appropriate for the project and its surrounding environment. The plan should be prepared according to standards.

The interaction between the project planning and the verification planning activities is important. The project planning activity will drive the verification planning activity, which will, in turn, provide input and feedback to the former. Important interactions are:

1. The needs and objectives of the verification program must support the project mission;
2. Time and resource requirements for the verification activities must be factored into overall schedules and budget.

WHAT DOES IT INCLUDE?

For a given project, the extent of the IV&V effort is determined by a trade-off between confidence in the quality of the system and the cost of IV&V; that is, how much risk is acceptable. Criteria for determining which verification activities should be performed for a given project are critical and must be identified prior to embarking on it. The first step in the preparation of the verification plan is to identify the verification goals, formulated from software requirements and software product standards. Once these goals are established, the extent of the IV&V effort may be determined, together with techniques and tools chosen to help achieve these goals. The IV&V effort has to match the budget, schedule and contractual constraints (e.g. documentation to be produced). The selection of techniques and tools is strongly influenced by availability, acquisition cost, implementation cost, time required for acquisition, feasibility of implementing each technique or tool, and the need for training of project personnel.

Since the benefits of IV&V are highly dependent on a reviewer's independent objectivity and evaluation, the requirement that the verification be performed by persons different from the design team is preferable and sometimes mandatory. The administrative/organizational separation between verifier and designer depends on the type of system to be verified and validated. V&V for a safety system is more stringent in this regard, and requires that those individuals who do the verification do not participate in the design or implementation. In any case, a verifier should have a technical competence comparable to that of a designer. Traceability is important, not only to document the V&V activities but also to record appropriate actions taken to resolve discrepancies. Thus a V&V program is, by its nature, oriented heavily towards documentation and the ability to trace changes in project documents.

WHAT ARE THE BENEFITS?

The benefits of IV&V are not easy to measure. How, then, do we determine whether or not IV&V is worth while? Some of the factors to be considered are:

1. Increased reliability;
2. Increased management visibility;
3. Early error detection;
4. Reduced life-cycle cost.

IV&V reduces expense and limits risk by exposing errors as early as possible in the life cycle. Errors discovered and corrected during development do not reach the user. Thus, operations are not impacted by downtime and re-runs, and unwarranted expense. According to experience made of several large software development organizations, if an error originates in the requirements phase, and if that requirement error is incorporated into the design, then the cost to correct the error during design will be one to two times more expensive than to correct it during the requirements phase. If the designed requirements error is incorporated into the implementation, the cost to correct it during implementation will be two to four times more expensive than in the requirements phase. If the implemented error enters the system test phase, the cost to correct it is four to eight times more.

In addition, verification, as applied to computer software, imposes such an organized, systematic development discipline that verification requirements have caused major changes in the practice of software developers. Manual programming practices have been replaced by planned systematic program development. Each phase of this development is considered completed only when the phase has been documented sufficiently that an independent person can easily understand and evaluate the documentation.

HOW DO WE KNOW IT IS NEEDED?

Independent verification and validation is mandatory in many safety-critical applications. Mission criticality is the most important parameter to decide if we need IV&V or not (IEC, 1991). Selection of the appropriate level of IV&V is governed by many parameters, the more important being:

1. Criticality of the application;
2. Impact of an operational error;
3. Available budget and staff resources.

Based upon the assessment of criticality, a minimum acceptable set of IV&V requirements will be formulated in the verification plan.

HOW MUCH TIME AND MONEY DOES IT TAKE?

IV&V may require considerable resources. The IV&V team must be composed of members maintaining a wide range of expertise and related experience. The potential benefits of IV&V are not free; the more comprehensive the effort, the greater the cost. Experience indicates that IV&V activities cost about 40% of that expended for software development. The major cost of IV&V is the labour required to implement the activities defined in the verification plan and to set up a suitable verification environment.

VERIFICATION AND VALIDATION PRINCIPLES

This section describes a number of concepts associated with the V&V process (Bologna and Rao, 1985; Wilburn, 1983). In general, they cover the V&V activities during the system development and implementation process and will affect one or more stages of the system development/implementation process as illustrated in IEEE Standard for Software Verification and Validation Plans (IEEE, 1986).

Integrated throughout software life cycle

The V&V process should be integrated into all phases of the system development life cycle rather than isolated into a separate testing stage which takes place long after the design has been developed. Traditionally, in the past, whatever verification took place was confined solely to the testing phase. Verification is most effective and efficient when applied from the beginning of the development program, and not only in a testing phase.

Applied to all products of software development

Within each of the software development activities there are many software products. Verification should be applied to all these products in order to accomplish a quality software product.

Software requirements specification mandatory

The software requirements document, which is the first product in the software development life cycle, is a necessary requirement for any verification program. The software requirements specification forms the foundation for determining the correctness of a software system. As its name implies, it specifies what the software is supposed to do. Unless the verifier knows this, it is essentially an impossible task to verify the program.

Systematic development methods required

Differences in the quality of the software are directly related to the degree of a systematic development methodology that was used. An orderly approach to system development supported by clear and concise documentation reduces the verification costs. The documentation structure must present a traceable, step-by-step approach to the development of the system and its application. The translation of information from one stage of development to the next must be sufficient to be understood by persons other than the originator.

Cannot be done using only one technique

Traditionally, testing has been the only technique of software verification. However, a single technique of verification cannot provide sufficient substantiation of the correctness and reliability of the software.

Accurate records of V&V activities

There are many documents that will have to be generated during the system life cycle which record the V&V activities. All these, as well as the system development documents, have to be managed according a specific project configuration management plan.

ORGANIZATIONAL PRINCIPLES

The primary responsibilities of the verification team are to verify that the software correctly performs the stated functions, to identify incorrect or incomplete design documentation, and to discover ambiguous or incorrect translations during the relevant stages of the design. The software verification team performs the verification activity, independent of the software design team, under the technical guidance of the chief software verifier.

Chief software verifier

The chief verifier is the team leader responsible for all technical matters concerning the verification of the software, including all associated internal and external interfaces, and ensuring that all parts of the software design and implementation are adequately verified. The chief verifier:

1. Supervises and consults with the verification team in software technical matters;
2. Ensures that defined parts of the design are adequately verified by the verifiers;
3. Determines and ensures the conduct of the required re-verification whenever a software design change has occurred, both during and after the verification process;
4. Ensures that all verifier comments are resolved;
5. Ensures that the results of verification testing and their review are adequately documented by the verifiers;
6. Ensures transmittal of all verification documentation and products to a retrieval file in accordance with the configuration management plan;
7. Ensures transmittal of all verification documentation and products to any other required groups;
8. Reviews and approves design/procurement of all verification support products such as test support hardware and software;
9. Checks the documentation compiled by the verifiers for completeness, clarity and correctness;
10. Maintains all records, documentation, forms, etc. until they are transferred to archival files.

Software verifiers

The verifiers are responsible for the parts of a project that have been assigned to them, which will include one or more of the following functions:

1. Verifying that the software design specifications are complete, accurate and a faithful translation of software design requirements into software design specifications;
2. Ensuring that the software implementation specifications (source code) are complete and accurate, and are a faithful translation of software design specifications into software implementations specifications;
3. Documenting discrepancies for transmittal to the design group for resolution;
4. Designing test cases, selecting test input data and determining the expected resulting output data for each of those test cases;
5. Preparing software test specifications, which shall document the rationale for test cases selected, their test inputs data and expected and actual output results;
6. Performing structural and functional testing in the host environment;

7. Evaluating the collected output results for correctness of functional performance of the entity;
8. Ensuring that adequate structural test coverage is provided by the selected test cases;
9. Identifying and submitting to hardware verification those software entities that have hardware interfaces that need to be verified;
10. Documenting the results of verification activities;
11. Preparing verification test results reports.

Interfacing groups and communications

A major part of the verification process is based on communications between the design and the verification teams resulting from the systematic documentation of the activities identified in the system life cycle. Communications between the software verification team and all interfacing groups shall be established with formal records of all comments, discrepancies and resolutions thereof, prepared and maintained for inspection and retrieval as needed.

CONCLUSIONS

The benefits of using independent software verification and validation are well known among the people working with safety critical applications. Less evident is how to decide when, if not mandatory, it is economically convenient to use it, or how it should be tailored to the unique needs of a specific project.

Verification and validation must be carefully planned before starting with the project and documented in the V & V Plan, that will define the management organization, standards and documentation, practice and convention used, problem reporting and corrective action, etc. Developing a good V & V Plan requires the application of sound technical and management principles. To ensure consistent, traceable and auditable high performance of the individuals involved in the V & V activities, several pragmatic issues such as quality of documentation, details and staging of activities, etc., should be resolved prior to the starting of the V & V activities.

REFERENCES

Bologna, S. and Rao, D. M. (1985), Verification and validation program for a distributed computer system for safety application, *Proceedings IFAC SAFECOMP '85*, 1–3 October, Pergamon Press, New York

Buckland, D. E. and Reifer, D. J. (1982), *Independent Verification and Validation Plan*, Report prepared by Reifer Consultants, Inc., 25550 Hawthorne Blvd, Torrance, CA 90505 for Goddard Space Flight Center, Greenbelt, Maryland 20771

Institute of Electrical and Electronic Engineers (IEEE) (1986) *IEEE Standard for Software Verification and Validation Plans*

International Electrotechnical Commission (IEC) (1991) SC65A, WG9, *Software for computers in the application of industrial safety-related systems*, IEC SC65A (Secretariat) 122

Redmill, F. J. (1988) *Dependability of Critical Computer Systems – 1* (Guidelines produced by The European Workshop on Industrial Computer Systems – Technical Committee 7 (EWICS TC7)). Elsevier Applied Science, New York

Wilburn, N. P. (1983), *Guidelines for software verification*, Report prepared by Hanford Engineering Development Laboratory for the US Department of Energy

7 Formal methods: use and relevance for the development of safety-critical systems
John A. McDermid

INTRODUCTION

At the time of writing (May 1990) there is considerable debate about the use and relevance of formal methods in the development of safety-critical computer-based systems. Some of the protagonists claim (or at least are said to claim by their detractors) that formal methods offer a complete solution to the problems of safety-critical software development. Others claim (or at least are said to claim by the formal methods protagonists!) that formal methods are of little or no use – or that their utility is severely limited by the cost of applying the techniques. The aim in this chapter is to try to cast some light on this debate and to discuss from a technico-philosophical viewpoint the benefits and limitations of formal methods in this context. It is, however, perhaps useful to expose my prejudices now by summarizing my views – *formal methods are both over-sold and under-used*.

In order to provide justification for this view it is necessary first to lay some terminological groundwork and to consider current practices. The term *formal method* is widely used, but with differing meanings. In this chapter we use it to refer to methods with a sound basis in mathematics. We use the term *structured method* to refer to methods which are well defined but which do not have a sound basis in mathematics for (completely) describing functionality. Technically the most significant difference between the two classes of techniques is that formal methods permit functionality to be specified precisely whereas structured methods only allow system structure to be specified precisely. (Interestingly, many formal techniques are weak at describing system structure and boundaries.) In practice, some formal techniques also explicitly address other, non-functional, aspects of systems (e.g. their timing behaviour).

It is possible to distinguish five types, or classes, of formal methods which can be roughly characterized as follows:

1. *Model-based approaches*, giving an explicit (albeit abstract) definition of system (program) state and operations which transform the state, but no explicit representation of concurrency (e.g Z and VDM);
2. *Algebraic approaches*, giving an implicit definition of operations by relating the behaviour of different operations without defining state, but again no explicit representation of concurrency (e.g. OBJ and PLUSS);
3. *Process algebras*, giving an explicit model of concurrent processes and representing behaviour by means of constraints on allowable observable communication between the processes (e.g. CSP and CCS);
4. *Logic-based approaches*, a variety of approaches using logic to describe properties of systems, including low-level specification of program behaviour

and specification of system timing behaviour (e.g. temporal and interval logics);
5. *Net-based approaches*, giving an implicitly concurrent model of the system in terms of (causal) data flow through a network, including representing conditions under which data can flow from one node in the net to another (e.g. Petri nets and predicate transition nets).

In practice, the distinctions are not always clear, and there are hybrid methods which incorporate facets of more than one approach. Most of the methods have set theory and predicate logic as their underlying basis, so there is some technical similarity between all the approaches. However, there are significant differences between the expressive power of the methods, and this was the essence of our classification above. In commenting on formal methods we will, where appropriate, identify the classes of method to which the comments apply.

Formal methods can be employed in two distinct ways. First, they can be used for production of specifications which are then the basis of a fairly conventional system development. Second, formal specifications can be produced as above, then used as a basis against which the correctness of the program is verified (proven). In the first case the mathematics is used, essentially, as a documentation medium. The benefits of the formalism include precision, abstraction, conciseness and manipulability. Manipulations might include consistency checking, automatic generation of prototypes or animation and derivation of properties by means of proof. In the second case similar benefits accrue, but, in addition, it is possible to prove the correspondence of program and specification – to show that the program does what it is specified to do – thus giving software development the same degree of certainty as a mathematical proof.

Structured methods are used fairly widely in industry. Formal methods are employed much less widely, but their use is on the increase. In practice, most industrial-scale applications of formal methods have involved model-based approaches where programs were developed 'conventionally' from formal specifications (the first case above). Formal verification of programs is much less common and the main examples, outside academia, are in the security community in the USA.

There are some examples of the use of formal methods for safety-critical systems, most notably by Rolls-Royce and Associates (Hill, 1988). Reports from such projects indicate that formal methods were effective and contributed to the success of the work. Thus there is some practical evidence that formal methods are of utility in producing safety-critical systems, although it is always difficult to isolate the factors that lead to successful projects. Also, the use of formal methods is advocated by a number of standards, most notably Interim DefStan 00–55 in the UK. This standard implies that the techniques are of central importance in the development of software for safety-critical systems.

The chapter is based on the premise that formal methods are, in principle, valuable to industry for at least some aspects of the development of safety-critical systems and that their introduction represents a signifiant step in the evolution of software development towards a true engineeering discipline. However, there are theoretical and philosophical limitations to the methods, and it is not entirely clear how relevant and useful they are for solving the particular problems encountered in the development of safety-critical systems. This is the main point which we hope to illuminate in this chapter. As well as discussing limitations of formal methods, in principle, the chapter sets out what the author sees as being the practical problem with formal methods, *vis-a-vis* application in the development of safety-critical systems, given their current state of development.

In the next section we set out the issues which have to be addressed in developing software for safety-critical systems, focusing particularly on how we gain confidence in the safety of systems containing software. In subsequent sections we discuss the (potential) role of formal methods in the software development life cycle and illustrate (inevitably briefly) the nature and capabilities of current formal methods. This enables us to return to our main concern: the utility and relevance of formal methods, both in principle and in practice, in the development of safety-critical computer-based systems.

THE DEVELOPMENT OF SOFTWARE FOR SAFETY-CRITICAL SYSTEMS

Even when used in a safety-critical application, software cannot, directly (of itself), cause loss of life but it may control some equipment that does so. Thus software can contribute to the safety (or otherwise) of a system. In practice, we often apply the term *safety integrity* to software to denote the extent to which the integrity (freedom from impairment) of the software contributes to the overall safety of a system.

Software in safety-critical systems

We might think that we simply require software in safety-critical systems to be highly reliable, but this misses a key point. First, software can fail frequently but still not lead to unsafe behaviour – if the failures do not cause hazardous consequences. (Reports indicate that there have been five 'anomalies' in the software controlling the trip systems in French nuclear power plants, but none of these have led to safety-related 'incidents'.) Second, reliable software can be unsafe – if in the rare event of failure there are catastrophic consequences. This suggests that we need to consider both failure modes and their consequences. However, for the purpose of discussing the effectiveness of formal methods, we need to focus primarily on failures. Although we cannot take reliability as the only measure of safety, or safety integrity, we must accept that reliability remains a valid measure and objective – so long as it is related to classes of failure which can lead to hazards.

Software is quite different to hardware in that its only 'failure modes' are through design faults, rather than any form of physical mechanism such as ageing. Some classes of software faults (e.g. timing faults) may only be exposed as hardware ages, so software can *appear* to age, but this is simply belated exposure of a latent design flaw (or perhaps a flaw in specification), not genuine ageing. In reality, therefore, software failures reflect human fallibility, and although we have good psychological models of human error in some situations (see, for example, Reason, 1979) we do not have good models of error in software development on which to base models of software reliability.

Further, software behaviour is discontinuous, that is, a small change in inputs can cause a very large change in outputs, timing or other properties, because the flow of control in the program (usually) depends on the input values. Perhaps more pertinently, slight changes in conjunctions of inputs can cause major changes in behaviour – even with non-faulty software. Consequently we cannot easily extrapolate to future performance from past performance, nor apply factors of safety to achieve adequate reliability levels as we might do in conventional mechanical or electronic systems. This means that it is relatively difficult to derive reliability figures for software. Specifically, for the reliability levels which some certification standards require (e.g. the oft-quoted 10^{-9} failures per hour) a statistical analysis shows that impractically long testing times would be required to give confidence that such levels of reliability had been achieved in a software-controlled system (Abdel-Ghaly *et al.*, 1986).

Because of the above two problems there is considerable risk associated with using software in safety-critical systems, and it is common (and good) practice to avoid the use of software in critical applications, or to design systems in such a way that the software cannot contribute to catastrophic failures. Nonetheless, there are applications where it is impossible or impractical to achieve the requisite functionality without making software a critical component of the system. A 'fly-by-wire' aircraft is probably the most obvious example where the functional requirements make it impractical to develop the system without computers and software, but the system is inherently safety-critical. Simplistically, we might think that we need to eliminate causes of failure that can compromise safety or, at least, to 'do the best we can' to eliminate failure causes. However, the issue is rather more subtle.

In practice, economics or other factors may dictate that we do not 'do the best possible'. For example, for a medical application, especially where there is a perceived market price for the product, we may have to develop a product to the stage where the life-saving properties outweigh the life-threatening ones, and this may preclude using the best technology. Similarly, bringing a product to market quickly may save lives, even though the product is not developed to the highest standards. To simplify our discussion, we largely ignore these constraints on the choice of techniques, although there is a substantial body of work on measures of safety based on the notion of 'willingness to pay' (see, for example, Jones-Lee *et al.*, 1985).

The decision to use software in such a context should be based on an analysis which shows that the risks are likely to be outweighed by the benefits but, in practice, such decisions are often made on an *ad hoc* rather than a systematic basis. In the following we assume that software is at least partially responsible for system safety, whether or not the decision to use software in such a context was arrived at in a satisfactory manner.

Goals and principles for achieving safety integrity

In this section we discuss the objectives of techniques for producing software with a high degree of safety integrity – although, following Laprie (1989), we more often use the term *dependable*, or *dependability*. Also we present some fundamental principles which, we believe, facilitate the assessment of the contribution to safety of various (alternative) software development techniques. To simplify the discussion, we will assume that the system to be produced is to be assessed by some agency independent of the developers. This is the case in many industries (e.g. civil aerospace) and probably should always be true where human life is at stake. We also assume that normal software engineering discipline is applied (see, for example, Macro and Buxton, 1987) and focus on the *additional* issues which affect dependable systems.

Goals

A characteristic of safety-critical systems is that a failure can be catastrophic. Thus in developing software for safety-critical systems we have to achieve two distinct goals:

1. To develop the software in such a way that it is impossible or extremely unlikely that its behaviour (execution) will lead to a catastrophic failure; and
2. To provide *evidence* that will convince both the developers and the assessment authority of the dependability of the software (that the software will not, or at least it is very unlikely to, cause catastrophic behaviour in its operational environment).

Note that the above points cannot be established for software in isolation, but we will deal with software as independently of its operational environment as possible. We used terms such as 'extremely unlikely' above without quantification. Ideally, we would like to attach a reliability figure or probability to these undesirable events. However, this is not necessarily straightforward as we noted above, and we will return to this point later.

As a consequence of the above observations we can see that we would like to achieve (and to demonstrate) for the software in a system that:

1. Its requirement specification does not admit (allow) executions which would lead to catastrophic failure in its intended operational context;
2. It is free from design flaws which could lead to catastrophic failure in its intended operational context; i.e. that it satisfies its specification or, at least, the safety-relevant portion thereof (note that this might involve taking into account new failure modes which are only apparent at the design, rather than the requirements, level);
3. It can protect itself against the failures of other components of the system (which are not trapped by other means, e.g. hardware memory protection), and from external threats or attacks which could cause catastrophic failure.

These are objectives, and it is useful to discuss the degree to which they are attainable.

Demonstrating to our complete satisfaction that we have achieved the first objective, i.e. adequate specifications, is generally accepted to be impossible (see, for example, Leveson, 1986 and below for discussions of this point). In essence, the difficulty is that we do not have any way of knowing that we have identified all the possible threats to, or failure modes of, the system, so we can never be sure that our specification(s) is(are) complete. However, it is possible to apply techniques which reduce the likelihood that the specification is catastrophically flawed (see below).

As indicated above, design is a fallible human activity, but it is rather less problematical than specification, so we can (usually) be rather more confident that we have got the design and implementation 'right' with respect to the specification than that we have got the specification 'right'. Clearly, the distinction arises because, once we have written the specification, we have bounded the issues which we need to address in the later stages, so we are less likely to make major omissions in the design and implementation. We have previously used the term *assurance* for the degree of confidence that we have in the specifications and design (McDermid, 1989b) and we amplify on the issue of levels, or degrees, of assurance below.

There are generally applicable techniques which can assist with the third point, e.g. solutions to the so-called Byzantine Generals problems (Lamport *et al.*, 1982) where each system component assumes that all other components can fail in any manner, including maliciously. There are also techniques (e.g. the work of Ezilchelvan and Shrivastava, 1986), which are effective in the face of rather less pessimistic fault assumptions. However, achievement of protection against failures is largely application dependent, so we will primarily concern ourselves with the first two points.

The limits to assurance

Assurance is based on a number of issues, including the level of trust we have in the individuals carrying out the development, etc. However, one of the main contributing factors to assurance is the *evidence* produced during software development, and this, in turn, derives from the verification and validation activities which we carry out throughout the software development process (see below).

It is common to equate validation with answering the question 'Are we building the right thing?' and verification with answering the question 'Are we building the thing right?' Clearly, this interpretation of the terms identifies validation as dealing with the first of our three demonstrable properties above, and verification as dealing with the second point. While these definitions are intuitively appealing, they are not very precise, and it is difficult to make the distinction in practice. For example, it is common to view proof of a formal refinement step (showing that a low-level specification corresponds to a high-level one) as an aspect of verification. However, there will normally be information added in the low-level specification which suggests that there is also an element of validation. While this difficulty may not be of immense significance, it is undesirable to have definitions which are hard to apply, and there appears to be a much more appropriate (helpful) distinction, based on the long-established (philosophical) distinction between *analytic* and *synthetic* reasoning. (The usage of the terms dates back to Leibniz and Kant.)

Analytic reasoning is something that can be carried out entirely within a logical framework (e.g. predicate calculus or differential calculus). Synthetic reasoning requires one to look at the 'real world' – e.g. the statement 'the author of this chapter wears spectacles' is a statement which can only be verified by inspecting the author: no amount of logical/analytical reasoning will check the validity of this statement. There is a strong link betwen validation and synthetic reasoning, and, similarly, between verification and analytic reasoning, but the terms are not identical. In essence, the problem arises due to the addition of information (design detail) in the software development process. Considering only functionality, verification is enough to guarantee validity of this additional information, assuming valid specifications. However, the same is not true for safety specifications (e.g. due to the need to take failures into account), and further synthetic activity is required to show the acceptability of the added information (that that lower-level specifications are adequate and appropriate). The justification for this view relates to the way in which failure behaviour is treated when we provide abstract descriptions of systems (see Dobson and McDermid, 1990).

More importantly, the synthetic/analytic dichotomy enables us to assess the capability of software engineering techniques, for safety-critical systems, fairly directly (see below). It is worth pointing out that, within a particular analytical framework, it is usually possible to judge 'how well we have done' against the theoretical capability of the framework when using a given analytical technique. However, with synthetic reasoning there is no equivalent 'yardstick' against which to judge efficacy, and the best we can do is to rely on experience.

Safety is a property of the 'real world', thus it is (ultimately) the province of synthetic (not analytic) reason. Design (and design verification) techniques work within a logical framework. Most obviously, formal verification/program proving are analytical techniques and cannot *of themselves* ensure safety of a software-controlled system. (This seems to be essentially the point that Fetzer, 1988, was making, albeit at excessive length.) We will return to this important point after we have illustrated the nature of existing formal methods.

Synthetic reasoning is inherently uncertain – we can never be certain that we have 'apprehended the real world' correctly (Wittgentstein, 1969). Thus the production of specifications for safety-critical systems is inherently uncertain, and so, therefore, is the production and assessment of the systems themselves. Our aim as responsible software engineers is to reduce the uncertainty (or increase the assurance) in the dependability of some critical item of software as much as possible.

Pragmatically, the ramifications of these observations about synthetic and analytic reasoning are that we may need to use a combination of formal verification, testing, and so on to achieve safety integrity, but before we can deal with specific software development approaches we need to assess the principles on which assurance is based. Also we must recognize that we deploy safety-critical systems when we have 'enough assurance', not when we know the system 'is safe'.

It is worth pointing out that the limitations of synthetic reasoning also affect safety-critical systems produced using other technologies (e.g. mechanical or electronic components). However, the problems are rather worse with software, for a number of reasons. Program behaviour can be discontinuous, so the normal engineering principles of extrapolation from known behaviour cannot be used. Further, there is no equivalent to the concept of a 'factor of safety' in software, so it is not practical to 'over-engineer' systems to overcome uncertainty about the real world. Arguably also, the 'synthetic gap' between programs and the 'real world' is worse than for other engineering artefacts, because the underlying model of program behaviour and the models of the behaviour of the processes being controlled will be in qualitatively different forms – discrete mathematics/theory of computation rather than continuous mathematics.

Fundamental principles of assurance

Assurance could, in principle, be based on reliability figures if they could be linked to catastrophic (rather than non-critical) failures. However, it is generally accepted that it is not practical to assess reliability at the high levels required for safety-critical systems (Littlewood, 1989). Further, we have previously argued (McDermid, 1989c) that deployment decisions for critical systems are actually made on subjective grounds (perhaps subjective reliabilities), not calculations of reliability based on frequentist data, because of the uncertainties introduced by the inherent limitations of synthetic reasoning. Thus we present the principles which, we believe, underlie the choice of software engineering techniques in terms of assurance.

Assurance can be thought of as confidence – based, of course, on objective evidence. Our fundamental tenet is that assurance arises from *comprehension* and *diversity*. Simplistically, we can say that the greater is our comprehension of some artefact, the greater is our confidence about the dependability of the artefact. There is nothing remarkable about this statement – it simply reflects the fact that confidence increases with understanding. Similarly, confidence increases with the number of independent ways that we have arrived at compatible or equivalent understandings of the system.

More practically, we recognize that in developing or evaluating a putatively safe system we may discover a flaw, or flaws. Clearly, discovery of a flaw reduces our confidence in the dependability of the system. Thus we can define assurance in the following way:

> Assurance that we have correctly assessed the dependability of an artefact increases as our comprehension of the artefact, and the number of ways we have obtained compatible understandings, increases.

Thus we need to base our discussion of which methods and techniques to use in achieving dependability on the criterion of which yields the greatest understanding of the system under development. For a simple artefact we may be able to gain sufficient comprehension of the artefact itself that we can *directly* assess its conformance to the specification (and the 'validity' of the requirements). For a more complex artefact we may find it impossible to gain adequate comprehension directly, or simply more cost-effective to gain assurance in the process. In practice, it is helpful to address assurance from both the product and the process points of view, i.e. from the point of view of what is produced and how it is produced.

Also, software tools are extensively used in developing dependable systems. The use of the tools is nugatory unless we can trust them. Consequently, we require assurance in the tools themselves! Thus assurance in tools is one of the factors influencing assurance of a 'target' system, and, for very simple artefacts, greater assurance may arise *without* the use of tools as the benefits of using them may be outweighed by the need to comprehend them (to gain assurance in their correct functioning). In practice, this probably means that manual techniques are more effective only for programs of a few tens (or hundreds) of lines of code.

The use of diversity in various forms of fault-tolerant systems, including design diversity, is becoming more common. The principle extends to the development process. For example, the use of more than one (independently developed) tool to carry out some analysis reduces the risk of common-mode failure, and increases confidence. Similarly, one of the psychological bases behind the value of formal techniques is that specifications, programs and proofs are redundant structures, and the risk of complete 'system' failure is reduced as failures (design or construction errors) in one form will probably be detected by comparison with the others. Thus we believe that diversity is a ubiquitous principle and that it can be applied to analysis methods, personnel, tools, and so on but we will return to this point in relationship to formal methods later in the chapter.

This discussion enables us to clarify the fundamental principle behind assurance.

> Assurance arises from comprehension of, and diversity in, the complete procurement process, including the artefact which is developed, and the methods and tools used in its development and evaluation.

This principle should be evident in the ensuing discussion, although we focus more on the issues of comprehension than diversity.

FORMAL METHODS IN THE SAFETY-CRITICAL SYSTEMS LIFE CYCLE

Our aim here is to discuss the development process for safety-critical systems and to indicate where, in principle, formal methods can be applied beneficially. It is hoped that this general discussion will become more clear and concrete when we discuss and illustrate particular formal techniques later in this chapter.

The software life cycle

We give here a brief overview of the nature and scope of the software life cycle. A fuller description of life-cycle concepts and the important concepts of process design can be found in McDermid and Rook (1991).

The software 'life cycle' is concerned with the development of software from initial concepts through delivery, use and so-called maintenance. It is helpful to produce a generic model of the life cycle in order to have a basis for discussing different software development paradigms. Therefore we base our model on an abstract view of the activities carried out in software development and maintenance.

The first observation which we make is that, except for trivial systems, it is not possible to proceed directly from the initial concepts to executable software. Instead, a number of intermediate system specifications are produced (e.g. requirements specifications). We refer to these using the generic term *descriptions*.

In general, development proceeds from concepts, through requirements, etc. and one representation is developed by some intellectual or automated process from the preceding representation or representations. We refer to this process as a *transformation*, although there is no implication that this is a purely automatable process, and *synthesis* would perhaps be a better term.

In an ideal world the transformations would yield a sequence of descriptions, resulting in executable programs which satisfied their requirements and the initial concepts. In practice, errors and infelicities are discovered during development (and maintenance) which cause iteration, i.e. repetition of the current transformation or rework of earlier representations. We use the term *verification and validation* (V&V) for the checking activities which may lead to iteration. We have already indicated the distinction between these terms above, so it seems unnecessary to repeat any discussion here, but it is relevant to consider a distinction between forms of verification in the context of formal methods.

It is common to use the term *formal verification* to mean verification based on the concepts of mathematical proof. More strictly, it means proofs where all the detail of the mathematical argument are presented. In other words, the statement:

$$(a+b)+c=(b+c)+a$$

would not be accepted in a formal proof without explicit statement of the order in which rules of commutativity, etc. were applied to reduce the two halves of the equality to the same (textual) form. We can have very great confidence in the correctness (with respect to the specification) of a formally verified system, but the cost of gaining this confidence is very high (at the current state of the art; see below). Consequently, the use of formal verification would only be justified where the cost of system failure is very high (e.g. in safety-critical systems). Also, the successful use of formal verification is contingent on proper tool support, and this affects our views on assurance as the proof tools tend to be complex.

An alternative style of verification, known as the *rigorous approach* (Jones and Shaw, 1990), involves the use of much less detailed proofs, or arguments, and 'obvious' truths (such as the equality above) would be accepted without any requirement to present an explicit argument in a rigorous proof. With the rigorous approach much of the benefit of formal proofs is gained at a much lower cost. It is probable that future, large-scale, software development projects will be based on the rigorous approach.

It is worth pointing out that this model can encompass a number of different development paradigms. In a contractual model each description would be completed before work on the next was started and would form the contract (or technical annex thereof) for the next stage. With incremental enhancement all the representations (with the possible exception of the requirements) may be evolving simultaneously. Further, 'maintenance' is encompassed in the model – we simply observe that maintenance involves iteration, updating various descriptions, once the system has been delivered.

It is interesting to note that many so-called methods are deficient in terms of the model presented above. This is usually where the method defines a notation but no transformation guidelines, or rules for V&V. The absence of guidelines for transformation is a limitation of many current formal methods.

It is possible to produce many different instantiations of this generic model representing particular development methodologies. We give one (still fairly abstract) instantiation in the next section as a basis for the main part of our discussion. Management activities are not captured in the model as presented. This important topic is discussed in some detail by McDermid and Ripken (1984) together with a much fuller discussion of the above life-cycle model. Further information on management issues can also be found in McDermid and Rook (1991) and in several other chapters in the *Software Engineer's Reference Book* (McDermid, 1991).

Typical development stages

As indicated above, there are many different approaches to software development adopted in industry. The following 'typical' model is intended to encapsulate the differing nature of the information being worked with at different stages in software development, without making commitment to any particular development methodology. It is intended that the model encompasses most real safety-critical systems developments, i.e. we have erred towards including stages which might not always be employed.

Five stages are identified in addition to the concepts 'stage':

1. *Requirements analysis* – description of the system and its operationl environment, particularly stressing the interface between the system and environment;
2. *System specification* – an 'external view' of the system to be produced describing the system inputs, the system outputs and their relationships without describing internal system structure;
3. *Architectural design* – a high-level, internal view of the structure of the system as it is to be produced ('the grand plan' of the system such as the architecture of a building);

Formal methods   107

4. *Detailed design* – details of algorithms and data structures needed to implement the system;
5. *Implementation* – the program source code (and the executable images).

Requirements Analysis and System Specification are in the domain of requirements and this is usually summed up as representing *what* the customer or user wants. The remaining three are in the design domain and this is usually summed up as representing *how* the system developer intends to satisfy the requirements. In practice, there may well be multiple stages of detailed design. We leave more detailed descriptions of the life-cycle stages to subsequent sections, but make some observations on the distinctions between the stages.

The what/how dichotomy is rather simplistic and, in practice, it is perfectly legitimate for customers or users to specify 'how' something should be done (e.g. to specify an algorithm). Similarly, the system developer may have valid views on requirements, arising from a knowledge of similar systems or of implementation costs. In general, it is more reasonable to say that requirements and design specifications will contain varying proportions of 'what' and 'how' information, and that the levels of description really represent degrees of commitment to implementation strategies (Dobson and McDermid, 1990). In particular, for safety-critical systems, requirements may place stringent constraints on system architecture in order to achieve some degree of fault tolerance, and the what/how distinction is a fairly poor guideline to the distinction between requirements specification and design documents.

For clarity, the following discussion takes a fairly 'pure' view of each of these stages of system development, but it should be borne in mind that any level of description may contain information which we might think of as being primarily related to one of the other levels.

The role of formal methods in the software development process

We discuss each of the above five stages in the development process and describe in more detail the characteristics of the descriptions and the role that formal methods can play in representing, producing and checking the description. To simplify discussion, we use the term 'target system' to describe the system being specified and implemented in cases where there might otherwise be ambiguity.

Requirements analysis

Requirements analysis is the first stage of the development process concerned with documenting the user's or customer's perceived needs by 'transformation' from the (by definition, undocumented) initial concepts. The distinguishing characteristic of requirements analysis is that it is primarily an information-gathering exercise which can only be validated, not verified (except for internal consistency).

The results of requirements analysis should describe both the *system* and the *environment* in which it operates. This is the case for two reasons:

1. The environment may change, impacting the functionality required of the system.
2. The boundary of the system is not known *a priori*.

It is hard to bound precisely that part of the environment which should be considered in requirements analysis, but it should cover at least those systems, individuals, etc. which interact directly with the system to be developed. In the case of safety-critical systems the environment model should cover sources of threats to the system and other systems or equipments in which hazards could arise due to failure in the target system. The need to represent the environment means that requirements descriptions must be able to represent concurrency explicitly (because the system and processes in the environment operate concurrently).

In requirements analysis it must be possible to describe *non-computable* systems. This is both because users may ask for unrealizable systems and it is desirable to be able to record their requests exactly, and because it must be possible to record partial requirements, or requirements based on the assumption of infinite resources, which may arise as part of the information-gathering process.

The results of requirements analysis are the primary basis for communication with the user and customer. For this reason, it is desirable that the representation should be as precise as possible (e.g. formal). It is also necessary that requirements be intelligible to the customers, as one of the primary forms of validation is review with the customer. However, it is rare for users to be educated to understand the necessary formalisms. Consequently, it seems that formal techniques either cannot be used at this stage or, if they are used, some interpretation of the formalism is required for communication with the customer. For example, it would be possible to use techniques of animation, specification execution or derivation of properties by proof techniques in validation of requirements. In this latter case we might wish to prove that no sequence of operations which could be undertaken by the system (if it satisfied its specification) could lead to it (and the environment) entering an unsafe state.

Technically, requirements analysis methods need to deal with causality (e.g. 'when this event occurs in the environment the system must perform the following actions') and other properties such as behaviour of the system under hardware failure conditions. One of the key differences between 'normal' and safety-critical systems is the need to be able to deal with causality in the presence of failure, and this is the reason that techniques such as failure modes effects analysis and fault tree analysis are used at this stage in safety-critical systems developments.

There are few formal methods oriented towards requirements, although the work of the Alvey FOREST project (Maibaum *et al.*, 1986; Potts and Finkelstein, 1986) is worth noting, as it deals with issues such as formally representing causality and giving guidelines for requirements capture.

There are a number of research problems which have to be overcome before formal techniques can be used widely for requirements analysis. Perhaps the most crucial of these is the development of a notation (or notations) which is (are) rich enough to specify functional, causal and non-functional (e.g. timing) requirements but which can be presented to a user in an acceptable manner without (substantial) loss of precision.

System specification

System specification is still in the requirements domain, i.e. it is primarily concerned with what the system should do, not how it does it, although this is not always an easy distinction to make in practice (see below). The primary distinction between this and the previous stage is that it describes only the system, not the environment, and it gives precise definitions of the system interfaces. In practice, the system specification may be an enriched sub-set of the requirement specification and it should encompass both the system interfaces and its functionality.

In the contractual model of the life cycle the system specification would be the basis of the contract for the development team. The implicit requirement for precision suggests that the specifications produced should be formal. Further, the need to specify what (not how) suggests that it would be desirable to use *algebraic specification techniques*, i.e. techniques where the behaviour of a system is specified implicitly by equations relating inputs to outputs (Zilles, 1974).

Algebraic specification techniques have been widely applied to small examples, but there is little evidence, as yet, that they are suitable for specifying large systems. It is worth trying to amplify on the problems of using algebraic specifications by means of a small example. Imagine a system containing a database which we wish to update. If we model the database directly (e.g. using a model-oriented technique) we can specify the conditions under which the operation can proceed (the object to be udated exists, the type is correct, etc.) quite simply. In an algebraic approach we would have to establish existence of an object by reasoning about the sequence of inputs to the system and determining whether the object had been created (successfully) since it was last deleted. This would make the specification rather more obscure and cumbersome than the model-oriented approach. In the author's experience problems of this nature arise with the algebraic approach, and such specifications tend to obfuscate rather than elucidate the problem being specified. Thus we have a conflict between the theoretical attractiveness of algebraic approaches and their apparent practical limitations.

As far as possible, concurrency should be specified implicitly, not explicitly, so that the system developers are free to choose what level of concurrency to use in implementing the system. This is certainly a contentious point, and other authors (e.g. Zave, 1982) would argue in favour of explicitly modelling concurrency. The primary argument in favour of the implicit approach is that it does not involve making premature design decisions; the contrary view primarily relates to clarity of specifications.

There is another important issue related to system specification which can be illustrated by example. It is possible in an avionics system that some interfaces (e.g. to radar sub-systems) would be specified very precisely during requirements (e.g. down to the level of the meanings of bits at the interface). However, interfaces to other devices (e.g. a head-up display) may be known in terms of the information to be displayed but not in terms of the data formats, etc. Defining these formats is a design exercise which should involve human factors experts. In producing a system specification the interface definition would have to be made precise, so it will inevitably contain design information. The extent to which the system specification will (implicitly) contain design information will depend on the nature of the system being built (recall our general comment above about the relationships between the different levels of specification).

The system specification should be verified against the requirements. In practice, this will probably be an informal exercise. Since design information may have been added it is also desirable that it is validated against the initial concepts. It is possible that techniques of animation or specification execution (Coleman and Gallimore, 1987) can be used in validation, although, as pointed out above, system specification may not initially contain enough information to allow execution of all aspects of the specification. For safety-critical systems further failure analysis may be appropriate, especially if it is possible that new failure modes can be deduced from the system specification which were not apparent at the requirements stage.

There seem to be two possible ways in which formal techniques can evolve to become more applicable for this stage in the software development process. First, algebraic techniques can be developed so that they are applicable to large-scale systems. This will almost inevitably involve schemes for modularizing specifications. Second, it may be possible to find ways of applying the more operational techniques so that they do not unduly compromise design freedom.

Architectural design

The architectural design describes the system interfaces, functionality and structure as we intend to implement it. The architecture is distinct from the previous stage in that it describes system structure and how the functionality will be achieved as well as what functionality is required. The level of detail contained in such a specification will vary from project to project. However, it is not the level of detail which characterizes the architectural design, but the fact that this is the first description of the system which is produced primarily from the developer's, rather than the user's, point of view.

Many different ways of producing formal specifications have been proposed. However, the concept of architecture outlined above seems to match closely the ideas of *model-oriented* specifications and *process algebras*. Arguably, an 'ideal' approach would use a process algebra for specifying concurrent structure and communication but employ model-oriented specifications to state the behaviour of the operations engaged in by the processes.

A primary characteristic of the transformation from system specification to architecture is that it may not be structure preserving. In other words, the structure of the design may have to be different from that of the requirement. This change in structure may be necessitated so that the system performs sufficiently quickly, so that the customer can afford it, or perhaps so that it has the appropriate fault-tolerance characteristics.

Ignoring, for the moment, the fact that software may not function correctly, we can consider the effect of reliability requirements on architecture. If the reliability requirements can be met by a single (simplex) processor (because the available processor chips are of adequate reliability) then the architecture may follow closely the structure of the requirements, with one 'design function' for each 'requirements function'. However, if this is not the case, then redundancy may have to be used, thereby causing replication of function and introduction of new functions (e.g. for fault detection and system reconfiguration). In this case more than one design function would map to a function in the requirements and there would be functions which had no (direct) requirements counterpart at all. If we add timing requirements then we may find further changes in structure due to the fact that no one processor can keep up with the data coming from a sensor. Thus the limitations of current hardware technology are a primary factor in determining the design, but there are many other issues such as reliability, failure behaviour, timing behaviour, and so on. We can draw a number of points from this observation.

First, we have given non-functional reasons for the change in structure. In other words, non-functional requirements such as performance, cost and reliability *drive* the design process. This is significant, because formal specifications do not, for the most part, enable this non-functional information to be recorded. There are, of course, exceptions to this and some of the specification logics deal specifically with timing.

Second, many formal methods support a concept known as refinement (see, for example, Jones, 1986), which enables us to define and verify the correctness of the relationships between two formal descriptions of the same system. However, the published refinement techniques are usually too restrictive to admit the sort of structural change identified above, although current research work (see, for example, McDermid, 1989a) is addressing this problem, among others.

Third, we need quite a permissive interpretation of equivalence between the levels of representation. It must be possible to take into account non-determinism, asynchrony, etc. which would mean, *inter alia*, that the order of the outputs would not be determined entirely by the order of the inputs. This may be particularly relevant where high-priority inputs to a system can cause it to change operational mode and therefore 'ignore' other, 'lower-priority' inputs. The notion of *behavioural equivalence* introduced in algebraic specification (see, for example, Sanella and Tarlecki, 1984) admits at least some of the requisite laxity in the meaning of equivalence, but it is still a research issue to determine an appropriate set of refinement rules for dealing with the change from system specification to architecture.

As will be apparent from the example above, it is also necessary to be able to represent concurrency within the architectural design. The primary problem associated with applying formal methods at this stage in the life cycle is that there is no method, or notation, which encompasses all the requirements identified above. At present, the would-be user of formal methods must choose the technique which best supports the characteristics which are most critical in his application area or to use an eclectic approach and to find appropriate ways of relating the different formalisms used.

Detailed design

It is the author's view that detailed design should proceed from the architecture by the conventional process of (structure-preserving) refinement. This is not a universally held view, indeed the phrase 'one man's design is another man's requirement' is often used in the software industry when discussing hierarchical specifications of systems. Given the above interpretation of the relationship between requirements and design, this would mean that the structure of the design could be changed in each representation. This is an unhealthy attitude from at least two points of view.

Technically, it implies that the architect did not have a complete (adequate) understanding of the system. This is particularly critical if the proposed changes involve modifying the process structure and hence impacting timing, etc. possibly to the extent that the system no longer meets its (non-functional) requirements. Clearly, problems with the architecture may be found in detailed design: these should be resolved by updating the architecture, not making low-level changes to the overall design.

Managerially, it implies that the project is not under adequate control. For example, modules common to several sub-systems may have been identified for separate implementation, and the basis on which this decision was made could be invalidated by allowing changes at this level. Thus, even if the restructuring preserves sub-system interfaces, it could have 'knock-on' effects on the rest of the project and invalidate project plans, project resourcing, etc.

This structure-preserving view of detailed design is consistent with (capable of being supported by) current refinement techniques (see, for example, Jones, 1989; Morgan, 1990). The classical refinement techniques apply for sequential systems. Some techniques for dealing with concurrent systems (e.g. CCS; Milner, 1980) support hierarchical decomposition of systems, which is akin to refinement. So far as the author is aware, there is no satisfactory formalism for dealing with the simultaneous refinement of both the concurrent and sequential aspects of a system. Again, in practice, it seems that in order to use formal methods of *all aspects* of detailed design and refinement to this level it is necessary to take an eclectic approach and to work out on an *ad hoc* basis how to relate the different forms of specification.

Implementation

There has been considerable work on formal treatment of the final stage of development, that is, formally relating a program to a low-level specification. Techniques include the so-called 'constructive' approach (e.g. Backhouse, 1986) and program verification environments (e.g. Gypsy; Good, 1984). The constructive techniques are methods based on the idea of deriving the program from low-level specifications, and are intended to be applied manually. The verification environments are based on similar mathematical bases (Hoare, 1969) to the constructive techniques, but, typically, are more concerned with giving automated assistance to proof of correspondence between a program and a specification. Techniques for formal implementation are most well developed for sequential programs, but some work has been carried out for concurrent programs. The techniques are expensive to use and most of their uses to date have been in highly critical systems, where the cost of failure justified the expense of applying the techniques in development. A considerable improvement in productivity using these techniques will be necessary before they can become more widely used.

The majority of these techniques are suited to the development of sequential programs, or at least programs which terminate. However, many critical applications where the use of these formal verification techniques would be justified on economic grounds are continuously running programs, monitoring the state of some (physical) process and taking the necessary remedial actions if the process is becoming dangerous (e.g. monitoring and controlling the flow of steel through a steel mill). Improvements in techniques for handling concurrency and continuously running programs will be necessary to use this class of programs in a satisfactory manner.

Weaker forms of verification may be valuable under some circumstances. For example, tools such as Malpas (Bramson, 1984) can carry out various analyses on programs, and these can be used to validate or verify the program. Capabilities of the tools include analysing control and data flow for undesirable features and establishment of the information flow in the program so it can be compared against the specification.

EXAMPLES OF FORMAL METHODS

The aim in this section is to give a brief overview of the nature of three of the different types of formal method in order to illustrate their characteristics and to try to substantiate some of the general points made above. Due to limitations on space, the analysis is inevitably somewhat superficial, so references are given to texts which give more comprehensive tutorial treatments of the methods discussed.

We discuss three methods. First, we illustrate Z, which is a model-oriented technique developed primarily at the University of Oxford. Second, we discuss the FOREST specification language, which is an example of a non-standard logic intended primarily for expression of requirements. Third, we give an illustration of the capabilities of process algebras through the medium of timed CCS. Finally, we briefly discuss the notion of refinement in the context of model-oriented specifications to illustrate the issues which have to be addressed in proceeding from specifications towards code within a formal framework.

Model-oriented specification

The Z specification language is based on set theory and first-order predicate calculus. A distinguishing feature of Z is the use of schemas and the schema calculus. Schemas are 'modules' of specifications, and the schema calculus gives a way of linking the modules to build up complex specifications from simple parts in a clear and elegant manner. Z was originated by J.-R. Abrial and has subsequently been developed by a number of staff at the Programming Research Group in Oxford. Some examples of the use of the language can be found in Hayes (1986) and a more definitive discussion of the language is given by Spivey (1989).

In order to illustrate the capabilities of Z we first present an elementary introduction to Z specifications, showing how they can be structured using schemas, but eschewing the details of the predicate calculus. This is followed by a rather more detailed example which shows the specification of some safety-relevant properties.

Basic Z concepts

In producing Z specifications it is conventional to build up a model of the state of the (computer) system being modelled, then to define operations which modify that state. Z has some built-in types (like types in programming languages) but allows new types to be introduced, without defining their structure (these are akin to abstract data types). An example of the introduction of a new type is:

[Declarations]

This introduces the type 'Declarations', and it is known as a given set or parachuted type (because it appears as if it floated down into the specification on a parachute!).

We can next define schemas which declare objects and define predicates representing constraints on the allowed values. The example below shows the form of a schema (the stylized box). The schema contains declarations of objects and predicates which constrain the allowable values taken by those objects. The schema below declares an object 'Decs' of type 'Declarations' and could contain any predicate expressible in the Z language relating to Decs (examples will be given later).

```
┌─ Form_of_Schema ─────────────┐
│ Decs : Declarations          │
│ ──────────────────────────── │
│ any old predicate referring to Decs │
└──────────────────────────────┘
```

The top half of the schema is known as the signature and the bottom half as the predicate part, or body.

A more realistic example schema, using the built-in type $\mathbb{N}$ representing natural numbers, might be:

```
┌─ Example ────────────────────┐
│ n : $\mathbb{P}\mathbb{N}$   │
│ ──────────────────────────── │
│ $\forall$ num : $\mathbb{N}$ | num > 23 $\wedge$ num < 43 • num $\in$ n │
└──────────────────────────────┘
```

Formal methods 115

This defines a set of natural numbers, denoted by the symbols ℙ ℕ. In the predicate part the inverted A is read as 'for all', the vertical bar as 'such that' and the dot as 'it's true that'. Thus we have 'for all natural numbers, num, such that num is greater than 23 and less than 43, it's true that num is a member of the set n'. Thus the schema constrains the set 'n' to contain every number in the range 24 to 42 inclusive.

An example which shows a constraint which we might actually be interested in specifying (!) is:

```
┌─ Primes ─────────────────────────────────────┐
│ primes : ℙ ℕ                                 │
│ ───────────────────────────────────────────  │
│ ∀ p : ℕ | p ∈ primes •                       │
│     ∀ f1, f2 : ℕ | f1 * f2 = p •             │
│         f1 = p ∧ f2 = 1 ∨ f2 = p ∧ f1 = 1    │
└──────────────────────────────────────────────┘
```

This defines the set of prime numbers – numbers which are only divisible by one and themselves. As a general rule, it is easiest to read such quantified expressions 'inside out' – the final predicate states the condition of interest and the quantifiers 'establish the context' for the predicate, i.e. define and bind the identifiers in the predicate. Thus, in this case, we have 'a number f1 or f2 is either the number 1, or p, where f1 and f2 are factors of p, that is, their product is equal to p, where p is any prime number'. This is also a good point to illustrate style. Arguably, the next definition is much more elegant, although we leave the interpretation of the predicate to the reader:

```
┌─ Nicer_Primes ───────────────────────────────┐
│ primes : ℙ ℕ                                 │
│ ───────────────────────────────────────────  │
│ ∀ p : ℕ | p ∈ primes •                       │
│     ∀ f1, f2 : ℕ | f1 * f2 = p • {f1, f2} = {1, p} │
└──────────────────────────────────────────────┘
```

We can now illustrate a more realistic usage of the basic Z concepts introduced so far.

Typical Z specifications

Typically, we wish to model the state of a system and then represent operations, which might eventually be realized as procedures in programs, which modify the state. There will usually be properties of the data compromising the system state which remain true regardless of what operation is carried out. These properties are referred to as *invariants* for the obvious reason that they do not vary (change) as the system executes. Thus we would typically define a system state in the following form:

```
┌─ Form_of_System_State ─┐
│ Decs : Declarations    │
│ ───────────────────    │
│ invariant over data    │
└────────────────────────┘
```

This now gives us a state over which we can define operations, but we need therefore to be able to identify the state before and after the operation. This is conventionally done by 'decorating' the objects in the specification which represent state after an operation with a prime ('). Thus in the above example Decs and Decs' would represent before and after states, respectively. We have a further convention that we can decorate a schema name with a Δ, as shown beow:

ΔForm_of_System_State

This is equivalent to:

```
┌─ Expanded_ΔForm_of_System_State ─┐
│ Decs  : Declarations             │
│ Decs' : Declarations             │
│ ──────────────────────────────   │
│ invariant over data before operation (Decs)  │
│ invariant over data after operation (Decs')  │
└──────────────────────────────────┘
```

The effect of the convention is to declare the before and after states for some operation so that the invariant applies in both states; in other words, it is truly invariant. We can also import the Δ-schema into a signature of another schema, and this is as if the declarations of the Δ-schema signature had been made 'in line' and the predicate is included in the predicate part.

To define operations, we need to say when they are applicable, as not all operations can validly be used in all circumstances, and what they do. The former notion is known as a *pre-condition* and the latter as a *post-condition*. We also need to define parameters to (and results from) operations, and this is done by decorating with a ? and a !, respectively. Thus the form of operations is:

```
┌─ Form_of_Simple_Operation ──────────────────────────┐
│ ΔForm_of_System_State                               │
│ Parameters? : Declarations                          │
│ Results!    : Declarations                          │
│ ─────────────────────────────────────────────────── │
│ pre-condition over Decs and Parameters?             │
│ post-condition over Decs, Decs', Parameters? and Results! │
└─────────────────────────────────────────────────────┘
```

where the pre-condition refers to before state and parameters (only those objects

Formal methods 117

from the signature with no decoration or decorated with a ?) and the post-condition relates before and after state to parameters and results. If we expand the schema inclusion then the above is equivalent to:

―― Expanded_Form_of_Simple_Operation ――――――――
Decs : Declarations
Decs' : Declarations
Parameters? : Declarations
Results! : Declarations
―――――――――――――――――――――――
invariant over data before operation (Decs)
invariant over data after operation (Decs')
pre-condition over Decs and Parameters?
post-condition over Decs, Decs', Parameters? and Results!
――――――――――――――――――――――――――

We can now give an example based on the built-in types in Z. In order to make the example more realistic we present a (vastly oversimplified) model of part of the operations of a bank.

First, we introduce a useful function for summing over members of a sequence. The notion of sequence is built into Z, as is the tail function which returns all but the first element of the sequence. The open form of schema shown below is known as an axiomatic schema and is used (here) to give auxiliary definitions useful in the main specification but which do not form part of the system state:

sum : seq $\mathbb{N}$ → $\mathbb{N}$
―――――――――――――――
∀ s : seq $\mathbb{N}$ •
  (#s = 0 ⇒ sum s = 0) ∧
  (#s > 0 ⇒ sum s = s 1 + sum (tail s))

Technically, a sequence is a function from an initial segment of the natural numbers, i.e. a range *1 ... N*, to the requisite values in the range, in this case natural numbers. Thus we can use function application (e.g. s 1) to extract values from the sequence. We will use the fact that sequences can be viewed as functions below.

The predicate deals with the two distinct cases: an empty sequence and a sequence of size greater than or equal to one. Clearly, the recursive definition for the latter case adds each member of the sequence, in turn.

We now model a bank which contains a number of accounts – they are represented as a sequence, just showing the current balance, which obviously is a gross simplification. We use a sequence for the accounts so we can identify them (by indexing into the sequence) which we could not do if we chose the rather more obvious form of model, a set.

```
┌─ Bank_State ─────────────────┐
│ accounts : seq ℕ             │
│ balance  : ℕ                 │
│──────────────────────────────│
│ balance = sum accounts       │
└──────────────────────────────┘
```

The invariant is that the balance held by the bank is the sum of the amounts held in the individual accounts (again this is a simplification). We now define an operation to transfer money between local accounts:

```
┌─ Transfer_OK ─────────────────────────────────┐
│ ΔBank_State                                   │
│ amount? : ℕ                                   │
│ from?, to? : ℕ                                │
│───────────────────────────────────────────────│
│ from? ∈ dom accounts ∧ to? ∈ dom accounts ∧   │
│ amount? ≤ accounts from? ⇒                    │
│     accounts' =                               │
│     accounts ⊕                                │
│     {from? ↦ accounts from? − amount?,        │
│      to?   ↦ accounts to? + amount?}          │
└───────────────────────────────────────────────┘
```

This operation transfers *amount?* from one account to another if there is a high enough account balance. The term before the implication is the pre-condition and that after it is the post-condition. The pre-condition checks first that the accounts are held at the bank, i.e. that the accounts identified (*from?* and *to?*) are members of the domain of the account sequence. It then checks that the account balance is high enough to make the transfer. The post-condition says that the sequence after the operation is the same as that before, except that the account identifiers *to?* and *from?* are now mapped to the new balances – which are the previous balances plus and minus the amount to be transferred, respectively. This is done using function over-riding (denoted by the symbol ⊕) which replaces the identified element of the function (in this case mapping from the account numbers *from?* and *to?*) but leaves the rest of the function unchanged. We can state a further property:

$$\text{Transfer\_OK} \vdash \text{balance} = \text{balance}'$$

The theorem says that the balance in the bank remains constant. Note that we could have specified this directly (as part of the predicate in *Transfer_OK*), but the fact that the amount is preserved is determined by the predicate that calculates the balance and the nature of the change made to the account. Thus this is a case where we can derive a property of a specification, that is, to show that preservation of the balance is a consequence of the specification. In principle, we can prove such a property but, for brevity, we have chosen not to demonstrate this here.

The pre-condition ensures that the operation does not take place when it would violate the invariant – but it does not say what happens in this circumstance. We can cover this case as follows:

```
┌─ Transfer_Fails ─────────────────────────────────────┐
│ ΔBank_State                                          │
│ amount? : ℕ                                          │
│ from?, to? : ℕ                                       │
│ ──────────────────────────────────────────────────── │
│ from? ∉ dom accounts ∨ to? ∉ dom accounts ∨          │
│ amount? > accounts from? ⇒ accounts' = accounts      │
└──────────────────────────────────────────────────────┘
```

We can express this operation more succinctly using another Z convention:

```
┌─ Shorter_Transfer_Fails ─────┐
│ ΞBank_State                  │
│ amount? : ℕ                  │
│ from?, to? : ℕ               │
│ ──────────────────────────── │
│   from? ∉ dom accounts       │
│ ∨                            │
│   to? ∉ dom accounts         │
│ ∨                            │
│   amount? > accounts from?   │
└──────────────────────────────┘
```

The definition of Ξ-schema constrains the before and after states to be the same, i.e. it implicitly contains a predicate where all elements of the before state are defined to have the same values as the corresponding elements of the after state.

We have defined the two parts of the operation separately, and we can now use the schema calculus to compose the operations to define the behaviour of a *Transfer* operation under any circumstances:

$$\text{Total\_Transfer} \triangleq \text{Transfer\_OK} \land \text{Transfer\_Fails}$$

This schema calculus expression says that *Transfer* and *Transfer_Fails* are both true – this is the interpretation of the logical and between the schemas. This is equivalent to the schema:

```
┌─ Expanded_Total_Transfer ──────────────────────────┐
│ ΔBank_State                                         │
│ amount? : ℕ                                         │
│ from?, to? : ℕ                                      │
├─────────────────────────────────────────────────────┤
│ from? ∈ dom accounts ∧ to? ∉ dom accounts ∧         │
│ amount? ≤ accounts from? ⇒                          │
│     accounts' =                                     │
│     accounts ⊕                                      │
│     {from? ↦ accounts from? − amount?,              │
│      to? ↦ accounts to? + amount?} ∧                │
│     (from? ∉ dom accounts ∨ to? ∉ dom accounts ∨    │
│      amount? > accounts from? ⇒ accounts' = accounts)│
└─────────────────────────────────────────────────────┘
```

where the signatures of the two schemas have been merged and the predicates are related by the operator between the schemas (we have the full logical capability of and, or, implies, etc. available). This definition now covers all possibilities explicitly. In principle, this is another point which we might wish to prove, but here we are dealing with an aspect of specification completeness, not with deriving a property of interest.

We note, however, that we could not have used *Shorter_Transfer_Fails* in the above schema calculus expression because of the way in which the predicate is formed would lead to conflicting constraints being specified. Thus we have to take care in using these constructs.

While the above examples are very elementary, they serve to show the basics of the Z specification style. We can now illustrate a rather more realistic use of Z for a safety-related problem.

Safety example

Our intention is to show the behaviour for a thresholding device such as might be used in temperature monitoring, where it is necessary to compare the values from a number of temperature sensors, to reject values which are out of tolerance and to calculate an average of the values which are within tolerance. Such a function might be useful in many situations (e.g. process monitoring), but it is not based on any specific system or device.

We first introduce some basic definitions for representing sensor properties:

[Sensor]

The parachuted type *Sensor* represents the set of all sensors known about in the monitoring system.

Formal methods 121

> upper, lower, bound, spread : $\mathbb{N}$
> ___
> lower < upper
> spread < upper − lower
> bound < spread

The data items *upper* and *lower* represent the limits on legal values for the sensors: any values outside the range *lower* ... *upper* indicate that the sensor has failed. The item *bound* is a limit on the difference between two successive values from a sensor representing the maximum allowance rate of change of value reported by the sensor. If any pair of successive values from a sensor are different by more than this bound then this will also be taken as evidence that the sensor has failed. Finally, *spread* represents the allowable divergence between any two functioning sensors. If some values do disagree by more than the allowed spread then their values are ignored, but the sensors are not assumed to have failed (this is intended to deal with cases where noise, etc. may affect values temporarily). The constraints represent the natural relationships among these data items. In practice, we would need to specify the exact values to be used.

We now define a number of data types corresponding to the range of allowable values, the rate of change of sensor values and the coherence of the data values from the complete set of sensors. These are simply used as results from functions which evaluate the above checks on data validity. The first is used for checks on range:

> status ::= legal | illegal

The second is concerned with allowable rates of change of sensor value:

> rate ::= sensible | fast

The third is used for assessing data coherence:

> coherence ::= ok | out

We are now in position to define functions which evaluate the checks on data validity identified above. The choice of types for the functions is determined by convenience in representing state (see below). The function *valid* evaluates the range check on data validity and assigns the value *legal* or *illegal* to the results as appropriate:

> valid : $\mathbb{N}$ → status
> ___
> $\forall$ n : $\mathbb{N}$ •
>   (n ⩾ lower ∧ n ⩽ upper ⇒ valid n = legal) ∧
>   (n < lower ∨ n > upper ⇒ valid n = illegal)

122 Safety Aspects of Computer Control

We have used implication here dealing with each case separately. As the terms before the implication are mutually exclusive there is no ambiguity in the definition of the function.

The function for evaluating legal rate transitions is very similar to the check on absolute sensor value, but clearly needs to check pairs of values:

$$\begin{array}{|l} \hline \text{rate\_ok} : (\mathbb{N} \times \mathbb{N}) \longrightarrow \text{rate} \\ \hline \forall\, n1, n2 : \mathbb{N} \,\bullet \\ \quad (n1 - n2 \leqslant \text{bound} \Rightarrow \text{rate\_ok}\,(n1, n2) = \text{sensible}) \land \\ \quad (n1 - n2 > \text{bound} \Rightarrow \text{rate\_ok}\,(n1, n2) = \text{fast}) \end{array}$$

The coherence of a set of values is determined in a similar way, but here we use an equivalence between the function delivering '*ok*' and the condition when the data set is acceptable. In this way the behaviour of the function when the data are not coherent is defined *implicitly*, as the only possibility is for it to deliver the value *out*, signifying that the values are incoherent.

$$\begin{array}{|l} \hline \text{coherent} : \text{seq}\,\mathbb{N} \longrightarrow \text{coherence} \\ \hline \forall\, s : \text{seq}\,\mathbb{N} \,\bullet \\ \quad (\forall\, id1 : \text{dom}\,s \,\bullet \\ \qquad \forall\, id2 : \text{dom}\,s \,\bullet\, s\,id1 - s\,id2 \leqslant \text{spread}) \Leftrightarrow \\ \quad \text{coherent}\,s = \text{ok} \end{array}$$

However, it will not be enough to check *coherence* and we will have to find a sequence representing those values which are coherent. In doing this, we may need to discard mappings from a sequence which contains incoherent values to create one containing only coherent values. However, simply discarding arbitrary values might render the result an illegal sequence (e.g. the domain might be 1, 2, 4, which is illegal as 3 is missing: remember that sequences map from an initial segment of the natural numbers). We therefore need a function to turn arbitrary pairs of numbers into a sequence:

$$\begin{array}{|l} \hline \text{mk\_seq} : (\mathbb{N} \nrightarrow \mathbb{N}) \longrightarrow \text{seq}\,\mathbb{N} \\ \hline \forall\, \text{pairs} : \mathbb{N} \nrightarrow \mathbb{N} \,\bullet \\ \quad \exists\, \text{map}, \text{res} : \text{seq}\,\mathbb{N} \mid \text{map} \,\S\, \text{pairs} = \text{res} \land \#\text{res} = \#\text{pairs} \,\bullet \\ \quad \text{mk\_seq}\,\text{pairs} = \text{res} \end{array}$$

The above function, *mk_seq*, has the required property as the mapping sequence, *map*, converts pairs to a sequence and the constraints on the size of the result constrains map not to discard any elements of the function *pairs*. We can now use this function in calculating a sequence of coherent sensor values:

$$
\begin{array}{|l}
\text{co\_seq} : \text{seq } \mathbb{N} \rightarrow \text{seq } \mathbb{N} \\
\hline
\forall\, s : \text{seq } \mathbb{N} \mid \#s > 0 \bullet \\
\quad \exists\, s1 : \mathbb{N} \nrightarrow \mathbb{N} \mid \text{coherent (mk\_seq s1)} = \text{ok} \wedge s1 \subset s \bullet \\
\quad\quad (\forall\, s2 : \mathbb{N} \nrightarrow \mathbb{N} \mid \\
\quad\quad\quad \text{coherent (mk\_seq s2)} = \text{ok} \wedge s2 \subset s \bullet \\
\quad\quad\quad \#s2 \leqslant \#s1) \Leftrightarrow \text{co\_seq } s = \text{mk\_seq } s1
\end{array}
$$

The function finds the largest sub-set of the sequence given as a parameter which is coherent (or one of them, if there is more than one of the same size). This is done by ensuring (via the third quantifier) that any other coherent sub-set is no larger than the one already found. If there is more than one coherent set of the same size then an arbitrary one will be chosen. Note that since a data value is always coherent with itself the function will, at worst, deliver a sequence of only one element. In this case, and with equal size sets with more than one element, the function is non-deterministic, and we do not know which element(s) it will select (this seems to be reasonable, as we have no way of knowing which is the 'best' value if there is no agreement between the values). This specification is not entirely straightforward, but this is probably a good illustration of the value of formal methods – it is very easy to see how an implementor given only an informal specification might implement such a function incorrectly.

We now have a rather simpler function which calculates the average value from a sequence. Since the values are integers the average will only be approximate. We have chosen to specify the bounds on legal average values rather than to indicate that the average should be rounded up or rounded down. This leaves freedom to the system designers and implementors. The definition uses the function *sum* introduced in the previous section.

$$
\begin{array}{|l}
\text{average} : \text{seq } \mathbb{N} \rightarrow \mathbb{N} \\
\hline
\forall\, ss : \text{seq } \mathbb{N} \bullet \\
\quad \#ss * \text{average } ss < \text{sum } ss + \#ss \wedge \\
\quad \#ss * \text{average } ss > \text{sum } ss - \#ss
\end{array}
$$

We have now completed the preliminaries and can define the system itself by introducing the state and some operations on the state.

We introduce an object to represent the sensors in the system. If we were wishing to produce a complete specification we would need to deal with the way in which the sensor values changed, but for our present purposes the intention is that the function sensors represents the current values of the sensors.

$$\text{sensors} : \text{Sensor} \rightarrow \mathbb{N}$$

The state of the computer system checking the sensor values can be broken down into two parts and the parts are treated separately to simplify the specification (see below).

First, we have a pair of functions which contain the latest values read from the sensors and stored in the system (*new_values*) and the previous set of readings (*old_values*). There is no invariant as the only property of interest would relate to the 'freshness' of the data and, within this example, we are ignoring timing (we will return to this point later).

```
┌─ SS_History ──────────────────┐
│  old_values : Sensor → ℕ      │
│  new_values : Sensor → ℕ      │
└───────────────────────────────┘
```

The second part of the state is concerned with the computer's model of which sensors are functioning correctly, and which are not. The set *failed* indicates those sensors which the computer system believes to have failed and *check_set* the current set of values, drawn from the stored sensor values, which the computer is going to use to calculate the average sensor value, i.e. those that come from working sensors and which are deemed to be coherent.

```
┌─ SS_State ────────────────────────────┐
│  failed : ℙ Sensor                    │
│  check_set : seq ℕ                    │
│  ─────────────────────────            │
│  #(dom check_set) ≤ #Sensor - #failed │
└───────────────────────────────────────┘
```

The invariant states that the number of values to be used as the basis of the check (calculated by an averaging mechanism) can never exceed the number of working sensors. Note that the number might be less than the number of working sensors due to coherence problems.

We can now define the first aspect of the operations to be performed by the system. Here we define the operation which reads the sensor values and updates the (short) history of values retained by the system. The definition is fairly straightforward and we see the value of treating the state in two parts as the *SS_State* and *SS_History* change values at different times (in all cases, not just this one).

```
┌─ Read_Sensors ─────────────────────────┐
│ ΔSS_History                            │
│ ΞSS_State                              │
│────────────────────────────────────────│
│ new_values' = sensors                  │
│ old_values' = new_values               │
└────────────────────────────────────────┘
```

We now consider the checks on sensor data validity. We first consider the overall limits on sensor values. The schema calculates which sensors (if any) which have now failed as *new_fail* – despite the name, this might include sensors that were previously known to have failed. The set *new_fail* is 'added' to the set *failed*. Changes to *check_set* are not specified – this does not matter, as we will specify how the value of *check-set* is calculated later.

```
┌─ Check_Limits ─────────────────────────────────────────┐
│ ΞSS_History                                            │
│ ΔSS_State                                              │
│────────────────────────────────────────────────────────│
│ ∃ new_fail : ℙ Sensor •                                │
│    {s : Sensor | valid (new_values s) = illegal} = new_fail ∧ │
│    failed' = failed ∪ new_fail                         │
└────────────────────────────────────────────────────────┘
```

Here we say that the set *new_fail* is exactly the set of sensors for which the function valid yields illegal (this is read rather like a quantified expression). Note that if a sensor previously deemed to have failed gives a sensible reading we do not automatically reinstate it. This reflects an attitude that a failed sensor may drift and occasionally give legal (but erroneous) values, and so its values should be ignored until it is explicitly reinstated. In this specification fragment we do not deal with reinstatement operations.

The rate of changes of the sensor values are calculated in a similar manner.

```
┌─ Check_Rate ───────────────────────────────────────────┐
│ ΞSS_History                                            │
│ ΔSS_State                                              │
│────────────────────────────────────────────────────────│
│ ∃ new_fail : ℙ Sensor •                                │
│    {s : Sensor |                                       │
│     rate_ok (old_values s, new_values s) = fast} = new_fail ∧ │
│    failed' = failed ∪ new_fail                         │
└────────────────────────────────────────────────────────┘
```

We can now determine the set of values which will be used for the check. Note that we do not discard sensors just because they are in disagreement with others –

this allows us to discard noisy readings which probably were caused by noise without discarding the sensor. Again, in a full specification we might care to record a history of disagreeing sensors and to discard them after too many disagreements.

```
┌─ Define_Check_Set ──────────────────────────────────────┐
│ ΞSS_History                                             │
│ ΔSS_State                                               │
├─────────────────────────────────────────────────────────┤
│ failed = failed'                                        │
│ ∃ map : seq Sensor; values : Sensor ⇸ ℕ |               │
│    values = failed ⩤ new_values ∧ ran map = dom values  │
│       check_set' = co_seq (map ⨟ values)                │
└─────────────────────────────────────────────────────────┘
```

The operation for defining the sensor value to be delivered is now straightforward, being defined by calculating the average of the *check_set*. In addition, we deliver the size of the *check_set* as a measure of confidence in the accuracy of the value.

```
┌─ Calc_Value ──────────────┐
│ ΞSS_History               │
│ ΞSS_State                 │
│ val! : ℕ                  │
│ size! : ℕ                 │
├───────────────────────────┤
│ val! = average check_set  │
│ size! = #check_set        │
└───────────────────────────┘
```

We can now define the complete operation of a single checking cycle for the system, assuming that the checks are executed periodically. This is done by the following schema calculus expression:

   Check_Cycle ≙
       Check_Limits ⨟ Check_Rate ⨟ Define_Check_Set ⨟ Calc_Value

The forward relational composition between schemas is similar to that between functions except that it maps states to state, not results to parameters. Thus the after state of *Check_Limits* becomes the before state of *Check_Rate*, and so on. Note that the ordering of the operations is the same as the order of their definition. This is no accident, as it helps to explain their behaviour – but note that it was much easier to understand the operation 'piecemeal' than it would have been if we had presented the complete predicate for the total operation 'in one piece'.

Clearly, there are potentially other operations of interest for such a system but, hopefully, the above gives a clear definition of at least some of the requisite functionality, i.e. the basic checking mechanisms.

Commentary

We will comment in detail on the effectiveness of such specification techniques below. However, it is worth drawing out one point here. In systems like the (hypothetical) one described above, time is a very important property and we would probably want to specify the frequency with which the sensor values are checked, and the length of time needed to carry out the checks. There is no built-in notion of time within Z, so there is no pre-defined way of doing this. However, it is possible to extend the Z language with notions of time, and we could have expressed timing constraints if we so wished.

The next two notations which we will consider are much more strongly oriented towards specifying temporal properties of systems and we will return later in the chapter to the general issue of what we can specify formally.

Logic specification

As indicated above, there are many logics that can be used in specifications. For our purposes it is interesting to illustrate the logic developed as part of the Alvey FOREST project (Maibaum *et al.*, 1986) and known as MAL – standing for Modal Action Logic. The logic is *deontic*, that is, it includes notions of *permission* and *obligation*. MAL specifications are concerned with agents and actions, so it is possible to specify, for example, that some agent is obliged to carry out some action. Coupled with a temporal capability, this gives the ability, in principle, to state that some action must be carried out within a given interval. This is intuitively appealing, as it is close to the basic notions of safety in many cases (e.g. nuclear trips and other shutdown systems). For simplicity, we only consider simple deontic specifications here and do not address the temporal issues.

The available specification logics are very different in form, although all embody the capability of making inferences about (permitted) behaviour from the basis of what has been specified. Thus the following example should be viewed as being illustrative, not representative.

Simple MAL specifications

MAL is a layered logic, that is, it is built up by adding a more sophisticated logical framework over a basis of first-order predicate calculus (the same underlying basis as found in Z). The layers and their uses are:

1. First-order predicate logic for specifying the static properties of data and other entities being modelled;
2. A modal logic for expressing the effects of performing operations;
3. A deontic logic for expressing permission and obligation for carrying out actions;
4. Action combinators for constructing larger actions from smaller ones;
5. A temporal logic for expressing timing constraints.

128 Safety Aspects of Computer Control

Our simple examples will largely be concerned with the first three layers.

Assuming that the reader is now familiar with the simple first-order logic concepts through the treatment of Z, we can start to explain the second layer, the action logic. In the action logic we can specify axioms of the form:

   pre-condition⇒ [action, agent] post-condition

This is very similar to the Z concepts, except that there is an explicit identification of the agent which engages in some action. The axiom means that, if the pre-condition holds and the agent carries out the action, then the post-condition holds. A simple and artificial example (ignoring the fact that we should first define the agent, action and predicates) might be:

   is_hungry⇒[eat, glutton] is_fat

Assuming that the glutton has a conscience we might also specify:

   is_fat⇒[diet, glutton] is_hungry

A benefit of the logic is that we can make deductions about logical possibilities, for example, that:

   is_hungry⇒[eat, glutton][diet, glutton] is_hungry

i.e. that the sequence of actions identified lead back to the state *is_hungry*.

Even the simple modal basis allows us to express interesting properties and to deduce relevant facts about sequences of operations. However, the deontic component offers much greater expressive power. The two basic constructions are:

   obl(action, agent)
   per(action, agent)

The permission operator, *per*, simply says that the agent may do the action, whereas the obligation operator, *obl*, says that the agent must do the identified action next (although there is no time limit without the temporal component). Thus in our example we might have:

   [eat, glutton] obl [diet, glutton]
   [diet, glutton] per [eat, glutton]

This defines a 'stricter regime!' where the glutton is permitted to eat after dieting but obliged to diet after eating. We can also put deontic terms into more general predicates, e.g.:

   obl [diet, glutton]⇔is_fat

In general, these logic components may be used as part of generalized predicates, including quantified expressions.

Following this elementary introduction to the basic MAL concepts (excluding operation combination and timing), we can now give a simple example of a MAL specification.

An example MAL specification

The specification is structured into sections introducing agents, data types (including types for the predicates used in the specifications) and variables, which also include definition of the actions which can be undertaken by the agents. There is a specification checking and proof system for MAL, and our example is presented in the syntax used by the MAL tools so that we can also illustrate the use of one of them. However, it should be stressed that this is only a partial specification intended for pedagogical purposes, not to give a complete problem specification.

The specification is intended to represent the structure of agents and the action of the agents for a triple modular redundant implementation of a trip system where each of the triplicated channels reads input from six temperature sensors. The output from the three channels goes via a voter to a simplex actuator. In MAL we have chosen to model each of the basic hardware components as an agent – this is the natural approach, as the hardware components are the only entities which can engage in actions. It is intended that the example be viewed as defining a computational structure in which the threshold calculations described in Z in the previous sections might be appropriate, i.e. they might represent the functionality implemented in the channels.

In MAL we first introduce the basic entities for the specifications, i.e. the agents and data items to be manipulated, together with (types of) predicates which represent the actions engaged in by the agents. There is also identification of other predicates which simply represent properties of the system.

We first introduce four types (sorts in FOREST's terminology) for agents:

AGENT
    Sensor, Channel, Voter, Actuator

These agents, or rather agent types, represent the four major units in the trip system. The connections between these components will become apparent through the axioms presented later.

The data section now introduces two basic data types representing the main data elements that pass between the hardware components (agents) and defines the set of sensors and channels, together with the voter and actuator. We have chosen to have six sensors, S1–S6, although this is a rather arbitrary decision (a different number would not have affected the example in a significant way). We also define two predicates representing 'calculations' carried out by the system, i.e. *in_limits* and *majority*, but only give their types, in the sense of stating the data over which they are defined rather than their properties in predicate calculus. These predicates are, however, conceptually similar to the operations defined in the Z specification shown above. The three predicates – *available*, *assessed* and *all_assessed* – are necessary to specify data flow through the components of the system and various synchronization properties. Finally, the predicates *reading*, *assess*, *arbitrate*, *reset* and *closedown* define actions which can be undertaken by the agents.

DATA
>   temp, threshold;
> S1,S2,S3,S4,S5,S6 -> Sensor;
> C1,C2,C3 -> Channel;
> V -> Voter;
> A -> Actuator;
>
> available : Sensor × temp;
> assessed : Channel × threshold;
> in_limits : temp × temp × temp × temp × temp × temp;
> signal : threshold;
> majority : threshold × threshold × threshold;
> all_assessed : ;
>
> (Sensor)   reading   :temp;
> (Channel) assess   :temp × temp × temp × temp × temp × temp × threshold;
> (Voter)   arbitrate   :threshold × threshold × threshold;
> (voter)   reset   ;
> (Actuator) closedown   ;

The predicates are intended to have intuitively obvious interpretations. *Available* indicates the availability of a new reading from the temperature sensor, *assessed* that a channel has made an assessment and has a threshold value (perhaps indicating that the temperature is outside the allowed limits) available. Both are true when data are available. The predicate *all_assessed* is true when all the channels have made an assessment, i.e. when *assessed* is true for each channel. These predicates are necessary to define the synchronization and flow of control between the various system components (agents).

In_limits is a predicate representing an evaluation over six temperature values to assess whether or not they are within the specified limits – this is, in effect, the predicate evaluated by each channel. It is true when the temperatures are inside the permitted range. *Signal* is true when an out-of-range temperature set is signalled from the channel to the voter. *Majority* is the analogue of the predicate *in_limits* evaluated by the voter.

The action *reading* delivers a temperature value from a sensor. *Assess* evaluates a set of six temperature readings and determines whether or not they (according to some averaging calculation) exceed the allowed threshold value – and signal a threshold value if this is the case. *Arbitrate* is a similar function to *assess*, dealing with the threshold signals coming from the three channels and *closedown* represents the action of shutting down the reactor (e.g. dropping the rods). Finally, *reset* enables the system to start reading temperature values again; it is slightly arbitrary that *reset* is deemed to be an action of the voter, but this reflects a view that, once the voter receives the inputs from the channels, the previous values are no longer needed. In practice, a rather looser synchronization may be appropriate.

We now introduce variables which enable us to state the axioms in the next section and define the semantics of the operations in which the agent types can engage. The temperature and threshold values with a numerical component represent the outputs from the sensors and from the channels, respectively. The identifiers introduced in the data section are also available for use in the axioms defining the system behaviour and clearly refer to parts of the physical system.

VARIABLES

    s: Sensor,
    c: Channel,
    t, tl, t2, t3, t4, t5, t6: temp,
    l, l1, l2, l3: threshold;

END

We can now specify the axioms which define the required behaviour of the system. The basic aim is to show the flow of data and control through the system, culminating in defining when the reactor is closed down. The axioms fall naturally into groups. We first state the axioms in each group then give an interpretation of their meaning:

/* Axioms for the trip system */

/* Axiom 1 */

all_assessed = > obl (reset, V);

/* Axiom 2 */

[reset, V]!all_assessed &
    !available(S1, t1) & !available(S2, t2) & !available(S3, t3) &
    !available(S4, t4) & !available(S5, t5) & !available(S6, t6) &
    !assessed(C1, l) & !assessed(C2, l) & !assessed(C3, l);

/* Axiom 3 */

FORALL s: Sensor (FORALL t: temp (!available(s,t) = > obl(reading(t), s)));

/* Axiom 4 */

FORALL s: Sensor (FORALL t: temp ([reading(t), s] available(s, t)));

/* Axiom 5 */

FORALL c: Channel ([assess(t1, t2, t3, t4, t5, t6, l), c] assessed (c, l));

/* Axiom 6 */

all_assessed <- FORALL c: Channel (assessed(c, l));

The above group of axioms is largely concerned with sequencing of the actions for the system as a whole. Axiom 1 says that when the *all_assessed* predicate is true, i.e. when all channels have assessed the input temperatures, the voter is obliged to carry out the reset action. Axiom 2 says that the consequence of carrying out the reset action is that no data are available from the sensors and that the assessed predicate reflecting the state of the channels is false for each channel (note: that '!' is used for $\neg$).

132 Safety Aspects of Computer Control

Axiom 3 says that all the sensors are obliged to read their associated temperatures when their output is not available. Axiom 4 says that after a sensor has engaged in the reading action the predicate *available* is true for the associated datum, indicating that it may be used by three channels carrying out the assessment. Axiom 5 represents a similar condition to Axiom 3 for the channels, and Axiom 6 says that *all_assessed* is true when all the channels have made their assessments.

None of the above axioms are very remarkable – they simply define the 'natural' sequencing of operations through the system. We can now consider the axioms that represent the channel behaviour:

/* Axiom 7 */

EXISTS t1: temp (EXISTS t2: temp (EXISTS t3: temp (
EXISTS t4: temp (EXISTS t5: temp (EXISTS t6: temp (
    FORALL c: Channel (EXISTS l: threshold(
        available(S1, t1) & available(S2, t2) & available(S3, t3) &
        available(S4, t4) & available(S5, t5) & available(S6, t6) &
        !assessed(c, l) = >
            obl (assess(t1, t2, t3, t4, t5, t6, l), c)))))))));

/* Axiom 8 */

EXISTS t1: temp (EXISTS t2: temp (EXISTS t3: temp (
EXISTS t4: temp (EXISTS t5: temp (EXISTS t6: temp(
    FORALL c: Channel (
        EXISTS l: threshold(
            !in_limits(t1, t2, t3, t4, t5, t6) = >
            [assess(t1, t2, t3, t4, t5, t6, l), c] signal(l)))))))));

The axioms here are rather clumsy due to the need to introduce variables for the temperature readings which pass between the sensors and the channels. Unfortunately, the MAL checker only allows single variables for each quantified statement, hence the need for the deeply nested existential quantifiers.

Axiom 7 says that when all the sensors have produced data values (temperature readings) then all the channels must assess the values and produce a threshold signal. In practice, it would probably be appropriate to specify that the action occurs when a sub-set of the data is available or after some time-out has occurred. Additionally, there may be a need to specify synchronization between the channels, i.e. that the channels work in 'lock-step'. For simplicity, we have not addressed such issues.

Axiom 8 states that if the temperature values are not within limits then the threshold value produced by each channel makes the predicate *signal* true, indicating the out-of-limits temperature values to the voter. It should be noted that we have not said how the predicate *in_limits* is defined, so we do not have a full definition of system behaviour.

Finally, we have the axioms defining the operations of the voter and actuator.

/* Axiom 9 */
EXISTS l1: threshold (EXISTS l2: threshold (EXISTS l3: threshold
           (assessed(c1, l1) & assessed(c2, l2) & assessed(c3, l3)
                = > obl (arbitrate(l1, l2, l3), V))));
/* Axiom 10 */
EXISTS l1: threshold (EXISTS l2: threshold (
     signal(l1) & signal(l2) & l1 != l2 = >
           [arbitrate (l1, l2, l3), V] obl (closedown, A)));

Axiom 9 says that the voter is obliged to carry out an arbitration when all the channels have produced values for assessment. Note that we cannot use the predicate *all_assessed* because we wish to identify that the values l1, l2 and l3 are actually used as a basis of the arbitration, i.e. we are identifying the flow of data from the channels to the voter.

Finally Axiom 10 says that if any two of the three channels indicate that the temperatures are outside their set limits then the *closedown* action must occur. The specification here is a little artificial, as the redundancy and voting is only useful if the channels might 'see' different temperature values (perhaps due to synchronization problems) or the channels may fail. Again for simplicity, in illustrating the use of MAL we have not included such details here.

In principle, we should prove that the specification has certain consistency properties, e.g. that it does not require one agent to carry out two actions at once (the semantics of obligation is that the agent must do the obliged action next). Also, we can derive properties of interest from the specification – for instance, it should be possible to show that the temperature values going out of range implies that the actuator is obliged to carry out the closedown action. The FOREST project has developed some tools, including a proof assistant, for investigating such properties.

We illustrate below the use of one of the tools, a simulator, which enables the user to 'animate' the specifications to investigate their consequences. The example is a fragment from the middle of a simulation using the above specification:

    assessed:
    in_limits:
    signal:
        signal(.(_5245,_5246))
    available:
    majority:
    EVENT
    s1 is obliged to do action reading([_5287|_5288])
    s2 is obliged to do action reading([_5287|_5288])
    s3 is obliged to do action reading([_5287|_5288])
    s4 is obliged to do action reading([_5287|_5288])
    s5 is obliged to do action reading([_5287|_5288])
    s6 is obliged to do action reading([_5287|_5288])
    v is obliged to do action arbitrate([_5287|_5288],[_5290|_5291],
    [_5293|_5294])

Permitted action-agent pairs are:
1 OBL arbitrate([_5265|_5266],[_5268|_5269],[_5271|_5272]) v
2 OBL reading ([_5280|_5281]) s6
3 OBL reading ([_5289|_5290]) s5
4 OBL reading ([_5298|_5299]) s4
5 OBL reading ([_5307|_5308]) s3
6 OBL reading ([_5316|_5317]) s2
7 OBL reading ([_5325|_5326]) s1

The five lines containing a predicate name followed by a colon give the value for each of the associated predicates. Here only *signal* has a defined value and the numeric identifiers (e.g. _5245) stand for internal variables used in the simulator. Note also that the translator from the above specification form turns all the variable names into lower case for use by the simulator.

The above fragment of the tool output shows a situation where each sensor is ready to make a temperature reading, and the voter is ready to arbitrate. This means that some values have already been read and the sensors have been reset. The simulator identifies the events that are obliged and those which are permitted (which should include those that are obliged). In this case, the two sets are the same, as we have not user permission operators in the specification.

We now show what happens if we interact with the simulator. As there is more than one possibility for the next action (there is no absolute timing relationship between the agents), the user is asked to select an agent/action pair to 'fire':

Choose a pair (enter number)>2.
FINISH [reading([_5280|_5281]),s6]
Satisfied axiom(s): 4 8
Satisfied axiom(s): 3 7
Meta rules checked.
assessed:
in_limits:
signal:
    signal(.(_6160,_6161))
available:
    available(s6,.(_6161,_6162))
majority:
EVENT
s1 is obliged to do action reading([_6202|_6203])
s2 is obliged to do action reading([_6202|_6203])
s3 is obliged to do action reading([_6202|_6203])
s4 is obliged to do action reading([_6202|_6203])
s5 is obliged to do action reading([_6202|_6203])
v is obliged to do action arbitrate([_6202|_6203],[_6205|_6206], [_6208|6209])
Permitted action-agent pairs are:
1 OBL arbitrate([_6180|_6181],[_6183|_6184],[_6186|_6187]) v
2 OBL reading([_6195|_6196]) s5
3 OBL reading([_6204|_6205]) s4

4 OBL reading([_6213|_6214]) s3
5 OBL reading([_6222|_6223]) s2
6 OBL reading([_6231|_6232]) s1

Choose a pair (enter number) > 2.

The simulator shows that the selected action – reading from sensor s1 – has finished and, as a consequence, four of the above axioms are satisfied. The term *Meta rules checked* means that consistency checks (such as no agent being required to engage in more than one action at once) are satisfied. More helpfully, the state definition now shows that a reading is available from sensor s6, so we can see that progress is being made. The simulator then asks for the next step to be identified – note that pair 2 has now been redefined and that the internal variable identifiers have also been updated.

Using the simulator in this way it is possible to 'step through' the specification to see that the specified behaviour is as expected. In this particular case we can see the cycle of the sensors reading values, the channels making the assessment and then re-enabling the sensors. Since we have not defined the predicate *in_limits* we would need to define the truth value of the predicate explicitly to cause the voter to be activated. We would also discover that, if the voter were enabled this way, it would be obliged to arbitrate and reset at the same time, and we would be informed of this problem (as noted above, this is an artificial aspect of the specification introduced to simplify modelling of the cyclic nature of the system activity).

We will return to discuss the relative strengths and weaknesses of the MAL approach later, but it is worth stressing that we have not only been able to specify required behaviour but, through the animator, shown that the system has the expected behaviour in defined circumstances. Thus simulation (and other forms of 'animation') can be an aid to validation of specifications.

Process algebra specification

The third illustration of formal techniques will be given in timed CCS – timed Calculus of Communicating Systems (Moller and Tofts, 1989). The notation is based on earlier work by Milner (1980), which defined a calculus for representing communication between processes and composition of processes as a way of constructing models of systems. The later development which we shall employ introduces the notion of time into the calculus, and makes it possible, for example, to specify delays between communication events.

The essence of all process algebras is to identify processes and the communication actions which the processes can engage in. Actions of processes are labelled so that corresponding actions – like sending and receiving data – can be identified. Typically, the algebras use conventions like '!' and '?' for output and input, respectively, or another form of 'decoration', i.e. 'ā' 'a'. The notations enable the syntax of possible communications to be defined by expressing alternative actions, repetition, and so on. In addition, they enable composite processes to be constructed (e.g. by composing processes in parallel). Our examples in TCCS will show most of these basic capabilities.

Basic concepts of TCCS

The three primitive notions in timed CCS are actions, processes and time. Variables (in the conventional sense) are treated as special forms of process. A system simply comprises a set of processes.

Processes, typically denoted by upper-case letters, correspond to the classical notion of process, that is, a sequential computation which may run in parallel with other sequential processes. Actions are typically denoted by lower-case letters. The language has the notion of complementation where actions denoted, say x, are complemented by $\bar{x}$. If a process engages in some action $\bar{x}$ then it can communicate with some other process which is ready to engage in an x action. The term 'engage in some action' can be thought of as being similar to 'call an entry' in a task in an Ada program. The complementation is very similar to the notion of calling an entry and accepting the entry call in a rendezvous. If no such action is possible then the system of processes deadlocks. Time is treated as a set of natural numbers and delays and other temporal properties may be specified in these time units.

Systems are specified in timed CCS by defining the actions in which processes can engage and, more particularly, the order and conditions under which the actions can occur. The ordering and conditions are defined by means of expressions representing the composition of processes either out of actions or other processes. The basic syntax for process definitions includes the following constructions:

$$P ::= \mathbf{0} \mid X \mid a.P \mid (t).P \mid \delta.P \mid P+Q \mid P/a$$

The constructions may be interpreted as follows:

0 is the null process which can do nothing. Strictly, we often require a process to end with a **0** but, typically, we omit the null process;
X represents a process bound to the variable X;
$a.P$ represents a process which can perform action a and then behave like the process P;
$(t).P$ is a delay and represents the process which will behave like P after t units of time;
$\delta.P$ represents an undefined delay, i.e. the process acts like P but is willing to wait any amount of time before proceeding;
$P+Q$ represents a choice between doing P or Q. The choice will be made on the basis of the first action;
P/a represents the process P with the action a hidden.

There are a number of other basic constructions, but the above will suffice for our example. We will also use one or two shorthands which we will explain as we go along.

Processes can now be defined using the above forms. As will probably be apparent from the available constructions, processes are often defined in a recursive style, e.g.:

$$P \hat{=} (t).a.P$$

is a process which waits t units, performs a, and then acts as P, i.e. it loops in computational terms. The process:

$$Q \hat{=} \delta.\bar{a}.Q$$

represents a process which can communicate with P. The system:

$$S \hat{=} P | Q$$

executes P and Q indefinitely. Since Q is prepared to wait any length of time to do $\bar{a}$ the system never deadlocks.

In general, we need to show that the timing constraints in a timed CCS specification are such that the system can proceed. In our examples we will rely on intuition to deal with such properties but, in principle, these are properties which can be resolved entirely within the formal framework.

Simple example in TCCS

Our simple example is, again, based on the model of a temperature monitoring and trip system illustrated above. In TCCS the example is conceptually more similar to the FOREST specification than the Z specification, as it is concerned with modelling the agents and their interactions, rather than saying what the individual actions should do. Nonetheless, there are still considerable differences between the FOREST and TCCS specifications, and we will draw out some of the points below.

There is a definition of the syntax and semantics of TCCS, but is quite common to use syntactic extensions and conventions in order to simplify specifications. We make use of some of these extensions and explain them as we use them. We have also employed slightly different expressions for some of the process definitions than those used by the originators of TCCS to simplify printing the specifications, but we believe that the example obeys the spirit of the TCCS definition, if not the symbol! Unlike MAL and Z, there is no well-defined declaration syntax requiring us to introduce objects before using them, and we introduce the specification of the processes progressively, explaining the properties of each process in turn.

We first introduce the processes which represent the sensors:

$$S_n \hat{=} (t_n).\bar{o}_n(h_n).S_n$$

This identifies a process family, S, each member of which, S_n, represents a temperature sensor (refer to the examples above for a detailed informal description of the functionality of the sensor). The action o_n represents the output of a temperature value for use by the monitoring channels. Each process waits t units of time before engaging in o_n, delivering a value h_n representing the measured temperature, then behaves like S_n. In other words, the process loops reading the temperature values and passing them on. Note that this is somewhat different to the MAL specification in that we have specified sensor behaviour as cyclic, with a fixed cycle time t, rather than stating that the system behaviour is cyclic but without indicating absolute timing properties.

We now need to define channels and to say how they communicate with the sensors (and the voter):

$$C_m \hat{=} (\prod_n {}_1^6 \delta.o_n (h_n).\mathbf{0}); (\beta).\bar{a}_m(\alpha(t_n | n \in \{1 .. 6\})).C_m$$

This rather more complex specification can be read in two halves: the part before the semi-colon and the part after. The semi-colon indicates a composition between processes. It can be thought of as a convenient abbreviation which prevents us from having to write a more complex expression composing actions with the '.' operator to define the overall process.

The first part uses the $\prod$ operator to compose a number of processes in parallel. The processes are indexed by the variable n and the number of processes is defined by the upper and lower bounds following the symbol, which are 1 and 6 in this case. Thus, in this example, the process C_m waits for each of the six temperature sensors (recall that δ represents an arbitrary wait) and takes a temperature value, known to the process as t_n, from each sensor. The null action $\mathbf{0}$ is needed for technical reasons but is often omitted from specifications. In effect, it just represents the fact that the six sub-processes which read the sensor values 'synchronize' before the process terminates. In practice, we would probably wish to specify a more complex communication structure where the channel processed the sensor values when it had received a majority of them (recall the Z specification, where we dealt with maintenance of a record of sensor states), or after some time-out had expired (see below).

The second part of the process definition represents the assessment of the six temperature values and the communication of the result to the voter. The function calculates a value based on the six temperature values received from the sensors. This value is then communicated by the action a_m to the voter, which we define next. The time (β) represents the delay involved in calculating the function:

$$V \hat{=} (\prod_m {}_1^3 \delta.a_m (y_m).\mathbf{0}); (\gamma).\bar{r}_m(\mu(y_m | m \in \{1 .. 3\})).V$$

The voter structure is very similar to that defined for the channels except that the voter waits for values from each channel. Again, a calculation function and a delay are specified. We next consider the actuator and introduce a process which nominally represents the reactor itself.

$$A \hat{=} \textit{Time-out}_t(r(q).A'(q), \bar{d}.\textit{Reactor})$$

$$A'(q) \hat{=} \text{ if } q=tt \text{ then } \bar{d}.\textit{Reactor} \text{ else } A$$

There are two extensions/conventions in use here. A time-out can be defined in TCCS as a process which waits an arbitrary length of time to do some operation, *or* carries out some other operation. It is such a common requirement to wish to model time-outs that they have been 'packaged' using the operator *Time-out*. In the example above the first parameter represents the normal action, the second the action which occurs if the time-out expires and the subscript t is the time-out period. Thus the actuator either does the action $r(q)$ with the value passed by the voter or, if the time-out expires, carries out *Reactor*. This shows the desirable design principle that the system fails safe. If the sensor system does not tell the actuator to keep the rods out of the reactor sufficiently frequently then the rods will be dropped.

The second extension deals with the definition of the behaviour of A'. This gives a logical defintion (which could be interpreted in programming terms) of the behaviour of A' which chooses either to drop the rods into the reactor (action d) if requested to do so by the reactor or behaves like A – again, this recursive definition effectively defines an iterative process. The behaviour of the process *Reactor* is nowhere defined. For the purposes of our example we can assume this to be specified elsewhere, perhaps in some totally different way (e.g. electronic circuit diagrams for the rod control actuators).

We could now define the whole system by combining the various processes in parallel. Since this adds nothing to our example, however, we omit the definition. Having obtained the definition, we could carry out a number of analyses (e.g. to determine whether or not the processes can deadlock). In our simple example it is relatively easy to see that the cyclic nature of the sensors is independent of the timing of the rest of the system, except that the sensors wait for their output values to be read. The channels and voter timing are dependent on the passage of data from the previous processes, and the actuator either waits for the voter or carries out the drop action after the time-out period has elapsed. Again, in order to give a complete and convincing treatment of the problem, we should specify failure behaviour within this framework.

We note considerable differences between the MAL and TCCS specifications. Some of this is due to our usage of the two notations, but it has been relatively easy to show the composition of multiple processes and the communication between the processes. We return to a comparison of the three approaches below.

Refinement

Space does not permit us to illustrate a complete refinement here, so our intention is to give a more detailed (but not too technical) discussion of the nature of refinement in order to clarify the concept. Our description essentially deals with refinement in the context of model-based specification – conceptually similar but technically different approaches are used with other formalisms (e.g. algebraic specifications).

Refinement covers both guidelines on how to proceed from a high-level to a low-level specification, and rules for verifying (checking) that this has been done in a consistent manner. It is normal to specify both data which will be stored within a computer system and operations which will modify or transform the data. Thus refinement rules have to deal both with refining data and with refining operations.

With data objects, the primary requirement for the verification rules is to show that all data which can be unambiguously represented at the high level can similarly be represented at the low level. This is usually referred to as *adequacy*. For example, a high-level specification may include the concept of a set, and a lower-level specification may choose to *implement* the set as a list. It is normal to define a function or relation which maps the values between the two levels. Demonstration of adequacy thus means showing that the relation or function gives an unambiguous mapping between the levels. In our (somewhat simplified)

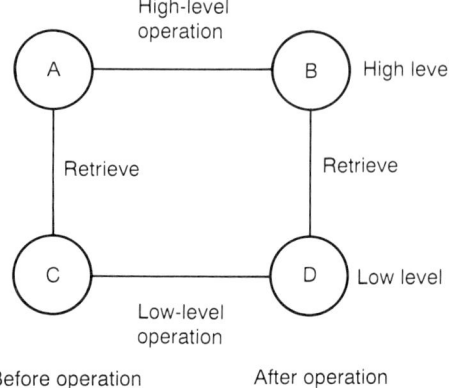

Figure 7.1 *Relationship between before and after states*

example this amounts to showing that every set can be represented as a list, and vice versa for every list that can be generated as the representation of a set.

The function or relation between the levels is given different names in different methods, but it is perhaps most commonly called a *retrieve* function, as it can be thought of as retrieving the high-level values from their low-level representation. In general, there will not be a one-to-one mapping between the levels, and it may be possible to represent *more* values at the low level than at the high level. For example, integers in the range 1 to 10 in a specification might be represented by full (machine-processable) integers in a program or lower-level specification. Further, values at the high level may be represented in more than one way at the low level – indeed, this is the case in our simple set example.

With functions/operations the requirement is to show that the operations at each level *do the same thing* – albeit after allowing for mapping between the data objects at each level. This is usually referred to as *satisfaction*. The concept of satisfaction can most readily be illustrated by considering Figure 7.1, which relates states before and after an operation.

Imagine starting with a low-level value (C) and mapping it to a high-level value (A) before applying the high-level operation to arrive at value B. It would also be possible to carry out the low-level operation first, then to map from D to B. Satisfaction requires that each route leads to the establishment of the same value at B. There are in fact many different definitions of refinement, although many of them are conceptually similar (but not identical) to the form illustrated in Figure 7.1. In practice, refinement rules typically incorporate a set of *proof obligations* which are criteria that must be met if a refinement is to be valid – more strictly, the obligations are theorems which have to be proven to show adequacy and satisfaction.

There are, in general, differences in amount of detail between two levels of specification, so verifying the proof obligations cannot show that the specifications are equivalent – merely that they are non-contradictory. This is essentially the point we were making earlier when we were drawing the distinction between the pairs: verification/validation and synthetic/analytic reasoning. More significantly, there is a considerable amount of freedom in defining a set of refinement rules (e.g. in the way they treat non-determinism), and this has led to many sets of refinement rules being developed, each with its own strengths and weaknesses. This does not mean that some techniques are right and that others are wrong, rather that they have different areas of applicability.

We have illustrated the concepts of refinement in the context of model-oriented specification. With the other approaches to formal specification the technical details of refinement are different from that of model-oriented specification, but the spirit is the same – verifying that we are adding detail, or otherwise enriching specifications, in a manner which is consistent with the initial specification.

Our brief discussion has also focused largely on the verification aspects of refinement, and not on the guidelines for proceeding from a high-level to a low-level specification. Typically, these guidelines will (or should) cover issues of functional decomposition, and also consider non-functional properties of systems. That is, the guidelines should recognize that non-functional issues such as performance, reliability, and so on can *drive* the refinement process. Unfortunately, current refinement approaches do not deal adequately with such issues, so, for example, there are no refinement rules which deal adequately with fault tolerance – an approach would need to show that the fault models plus fault-recovery mechanisms at one level 'satisfied' those at the next higher level. This remains an area of research.

Summary and comparison of approaches

There are a wide variety of types of formal methods, each with different characteristics, which means that generalizations about formal methods may be more misleading than helpful. It is also rather difficult to appreciate what the methods are like in use from simple definitions and descriptions. By way of analogy, consider how difficult it is to appreciate the utility of a programming language without trying it out on a few problems. This is why we have taken the trouble to give fairly extensive examples of three rather different types of formal method. We are now in a position to make some comparisons, although we steer clear of value judgements regarding utility, as this is the province of the next section.

First, we can now see clearly that the three methods permit us to do quite different things. Z enabled us to give quite detailed specifications of the required behaviour of the actions to be carried out in the system, but was rather poor at modelling communication and has no way of representing concurrency. In contrast, MAL and TCCS are much clearer about system structure (including potential for parallel execution) and communication, although they are relatively weak at defining functionality. The differences between MAL and TCCS largely stem from the fact that MAL is intended to define allowable behaviour, in the sense of a set of requirements, and the TCCS specification is much more at the design level, being concerned with showing more concrete process structures. Similarly, MAL and TCCS allow us to make statements about timing behaviour, whereas Z does not.

Some of the above differences are partly a reflection of the way in which we have used the notations. For example, it is possible to specify timing in Z. Indeed, the author has helped to develop some timing extensions to Z and has used them to specify safety properties (Clarke *et al.*, 1990), but we believe we have accurately characterized the 'natural' way to use the core specification languages in each case. Thus we must conclude that different methods have quite different expressive powers.

Second, we believe that it is quite difficult to use the techniques outside their natural domains. This does not mean to say it is impossible. As we indicated above, it is possible to extend the techniques to deal with additional properties of systems but it is not entirely straightforward – for example, adding a deontic component to Z would be quite difficult, especially when it came to defining the semantics for the extended notation. However, since the methods illustrate different facets of systems, then they can be used together – assuming we can map adequately between the notations (e.g. to relate a Z action specification to a TCCS process action). Thus we believe that it is both possible and beneficial to use an eclectic approach to specification, although this is rarely (if ever) done in practice.

Third, the mathematics, although valuable for its precision, does not stand on its own. In the example it was essential to use prose to define what it was that the specifications were meant to relate to – 'in the real world'. It is always necessary to support formal specifications with prose and, without this, we have no way of knowing what the specifications mean. More technically, we know what they mean in terms of the underlying logic but we do not know what they mean in relation to the systems we hope to build. This is a general property of formal approaches, not just a characteristic of our examples, but one which we hope is adequately borne out by the examples.

Fourth, there is considerable difference in the conciseness or verbosity of the notations. Again, this is partly an effect of the examples chosen and the way the problems have been addressed but, for example, we can conclude fairly unequivocally that timed CCS is a much more compact notation than MAL for describing multiple communicating processes. This is important, as conciseness influences intelligibility, although there is not a simple relation. Extremely terse and verbose notations may be equally hard to read and, ideally, we require concise notations so we do not have much to read, but which are still as easy to read as ordinary English prose. This is, of course, a difficult compromise to achieve, and we will leave the reader to draw his own conclusions about which (if any) of the three notations used above satisfy this requirement.

Finally, it is important to stress the point that the methods are genuinely different in their capabilities, and any generalizations about formal methods (other than this one!) may be quite misleading and inappropriate to some particular class of method.

STRENGTHS AND WEAKNESSES OF FORMAL METHODS

In the introduction we made a number of comments regarding the strengths and weaknesses or limitations of formal methods. We now return to these issues and endeavour to substantiate them as far as possible.

Strengths

We identified in the introduction a number of (purported) benefits of using formal methods. Our aim here is to amplify these points and to provide a justification for our views based, as far as possible, on the insight gleaned from the above examples. We asserted that the benefits of using formal methods for specification included precision, abstraction, conciseness and manipulability. We address these points, and a few subsidiary topics, dealing with them first as issues of principle, then assessing how close current methods come to these ideals.

Some of the points made below are not clear-cut. To avoid circumlocution we state the positive view here and explain any contrary views later.

Strengths – in principle

Specifications are primarily media for communication. That is, they are intended to convey information from the producer of the specification to the reader, i.e. from the specifier of a module to the implementor. Alternatively, they can be viewed as a means for documenting agreements, i.e. the specifier and implementor agree that the specification defines the interface to the module which is to be built. This is still a form of communication, although it implies different degrees of responsibility for producing and verifying the document. A communication medium should be (or facilitate specifications which are) clear and unambiguous. This is not equivalent to saying that they are precise, abstract or concise, but there are relationships between these five properties, as we will now show.

Ambiguity is easily dealt with. Formal notations are simply 'sugared mathematics', and hence they have an unambiguous meaning, that of the underlying mathematical structures. More accurately, the more sophisticated mathematical notions are built on more primitive notions (e.g. sets and propositional logic), and this means that there is a well-defined *interpretation* of the formal notations, and this is enough, in principle, to ensure consistent interpretation of specifications. We can now focus on the issue of clarity.

Formal specifications are (or can be) very precise definitions because the semantics of the notations are well defined and those of other media (e.g. English) are not. Other notations (e.g. those used by structured methods) are also precise but they are less expressive (e.g. showing structure, not functionality), so formal methods give more *useful* precision than other approaches to specification. The direct benefit of the precision is that it reduces (or even eliminates) the risk of ambiguity and misinterpretation of specifications. Thus precision is a property of formal methods (or notations) and it is a major contributor to the production of unambiguous specifications. It should also be pointed out that this precision has a major pragmatic benefit in reviews. It is often possible to have very detailed and constructive reviews when they are based on formal methods because there is no argument about what has been said, only about whether or not what has been said is what should have been said. (This point was borne out by the examples included in this chapter, as errors were detected very quickly when they were reviewed by the author's colleagues, although the reviewers knew little about the problems being addressed.) In other words, precision aids validation as well as communication.

The nature of the abstractions made possible by use of appropriate formalisms should be clear from the examples given above. Abstraction is one of our primary intellectual weapons for coping with complexity, and it aids clarity by 'drawing away from' details which are not germane to our interests. This is perhaps illustrated most clearly by our use of timed CCS – the properties of interest related to communication and timing structure – and we were able to deal with those issues without making significant commitments to descriptions of functionality. Thus, in this case, we were able to abstract away from (almost) all functional details, making the communication and timing structure clear.

Clarity also arises from conciseness. As we indicated above, formal notations vary in their ability to represent concepts concisely but, hopefully, the examples serve to show that they can be used to produce very compact descriptions. More importantly, they can be much more compact than equally clear natural language descriptions while (normally) being more precise. To some extent, this is borne out by the examples above (compare the length of the specifications with that of their prose explanations), but, obviously, the examples are a little biased by the fact that it was necessary to give a more tutorial level of description than would normally be the case.

The properties of abstraction, precision and conciseness all contribute to clarity, as does good structure. In principle, there is no reason why formal methods shold not yield good structure, but this does not seem to be an inherent property of the formalisms. This is perhaps an area where the structured methods are more effective.

In the introduction we stated that a valuable property of formal specifications is that they are manipulable, that is, there are well-defined rules for analysing and perhaps transforming formal specifications. As illustrated by our examples, this property can be used to show consistency of specifications and to derive important consequences of specifications (e.g. that processes cannot deadlock or that a trip system is obliged to drop the control rods if the temperatures sensed go outside the valid range). Thus manipulability also aids in validation and it gives further abstractions – the derived properties – which can also help make specifications clearer.

In general, it is possible to represent the mapping between a specification and the corresponding program within a formal framework. Obviously, a very important aspect of manipulability (which we have not been able to illustrate) is the possibility of verifying that the implementation, or at least the source code, satisfies the specification. More generally, it is possible to reduce the verification of the mapping between levels of specification and between specifications and programs to a matter for formal proof. Thus, in principle, formal methods offer very high confidence that the programs correspond to their specifications.

Finally, it should be noted that formal methods are, in effect, a *lingua franca* – they will be (should be) interpreted in the same way by readers of different backgrounds, whether the distinctions are between their mother-tongues or their professional disciplines. This truly is a property we require of a language for communication.

Strengths – in practice

It is interesting to consider the extent to which the above strengths are realized in practice. We discuss weaknesses below, so our aim here is not to be directly critical but simply to observe which of the above supposed strengths are manifest in practice. The simple answer is all, to some extent!

Formal methods are perhaps most effective as a form of communication and for agreeing and documenting (design) decisions. The properties relating to ambiguity, clarity and so on are not fully substantiable (see below), but, nonetheless, they do offer an effective medium for communication – between cognoscenti.

These observations are borne out by industrial experience. The use of formal methods in industry is not widespread but, where they have been applied, the evidence is encouraging. It is always difficult to make valid comparative analyses of the effectiveness of software development technology but, for example, IBM Hursley report a reduction in development costs of 9% through the use of Z on CICS. (This figure has been widely stated at meetings on software engineering by IBM staff but, to the author's knowledge, the claim has yet to be published in the literature.) They also report a significant improvement in fault rate, although the formally specified version of the product is not yet on full release. In the context of safety-critical systems probably the most notable examples of the use of formal methods are by Rolls-Royce and Associates and by RSRE on VIPER. In both cases significant quality benefits were attributed to the use of formal methods.

Thus there is relatively little evidence about the use of formal methods on real industrial projects of any nature, and even less on those involving safety-critical software. Nonetheless, what evidence there is indicates that the strengths discussed above are found in practice, albeit with some limitations. The greatest limitations, in principle, probably relates to the issue of ambiguity. The biggest problem in practice relates to manipulability largely due to the paucity of effective tools. We return to these two points below.

Weaknesses

Unfortunately, the existing formal methods do not fully live up to the ideal described above. This is mainly due to the state of development of current methods and their support tools, but there are also some issues of principle which run counter to those set out above, or which at least indicate limits to what they mean in practice for formal software development.

Weaknesses – in principle

The most fundamental weakness (or limitation) relates to the distinction between synthetic and analytic reason which we introduced earlier. We may be able to reduce software development (from a top-level formal specification to an executable program) to a purely analytical process, but validation of the top-level specification is inevitably a synthetic activity. In other words, we may be able to carry out development from the specification with 'mathematical certainty' but we will always have doubts about the veracity of the initial specification.

Clearly, it is extremely valuable to remove doubts associated with software development but, unfortunately, most evidence suggests that the primary source of (significant) software errors is the specification – and safety-critical systems are, if anything, more prone to this sort of problem (Leveson, 1986). At best, this means that the mathematics, of itself, is insufficient to assure safety. Perhaps more significantly, we are now faced with a value judgement about the level of effort we should put into formal development as against the effort we should place on means of validating the top-level specification. It should be noted that we can use proof techniques to assist in validation (e.g. by deriving safety properties from a specification), but this simply reduces the 'gap' between formalisms and the 'real world', and does not eliminate it. Thus we know that we cannot simply rely on formalism to achieve and demonstrate safety. We will return to this general issue from a more pragmatic perspective after considering ambiguity and the nature of safety properties.

Another major (although less clear-cut) limitation relates to interpretation of specifications. Formal specifications do not just have an interpretation in terms of the underlying mathematics, they are also interpreted by software engineers in terms of a computational model and by system users in terms of a model of the use of the system in its operational environment. The issue of ambiguity then becomes not one of the existence of a unique model for the specification in the underlying logic but of compatibility of interpretations made in different domains by individuals with differing backgrounds and knowledge. Formal specifications are still less ambiguous than most prose, but they cannot be said to be free of ambiguity in any absolute sense, as they are open to interpretation. This weakens (but does not negate) this strength of formal methods.

Another fundamental issue is that so-called 'non-functional' requirements and properties such as safety and security cannot be adequately articulated within a first-order framework. This is a somewhat subtle technical point with is best illustrated by an example.

Consider the requirement for a system to tolerate single-point failures. At the level of system architecture this may be interpreted to mean the failure of single processor/memory units. At the level of software module specification this may be treated as failure of a procedure invocation, and at a lower level if may be interpreted as the failure of a single logic gate or transistor. In other words, the requirement is re-interpreted in terms of the relevant abstractions at each stage in the development process. Thus we view properties such as safety (which may encompass notions of fault tolerance) as being higher-order in that they are really specifications which apply to other specifications.

In order to link formal specifications to the 'real world' and to guide the interpretation of the specifications, we give prose descriptions of the basic entities specified and other fundamental notions. In a prose specification we always have to work with such informal descriptions. With a formal specification we can work largely within an analytical framework (subject to the need to re-interpret parts of the specification such as the notion of fault) once we have established the primary links between our specifications and the 'real world', so there is reduced scope for errors of misinterpretation. Thus the true limit of formal methods with respect to ambiguity and precision is that they can only reduce the scope for misinterpretation and other failings of specifications, not eliminate them.

We next address another issue of principle, which was not treated under the heading of strengths above, and which has some practical ramifications. Once we realize that there is no such notion as absolute safety we have to recognize that we are primarily concerned with gaining assurance (or confidence) in safety, not a guarantee. As we indicated earlier in this chapter, assurance arises from comprehension and diversity both of (or in) the product and the process. If we carry out formal proofs as well as producing formal specifications then we are producing artefacts of considerable complexity – in other words, the proofs themselves are highly complex and difficult to understand. This leads to the question: Does the use of formal proofs increase or decrease our comprehension and assurance in a software system?

It is hard to answer this fairly from the point of view of principle because it is difficult not to be influenced by the capability of current program-verification tools, so we defer discussion of this point. There is one further issue of principle, however, regarding formal proofs which we should raise. Certain properties of specifications and programs (e.g. whether or not they halt) are formally undecidable. This means that it is impossible to write a program (e.g. a theorem prover) that can decide (calculate) whether or not the undecidable property holds (e.g. that the program will halt). It is not often that such problems are encountered in practice, but it is important to be aware of the perhaps surprising result that there are some properties which simply cannot be proven within a formal framework.

Weaknesses – in practice

There are many weaknesses or limitations of current formal methods. Our aim here is to give a brief survey of the most critical issues and to attempt a fair assessment of the likelihood that these problems will be resolved in the near future. As far as possible, the comments build on the insights gained by studying the examples set out above.

The most striking aspect of the example specifications is the forbidding symbology and, to a lesser extent, the arcane terminology. The mathematical abstractions embodied in notations such as Z and timed CCS facilitate brevity and precision, but they do not necessarily contribute to clarity. Indeed, there are many who would argue that the objectives of clarity and precision (or clarity and conciseness) are fundamentally opposed. In part, this is an educational issue to which we will return below, but there seems to be some substance in this criticism. Even seasoned users of formal methods often have difficulty in reading someone else's specifications, at least until they get used to the style. In the author's view this is because, in practice, we rely a good deal on the informal interpretation of the specifications, not their interpretations in terms of the underlying logic, in order to gain comprehension.

A somewhat related issue is that there is a high 'guff-to-stuff' ratio in many formal specifications. In other words, it is often necessary to set out a lot of basic background mathematics which has no direct bearing on the problem in hand before we can directly specify the system of interest. In our examples this is perhaps most apparent with the Z specifications, although the author believes that this is a property of the type of problem specified, not the Z notation itself. This problem is also clearly manifest with verification environments such as m-EVES (Craigen et al., 1987), where it is often necessary to prove many elementary mathematical theorems in order to build a basis on which to reason about the program properties of interest. This directly affects clarity and comprehension, as discussed above.

It could be argued that the formal specifications are not particularly precise as the notations and semantics for the methods are not particularly well defined. This is not an entirely fair criticism with the examples chosen but it is certainly the case that there are many variants of Z and ways of applying timed CCS. Also, some notations are considerably less well defined than the examples we have used, so it is not always clear what is meant by a formal specification in practice, although they can, in principle, be made precise. In the case of Z we have the ability to extend the language (e.g. by adding new operators) and there is no way of guaranteeing that these syntactic extensions are valid semantically. Thus current formal techniques are less well defined than they might be, and there are some difficult compromises between expressive power, flexibility and precision of definition.

Although the above problems are, to a large extent, practical issues, they will not be solved in the short run, although it is to be expected that technical progress will eventually yield re-usable specification libraries and more 'user-friendly' notations (e.g. by linking formal and structured methods). It is also to be expected that formal methods will 'stabilize' and the quality of their semantic and syntactic definitions will improve (there is already evidence for this: e.g. there are moves to standardize VDM and Z, which are two of the leading model-based specification approaches).

As the examples show, we have specification languages which are effective at representing functionality and certain aspects of concurrency. We have also seen that they are capable of representing some timing properties and more sophisticated notions such as permission and obligation. However, there are limitations. The concept of time is very abstract and it is quite difficult to handle absolute clock time within the available specification formalisms (in fact there are considerable philosophical difficulties here, especially when we need to deal with time in distributed systems, where we cannot guarantee clock synchronization). There are no well-defined ways of handling faults, or fault tolerance, although this is an area where there is now some research being undertaken.

A related (and rather stronger) point is that current refinement techniques do not deal with timing and failure behaviour. That is, we do not have well-defined rules for carrying out refinement in such a way that we can guarantee that the implementation we produce satisfies the timing and/or failure specifications. As almost all safety-critical systems have to satisfy timing requirements and achieve safety even in the presence of failures this is a major drawback, although it is much less of a problem in 'mainstream' developments. There seems to be no reason, in principle, why the above problems should not be solved in the reasonably near future, although the issues of refinement are quite subtle, and it would perhaps be unwise to rely on solutions appearing within the next ten years.

A further major issue is how much we have to trust tools. Clearly, it is necessary to trust some of the tools we use (e.g. loaders). The crux is the extent to which we have to trust complex tools, especially those which may be more complex than our application. In fact it is quite likely that any compilers and theorem provers used will be more complex than the application program. In many circumstances we have some form of independent check on the tool, e.g. we carry out testing on loaded code which gives an independent check (albeit probably far from exhaustive) on the compiler and loader. However, to a large extent, the tools have to be trusted except insofar as the testing and execution of the application gives an independent check. This is particularly worrying for tools such as theorem provers, which are often complex heuristic programs. Proving compilers and theorem provers (or proof checkers) is a difficult task, and certainly beyond the state of the art – although again these are problems which are being researched. There is also a recursive problem – to what extent do we trust the tools used to verify the verification tools and so on? Thus the use for formal methods and their support tools reduces certain classes of risk (e.g. that the specifications are inconsistent), but it does not remove all risks and introduces others, particularly in the area of trust in tools. Again, it would seem unwise to rely on having solutions to these problems within a decade, if not longer in this case.

Finally, we should not forget education and training. It is clear that few practising software engineers have the necessary skills to use formal methods. Perhaps more significantly, there are few engineers with both the application domain knowledge necessary to help validate the specifications and the skills to write or read them, and this exacerbates the validation problem. It is relatively easy to give engineers a level of understanding of formal specifications which will enable them to read the specifications with confidence, but it requires considerable skill and experience to write good specifications. Much of the skill in fact lies in finding good abstractions, and simple understanding of the notation is far from adequate to guarantee the production of good specifications. Unfortunately, principles of developing abstractions are not, as yet, something that even the formal methods experts know how to teach. However, it is perhaps relatively easy to overcome this problem if industry is willing to make the investment in staff time for education and training.

Summary

It is, hopefully, clear that there are benefits from the use of formal methods and that some of the theoretical benefits are borne out in practice. However, there are limitations, in principle, to what can be achieved with formal methods. At present, there are many more limitations, reflecting immaturity of the techniques themselves and inadequacies of the support tools, than there are philosophical problems. The difficult question which arises from this analysis is 'to what extent should formal methods form part of the development method for developing safety-critical systems, given their strengths and limitations?' We address this point in our conclusions.

CONCLUSIONS

Our main aim here is to draw the discussion to a close by substantiating our claim about formal methods being both under-used and over-sold, and to consider when and to what extent it is appropriate to use formal methods in the development of safety-critical systems.

When and how to apply formal methods

Given the above discussions, it should be clear that we are now entering the realm of value judgements. There is simply not enough information on which to base an objective evaluation of the relative contribution of formal methods (and other technologies) to the software and system development process. The following therefore represent the auhor's views based on a mixture of experience and assumptions about the prevalent classes of errors made in system development. It is worth noting, however, that there would be considerable benefit in carrying out experiments where different techniques were used to develop the same system to gain at least some evidence on which comparative judgements of method effectiveness could be based.

Turning now to personal judgements, I would use formal methods to produce top-level specifications for systems, but carry out development by a systematic application of stepwise refinement (informal variety), perhaps supplemented by formal refinement where there are adequate techniques. Moreover, I would use an eclectic approach to specification. For example, I would use a notation such as timed CCS to represent concurrent and communication structure but specify the effects of the individual actions in another formalism such as Z. I would also derive a number of theorems, e.g. stating that the system will not deadlock, or giving a top-level statement of safety policy. I would reason about these (putative) theorems formally, but not use theorem provers to assist in these endeavours. I would also link the formal techniques, so far as possible, to standard safety techniques (e.g. fault tree analysis). It would seem quite possible to apply such techniques in a manner analogous to the use of fault trees on programs (Leveson and Harvey, 1983).

In summary, I would supplement existing good practices with the use of formal specifications in order to gain clarity in top-level specifications, to aid consistency checking of specifications and to assist in validation through derivation of key properties from the specifications.

Claim and counter claim

Many formal methods protagonists clearly appreciate and articulate the limits in principle and in practice associated with formal methods. Unfortunately, however, there are many counter-examples to this good professional practice – although much of the evidence is somewhat anecdotal. Nonetheless, there clearly are occasions where unsubstantiated claims are made and, for example, the limitations of current techniques in terms of their expressive power or the capabilities of the support tools are 'glossed over'. Perhaps the best recent example of this is the claims made for VIPER, a formally specified microprocessor, where recent analysis has shown that the originators' claims were in excess of what they had actually achieved (Bennett, 1990).

It is perhaps also worth noting that the theoretical problems of synthetic versus analytic reasoning also affect real system developments. As long ago as 1976 Gerhart and Yelowitz pointed out cases where formally verified programs had failed. In the examples cited the problems were that inappropriate proofs had been carried out, not that the proofs themselves were flawed.

On the other hand, many 'opponents' of formal methods say that the techniques are fundamentally flawed, or have no relevance, or.... Again, it is hard to separate fact from anecdote but some major textbooks on software engineering (e.g. Macro and Buxton, 1987) argue quite strongly that the techniques are still research topics, so they cannot (even should not) be applied in industry, and that they have intrinsic limitations, essentially because of the problems of verifying refinements which were alluded earlier in this chapter. There are already (limited) counter-examples to the first point. The second issue is much more substantive. However, the key issue is not the substantiveness of the point but judging the extent to which the observed limitations actually matter in practice. The limitations do not affect the value of formal specifications *per se* as a documentation and communication medium. However, the issue of verifying refinements is a valid objection – but one that says we need to supplement proofs of refinement with other checks, not that the approach is fundamentally flawed. Nonetheless, it is clear that we do not yet have adequate refinement techniques and that this is still a difficult research topic.

It would be easy to re-open the whole debate on use and relevance and I do not wish to do this. I hope I have now produced enough evidence to show that formal methods can be used effectively in industry. Since their use has been limited to date, my assertion about the benefits of wider use seems to be clearly true! The examples given above show that the techniques are sometimes over-sold and it would appear to be very easy to over-state their value. The theoretical benefits are very great and fairly clear, but the limitations are far more subtle, and so it is rather more difficult to articulate them clearly and accurately. Also there is a temptation in trying to stimulate the use of formal methods to stress their value and to 'skate over' the limitations. This may not be deliberate over-selling but it has a similar effect. Thus I stand by my assertion that *formal methods are both over-sold and under-used*, but recognize that this is a simplification of a complex situation.

ACKNOWLEDGEMENTS

Acknowledgements are due to a number of my colleagues who have helped me formulate the above ideas and to develop the example specifications. In particular, thanks are due to David Scholefield, David Stokes and Peter Whysall, who have helped in developing and checking the specifications. Special thanks are due to Ian Toyn, who developed CADiZ, the Z specification checking and typesetting tool, which was used to check and typeset this chapter. Without Ian the chapter might have been written, but it certainly could not have been printed! Of course, responsibility for any errors or omissions remains mine.

REFERENCES

Abdel-Ghaly, A. A., Chan, P. Y. and Littlewood, B. (1986), 'Evaluation of completing software reliability predictions', *IEEE Transactions on Software Engineering*, **SE-12**(9)

Backhouse, R. (1986), *Program Construction and Verification*, Prentice-Hall International, Englewood Cliffs, NJ

Bennett, P. A. (1990), *VIPER: A Perspective*, The Centre for Software Engineering Ltd

Bramson, B. D. (1984), 'Malvern's program analysers', *RSRE Research Review*

Clarke, S. J., Coombes, A. C. and McDermid, J. A. (1990), *The Analysis of Safety Arguments in the Specification of a Motor Speed Control Loop*, University of York, Dept of Computer Science, June

Coleman, D. and Gallimore, R. M. (1987), *Software Engineering Using Executable Specifications*, Macmillan, London

Craigen, D., Kromodimoeljo, S., Meisels, I., Neilson, A., Pase, W. and Saaltink, M. (1987), 'm-EVES: a tool for verifying software', CP-87-5402-26, I. P. Sharp Associates Ltd

Dobson, J. E. and McDermid J. A. (1990), *An Investigation into Modelling and Categorisation of Non-Functional Requirements (for the Specification of Surface Naval Command Systems)*, University of York, Dept of Computer Science

Ezilchelvan, P. D. and Shrivastava, S. K. (1986), 'A characterisation of faults in systems', *Proc. 5th IEEE Int. Symp. Reliability in Distributed Software and Database Systems*, IEEE Press, Los Angeles, January

Fetzer, J. H. (1988), 'Program verification: the very idea', *CACM*, **31**(9)

Gerhart and Yelowitz (1976), 'Observations of fallibility in applications of modern programming methodologies', *IEEE Transactions on Software Engineering*, May

Good, D. (1984), *Mechanical Proofs about Computer Programs*, Technical Report 41, Institute for Computing Science, The University of Texas at Austin

Hayes, I. (ed.) (1986) *Specification Case Studies*, Prentice-Hall International, Englewood Cliffs, NJ

Hill, J. V. (1988), 'The development of high reliability software – RRAs experience for safety critical systems', *Proc. of BCS/IEE SE Conference*, Peter Peregrinus, Stevenage

Hoare, C. A. R. (1969), 'An axiomatic basis for computer programming', *CACM*, **12**(10)

Jones, C. B. (1986), *Systematic Software Development Using VDM*, Prentice-Hall International, Englewood Cliffs, NJ

Jones, C. B. and Shaw, R. C. F. (1990), '*Case Studies in Systematic Software Development*', Prentice-Hall International, Englewood Cliffs, NJ

Jones-Lee, M. W., Hammerton, M. and Philips, P. R. (1985), 'The value of safety: results of a national sample survey', *Economic Journal*, 49–72

Lamport, L., Shotask, R. and Pease, M. (1982), 'The Byzantine generals' problem', *ACM Trans. on Programming Languages and Systems*, **4**(3), 382–401, July

Laprie, J.-C. (1989), 'Dependability: A unifying concept for reliable computing and fault tolerance', in Anderson T. (ed.), *Dependability of Resilient Computers*. BSP Profesional Books

Leveson, N. G. and Harvey, P. R. (1983), 'Analyzing software safety', *IEEE Transactions on Software Engineering*, **SE-9**(9), 569–579

Leveson, N. G. (1986), 'Software safety: what, why and how', *ACM Computing Surveys*, **18**(2), June

Littlewood, B. (1989), 'Predicting software reliability', *Proc. Trans. Royal Society*, **327**

Macro, A. and Buxton, J. N. (1987), *The Craft of Software Engineering*, Addison-Wesley, Reading, MA

Maibaum, T. S. E., Khosla, S. and Jeremaes, P. (1986), 'A modal [action] logic for requirements specification', in Brown, P. J. and Barnes, D. J. (eds), *Software Engineering 86*, Peter Peregrinus, Stevenage

McDermid, J. A. (ed.) (1989a), *The Theory and Practice of Refinement: Approaches to the Formal Development of Large Scale Systems*, Butterworths

McDermid, J. A. (1989b), 'Assurance in high-integrity software', in Sennet, C. T. (ed.), *High Integrity Software*, Pitman, London

McDermid, J. A. (1989c), 'Towards assurance measures for high integrity software', *Proceedings of Reliability 89*, The Institute of Quality Assurance

McDermid, J. A. (ed.), (1991), *Software Engineer's Reference Book*, Butterworth-Heinemann, Oxford

McDermid, J. A. and Ripken, K. (1984), *Life Cycle Support in the Ada Environment*, Cambridge University Press, Cambridge

McDermid, J. A. and Rook, P. (1991), 'Software development process models', in J. A. McDermid (ed), *Software Engineers' Reference Book*, Butterworth-Heinemann, Oxford

Milner, A. J. R. G. (1980), 'Calculus of communicating systems', in Goos, G. and Hartmanis, J. (eds), *Lecture Notes in Computer Science No. 92*, Springer-Verlag, New York

Moller, F. and Tofts, C. (1989), *A Temporal Calculus of Communicating Systems*, LFCS, December

Morgan, C. (1990), *Deriving Programs from Specifications*, Prentice-Hall International, Englewood Cliffs, NJ

Potts, C. J. and Finkelstein, A. (1986), 'Structured common sense', in Brown, P. J. and Barnes, D. J. (eds), *Software Engineering 86*, Peter Peregrinus, Stevenage

Reason, J. (1979), Actions not as planned: the price of automatization', in Underwood, G. and Stevens, R. (eds), *Aspects of Consciousness*, Academic Press, New York

Rook, P. (1991), 'Project planning and control', in McDermid, J. A. (ed.), *Software Engineer's Reference Book*, Butterworth-Heinemann, Oxford

Sanella, D. and Tarlecki, A. (1984), *On Observational Equivalence and Algebraic Specification*, Department of Computer Science, University of Edinburgh

Spivey, J. M. (1989), *The Z Notation: A Reference Manual*, Prentice-Hall International, Englewood Cliffs, NJ

Wittgentstein, L. (1969), *On Certainty*, Blackwell, Oxford

Zave, P. (1982), 'An operational approach to requirements expression for embedded systems', *IEEE Transactions on Software Engineering*, **8**(3)

Zilles, S. (1974), *Algebraic Specification of Data Types*, Report No. 11, Project MAC, Massachussets Institute of Technology

8 Use of Ada in safety-critical systems
Ian C. Pyle

NATURE OF A SAFETY SYSTEM

The most important thing about safety is that it is fundamentally determined by *control systems*, and only weakly related to software correctness. Safety involves control: there must be some means of controlling the sources of potential dangers. We therefore first discuss computer-based control systems in general, in order to establish the context for the safety or danger that might arise during their use. A safety system is a special kind of control system; a protection system (as envisaged in the Health and Safety Executive Guidelines, 1987) may be a further special kind of control system.

Unless some activity in a plant under control has the possibility of harming life, limb or the environment, then the issue of safety never arises. Sometimes it will not be safe to cause or permit the plant to act in a particular way, whereas at other times it will be safe to do so. The fundamental determinant of safety is the discrimination by the control system (or protection system) between these situations.

The behaviour of a computer-based control system is determined by its software and hardware. Safety therefore depends on their effectiveness, which means that the hardware must be available, with sensors and effectors that relate plant status to logical control, and with processors to execute the software sufficiently quickly for the control loops to be stable. The control algorithms, expressed in the program executed, close the control loops (see Figure 8.1).

Traditional control systems have been based on simple control loops, in which the control algorithm is no more complicated than PID (Proportional–Integral–Differential). Software gives opportunities for unlimited complexity but also brings new kinds of failure mode, which are manifestations of faults in the specification, design or implementation of the automatic behaviour of the control system. Fortunately, alongside this risk comes an even more important improvement – software in control is perfectly replicable, and is fully susceptible to analysis.

Thus if the behaviour of a software-based control system is 'wrong' in a particular situation, then it can be trusted to behave in exactly the same (wrong) way whenever that situation arises. Equally, it can be trusted to behave consistently in the same (right) way in all situations in which it has been shown by testing to have the 'right' behaviour. Any faults in the software are *systematic* faults, in contrast with the *random* faults exhibited by hardware. Since software does not wear out, there is no need for repeated testing of the same situation: all testing of software is effectively 'full-life' testing, checking the behaviour of the

Use of Ada in safety-critical systems   155

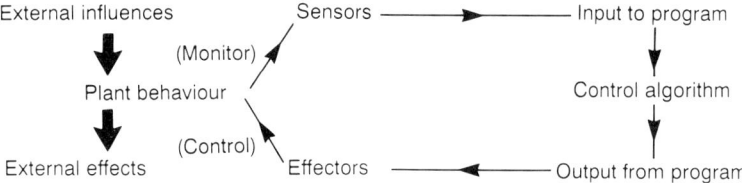

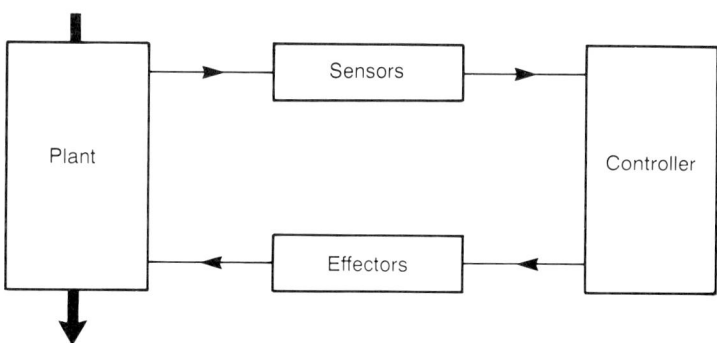

Figure 8.1

system in a particular situation, whenever and however often that situation arises.

Safety-critical systems require software that imposes context-dependent limits on the operation of certain output devices: a central kind of requirement for safety is that (depending on the circumstances) the system must detect situations when it must *not* carry out a particular action of which it is capable.

Software is thus responsible for the behaviour of the plant. Safe behaviour depends on the software making the appropriate discrimination between safe and dangerous conditions, and controlling the plant properly. Because of this fundamental responsibility, any residual defect in the software could imperil the safety integrity of the plant. This is the nature of automatic control: if the automaton is in control, then we rely on the automaton taking proper decisions and actions.

The risk in practice is of unexpected situations arising, in which the behaviour specified is not as the designer would have wished had that situation been anticipated. The deficiency is in the foresight of the specifier or designer – their failure to anticipate circumstances that might occur in the real world, after deployment of the control system.

Software is not inherently either safe or dangerous. However, it can be used to control devices that are inherently dangerous, rendering them safe. (Fortunately, it cannot work the other way, making safe devices become dangerous!) Thus we see that the property of safeness or danger resides in the plant controlled by the computer concerned, not in the software.

The power of a computer is limited by the nature of the peripheral devices that are connected to it; we are considering here systems in which there are potentially dangerous devices directly or indirectly under software control. Such devices have the intrinsic power to harm life or property, but this power is protected from misuse by interlocks and guards that are dependent on software. For example, computer-controlled machine tools could cause direct harm, and computer-controlled collision-avoidance systems (e.g. traffic lights) could cause indirect harm (by giving green in both directions). Similarly, a computer-controlled train could cause harm to its passengers and to anyone or anything on its track by virtue of its physical movement and momentum. In the intended mode of operation, interlocks ensure that the potentially dangerous functions occur only when nothing is present that could be harmed.

Classification of danger

We can classify the potential dangers in terms of controllability, independently of any other classification (by severity, frequency or tolerable risk, etc.) There are three classes of danger, which we call immediate, indirect and persistent.

The simplest kind of danger (as far as control is concerned) is the immediate danger that arises from an adverse effect on a victim of a directly and explicitly controlled item of the plant – for example, a high-voltage source (without capacitance). The target computer controls the switching on and off of the voltage, so ensures safety by sensing the environment when controlling the plant. To avoid this kind of danger,

do not start the hazardous action *until it is safe* to do so.

At the other extreme, we have indirect danger, where the victim is at risk from some action by an item of the world not directly controlled by the target computer but indirectly influenced by the plant. An example of this is a level crossing, where the train causes the danger but the plant extends only to the signals. In this case the system is made safe by the use of guards on potential victims (the barrier gates of the level crossing), so that safety is ensured by the target controlling the guards that control whether potential victims can get into the danger area. To avoid this kind of danger,

keep possible victims away from the hazardous place *while it is dangerous.*

The intermediate case arises when there is persistent danger, arising from a directly controlled item of the plant with inertia. Such an item may continue to be in a dangerous state after the target computer has commanded it to become safe.

An example is rotating machinery, where there may be control of the power input and the brakes but is still dangerous after power has been cut off and the brakes applied. In this case the system is made safe by both the above techniques, controlling the plant so that it only starts being dangerous when victims are absent, and controlling the presence of victims by guards so that the system cannot become dangerous given the state of the plant. To avoid this kind of danger,

> *do not start* any hazardous action *when victims are present*, and *keep victims away* from the hazardous place *until it becomes safe*.

Summarizing:

Harm = dangerous action in presence of susceptible subject
Danger = potential harm
Guard = means of preventing subject from being susceptible
Interlock = means of inhibiting action when it would be harmful

Availability

In certain kinds of system the requirements for availability affect safety. This is a significant motivation in the HSE guidelines for system configuration: ensuring that there are safety-related systems in the overall configuration to be capable of maintaining the plant in a safe state or of bringing it to a safe state when required.

We should note which inputs to the controller from the plant or its environment are involved in each of the safety-related interlock conditions, and consider the effect (fail-safe or fail-dangerous) of malfunction of each. This analysis may precipitate the introduction of some additional sensors in order to detect situations that are important for safety, or to the redesign of sensors to reduce the risk from malfunction.

We must record all the safety-related inputs to the controller, grouping them according to the danger they protect against, and associating them with the corresponding interlock formulae. It is preferable that each input be involved in, at most, one interlock; if it is involved in more than one, this should be explicitly noted, for the dependency implications in change control.

The particular relevance of Ada to this topic is the attention given to run-time error detection by the exception mechanisms in Ada, including application-specific exceptions. This means that malfunctions are acknowledged to be possible during the execution of the control program, and the designer is led to formulate appropriate recovery action. Recovery from a malfunction is only feasible if there is an alternative way of achieving an acceptable effect, which might involve reallocating functions among the hardware (i.e. reconfiguration), or reloading software.

The danger of this approach, of having automatic substitutes for faulty components, is that the substitute itself may be faulty, and in the normal course of events it is less extensively exercised. This same argument is used against having exception handlers at all in an Ada program: since the exception handler is only operative in rare circumstances (on detecting something unusual that never should happen in normal operation), it is quite likely to be faulty itself. The counter-argument is that the uncommon paths are certainly where the undetected errors are likely to lie, but this applies whether or not the notation of exceptions is used to improve the visibility of the normal and exceptional situations.

Thus safety is not an absolute property, but dependent on the context of use (see Bennett, 1984). The role of software in connection with assuring safety is twofold: it must be correct with respect to the control of the critical devices, and it must implement interlocks for those devices to ensure that their use is safe. Such interlocks depend on the ability of the system to detect and distinguish properly between the safe and dangerous circumstances, in order to restrict the potentially dangerous functions to safe situations. In addition, software can enhance safety by coordinating the use of built-in tests and redundant hardware.

AVOIDANCE OF DANGER

The fundamental problem of safety in a controlled system concerns the richness of the interaction between the bare plant and its environment. The bare plant is (and has to be) capable of carrying out certain actions which are, in some circumstances, desired and in others definitely to be prevented. Thus it is capable of interacting more richly than is desired with its environment. The responsibility of the safety controller is to ensure that the plant carries out these dangerous actions only when the circumstances are suitable: by using interlocks and guards.

Depending on the nature of the plant and its control system, various effects must be taken into account for their potential impact on safety. In any physical system there is a risk of deterioration (random hardware failures), which can cause the physical unit to fail. In an inertial system there is a delay before control signals are effective (latency). In a communication system there is latency and fallibility; and in a system involving human interaction as well as automatic information handling, problems of latency, fallibility and perversity may arise.

Another important distinction is between *static* and *dynamic* safety. The plant may have a safe stable state into which it can be set if the control system fails. But if it does not have such a state, the requirements for *availability* of the control system take precedence over the specific considerations of safety. Software and Ada are particularly significant in the design of a control system to achieve static safety. However, to achieve dynamic safety, the control system must be structured first, for high availability (by replication of unreliable components, coordinated by software), and second, for safety using the software techniques we describe.

In accordance with the principles of the HSE guidelines, a safety protection system may be separate from the control system. This does not remove the obligation to have safety interlocks in the control system, but provides diversity in the overall safety of the plant, by having it explicitly in the safety protection system as well as incidentally in the control system.

Safety interlocks

We will presume, since otherwise safety is not at issue, that the plant is capable of some actions that are dangerous, in that they can harm potential victims. Note that the actions of software are never dangerous in themselves, and that we disregard potential dangers of the target computer(s) themselves. (If we wish to protect users from the risk of the computer falling over on top of them, we must make sure that appropriate sensors and effectors exist, and consider the housing of the physical computer as part of the plant.)

The essence of designing for safety (in a computer-based system) is to ensure that the potentially dangerous actions of the plant can only take place when it is safe to do so. This means that possible dangerous actions of the plant must be constrained by suitable interlocks, or the possible victims must be constrained by suitable guards. The interlocks and guards depend on the existence of suitable sensors and effectors in the control system.

The first-level analysis, carried out when the requirements are established, must therefore be the check that appropriate interlocks and guards can be set up. We must identify the potential dangers in the plant, establish the criteria for safe use of dangerous equipment, ascertain that sensors can provide the information needed to discriminate between safe and hazardous modes of operation, and ensure that every danger can be protected by a combination of interlock and guard.

Control and availability

The behaviour of a computer-based control system, while determined by its software (in terms of the elementary actions of the actuators in the plant), is dependent on the continued availability of the computer(s) that execute the software. Depending on the nature of the control required (continuous or supervisory) and the intrinsic behaviour of the plant, it may be necessary to give special attention to availability in designing the control system. This could involve the use of several computers in parallel, to provide mutual back-up and stand-by facilities.

The safety of a controlled system depends on the control systems (at least the protection system) being available and working properly. Thus malfunction and unavailability of the control system are potential sources of danger. The HSE guidance on configuration and diversity is intended to take account of this kind of risk. However, a control system that relies on redundancy to mitigate the effects of malfunction or unavailability is likely to depend on software to coordinate the redundant parts; Built-in Test Equipment (BITE) is likely to be driven by software, causing the equipment found faulty to be de-activated and possibly replaced by spares. Here software provides a positive enhancement of safety.

High availability can only be achieved by careful design of the system (taking the software and hardware together), to ensure that appropriate steps are taken when failures occur. This means that the software must be designed to deal with the possibility of plant and control system failures, by including detection mechanisms for the possible faults, and providing graceful degradation of the system when they are detected. There are random and systematic faults. Faults may arise randomly because of failures in the hardware or sub-systems. Although we cannot predict the occurrence of any individual random fault, we can make statistical estimates, based on past experience of the same or similar equipment. Systematic faults arise as a consequence of deficiencies in the software or hardware design (which may be the result of deficiencies in the specification), and are exposed whenever particular (unpredicted) situations arise. Failures of this kind will occur consistently (reliably!) when the same combination of circumstances occur, whether during testing or operational use. Prediction of their likelihood is therefore much more difficult, since it is based on the extent to which the operational situation was not anticipated during the development: dependent on the people and environment of the development, not on the particular system.

Summary

A non-trivial safe system must have some potential to cause danger to life, limb or the environment. The software that determines the behaviour of its controller must take account of the conditions under which the potential danger would be actual. Thus there must be some output controlled by the software that affects the hazardous devices in the plant, and input sensed by the software that indicates whether a particular action by the equipment under control is safe or dangerous at the time; in other words, whether there is a susceptible victim in the environment of the plant.

The software handling the raw input–output must be protected from interference from any other activity in the computer, and the whole causal chain (Figure 8.1) of input, control algorithm and output must ensure that no dangerous action can take place when a victim is susceptible to harm.

ROLE OF ADA

On the assumption that the control system is sufficiently complicated to justify the use of computers, the style of software may be one of two kinds: interpretive or compiled. Interpretive software is used in a variety of general-purpose controllers (e.g. programmable logic controllers (PLCs), relay ladder emulators) and in the interpretation of the rules in knowledge-based systems. In general, the response time of the plant to the controller is of order seconds or more, so is not a significant constraint on the speed of the controller. Compiled software, in contrast, is used when the control algorithm itself has to be specified, when multiple control loops may interact, or when the speed of the controller is significant in relation to the response time of the plant.

Ada is not intended to be interpreted: the language was designed with the intention that programs would be compiled (and thereby checked extensively before operational use). An interpreter could be written in Ada, as a general-purpose controller whose specific parameters were provided by the PLC or ladder definitions, but this is not the primary role intended for Ada (and not one in which it would contribute to safety). Ada is intended to be used for compilation into imperative software, particularly for explicitly programmed input–output (handling the sensors and effectors in Figure 8.1) and for dealing with unintended conditions that might arise (exceptions), with powerful means of achieving software integrity through its visibility rules. All these contribute to the safety of the system whose controller's behaviour is expressed in Ada.

In addition to the intrinsically safe features of Ada, its known unsafe features (which have been more intensively analysed than those for any other language: see Wichmann, 1988) can be regulated by the use of certain design rules. Various authors (e.g. Holzapfel and Winterstein, 1988; Carré and Jennings, 1988) have advocated linguistic restrictions (i.e. sub-sets of Ada) to achieve this, but most imply a fundamental rule for safety – that there should be no input–output. Clearly, if the computer controls no output, it can cause no danger. Such rules give trivially safe systems; in particular, they are inapplicable to equipment that depends on the controller for its continuously safe operation.

Program structure

The concepts of Ada provide the fundamental structure of a safety-related program, recognizing that it needs both careful construction and comprehensive checking. In an Ada program the software concepts are encapsulated into packages, which may be categorized in a number of ways. In a safety-related system the importance of each safety or protection control loop of the plant is categorized (see MoD, 1987; IEC, 1989a) according to the likelihood of failure and severity of failure if it occurs: for example, in avionics safety there are *critical*, *essential* and *normal* categories. When software determines the behaviour, we follow MoD (1987) and refer to the *risk factor* of each software unit on this same basis. The risk factor might be directly related to the functionality of the software that controls the loop, or it might arise from the position of a package in the layers of software on which safety-critical functions rely. Thus any package that is *used by* a critical control loop must be categorized as critical, since a deficiency in any underlying package would be as serious as though it were in a package that uses it. Similarly, any package that is *used by* an essential (non-critical) control loop must also be categorized as essential (see Pyle, 1988).

The risk factor of the control loop handled by each package should be stated explicitly (as a comment in the header of the package specification). The over-riding principle of correctness and safety is that:

> Safety-critical parts must be small enough to analyse; those program parts must be adequately isolated.

The significant difference in the software structure is therefore between:

1. Packages that handle safety-related devices (whether critical or essential);
2. Packages that ensure proper isolation; and
3. Other packages.

Since the packages must be written in ways that take account of these differences, the above categories are the relevant ones for software development in Ada. We call this the criticality categorization of the packages. Category 1 refers to packages handling input–output for potentially hazardous devices; category 2 to the packages that protect these from interference; and category 3 for the rest. In addition, since the safety category of a package determines the kind of checking to be applied, there is a further categorization based on the ease of verification of the packages. The general principle is to keep the category 1 packages as simple as possible, so that they can be rigorously checked by formal analysis and intelligent inspection. The category 2 packages ensure that other packages cannot subvert these checks. Thus the criticality category determines the allowable contents of the package and the associated checking/verification regime.

This approach uses the linguistic structure of Ada to ensure that the critical packages (category 1) are kept simple, protected by other packages of trusted software (category 2) that handle anything which might have an adverse effect on the critical software, with the general software in category 3 packages which do not contain any input–output or facilities that could bypass the category 2 protection.

This scheme is based on each package having a specific responsibility, which for categories 1 and 2 is explicitly formulated as a 'claim'. The designer identifies the individual responsibilities and the checker independently confirms them. The evidence of the checker is used by the assessor for certifying that the system is adequately safe.

The design rules are formulated in terms of Ada constructs, so may be interpreted as recommended sub-sets of Ada for the different categories of package. Note that these are sub-sets for programmers, not for compilers.

Design rules concerning Ada features

We have discussed the risk factors and criticality categorization of the software units; each package should state them in a comment in the header of the specification. Appropriate design rules which determine the allowable contents of the package (and the associated checking/verification regime) can then be determined. For checking purposes, it is important that certain packages and internal sub-programs have a *claim*: a definition of the intended properties of the unit (e.g. invariant, pre-condition and/or post-condition).

The Ada features that are intrinsically significant for this safety package categorization are:

Tasks (callable entries and interrupts)
Exceptions
Access types
Representation specifications
Machine code
Unsafe conversion and de-allocation

Table 8.1 Critical package constituents

	Category		
	1	2	3
Claim	Must	Must	May
Machine code	May	No	No
Rep. Spec.	May	No	No
Interrupt entry	May*	No	No
Normal entry	No	May	No
Unsafe	No	May	No
Task w'out accept	No	May	May
Exception	May*	May	May
Access type	No	May	May
Alias	No	May	May
Go to	No	No	May

We also make recommendations concerning aliasing and the use of *go to* statements, to facilitate the checking (basically for stylistic reasons). We summarize the position on these in Table 8.1.

The table entries indicate whether packages of the designated category must, may or must not contain the particular Ada features. The asterisks in column 1 mark important contentious entries: some authors reject the use of interrupts and exceptions in safety-related systems. We have developed the present approach based on the use of interrupt-based input–output and exceptions to frustrate and report attempts to perform a potentially dangerous action when it would be actually dangerous.

Principal package constituents

Note that any machine code or representation clause puts a package into category 1; such packages must have a claim, and the package must be independently, rigorously and (as far as possible) formally verified, to ensure that the claim is met. Such packages must not include any of the other complicating features, both to facilitate the analysis and to avoid any further risk arising from mistakes in the code generator in the compiler (in the translation from the linguistic semantics of the Ada program to the executable binary code).

Unsafe programming and tasks with callable entries (i.e. passive tasks) put a package into category 2; such packages must also have a claim, and the package must be independently checked statically to ensure that the claim is met. (Note that the unsafe programming and task interactions can cause problems in the package containing them, but not in any packages it depends on.)

General packages, in category 3, should then contain no entries, representation specifications, unsafe programming, machine code or unsafe de-allocation.

Claims

We recommend that all packages in categories 1 and 2 contain a *claim* about their intended semantics. Ada package specifications, sub-program specifications and task specifications define the *syntax* of the respective constituents, but not their semantics (and certainly not their performance). Various schemes have been advocated for providing formal semantics for Ada programs (see Goldsack, 1985), mainly by introducing special annotations. These use the Ada comment convention to 'hide' the semantic information from an Ada compiler, while allowing it to be seen by an analyst or analyser. Thus they significantly extend the language (possibly as well as restricting the conventional Ada part) by introducing new rules concerning the annotations.

ANNA (Luckham *et al.*, 1984) is a notation for annotating Ada programs based on the predicate calculus. An annotated package contains Boolean expressions that state the invariants for the data objects in the package and for the sub-programs that are visible in the package. It does not deal with tasks. Asphodel (Hill, 1988) similarly annotates Ada text, but uses different typefaces in the printed form to distinguish the semantics. Formal specifications in Asphodel include the assumptions about properties of generic parameters and sub-programs used, as well as pre-conditions, post-conditions and invariants. SPARK (Carré and Jennings, 1988) has mandatory annotations, which specify dependencies, input–output relationships; they may also include proof rules.

The purpose of formalizing the semantics is to permit automatic checking of the consistency between the executable parts of the program and the claimed intentions. Such formal semantic specification is desirable in any case, and particularly so for the critical software. It allows the V&V contractor to make automatic checks on the respective bodies that are produced by the developer, as well as to assess the coverage of the test sets produced to check the implementations.

This strategy is related to (but different from) the approaches of other workers on safety systems in Ada, in which a single sub-set of Ada is used throughout the program. The difference in the approaches is that here we concentrate on the safety of the *system*, not only the software, and accordingly recognize that the output operations are essential for effective operation. They cannot therefore be banned in the interest of safety.

Aliasing

It is possible in a number of situations for the same variable to be identified by more than one name. Obviously, if two variables are given the same explicit address by representation clause, they will be the same. Several other cases can occur: for example, a variable given as an actual parameter to a sub-program may be referenced inside the sub-program by both the actual and the formal names (if the sub-program is declared within the scope of the actual name); an array element may be referenced by using different expressions for the index, which may have the same value; and several variables of the same access type may have the same value, in which case they would denote the same variable. This situation is described as *aliasing*, and is important in analytic checking of software because, in certain respects, there can be unexpected (and undesirable) consequences.

A sequence of statements appears to show visibly which variables are changed when the statements are executed: those whose names occur on the left-hand sides of assignment statements, or in call statements as actual parameters of mode *out* or *in out*. For the purposes of checking, it is often important to know which variables are *not* changed when particular statements are executed: all variables out of scope, for example. Were it not for aliasing, the rule would be very simple: only those variables in the above positions are changed, others are not.

However, because of the possibility of aliasing, a variable may be changed even though its name does not occur in any susceptible position. Disjunction of name does not imply disjunction of the referenced variable. Consequently it is much more difficult to analyse software in which there is aliasing, and automatic analysers may not be able to cope with it. Rules for guidance have therefore been framed to avoid aliasing in order to simplify analysis. It is not that aliasing is intrinsically bad, but that it hinders checking.

Specific rules to avoid or cope with aliasing in Ada are:

1. Do not use *rename* declarations (which explicitly introduce aliases).
2. If representation clauses are given for the addresses of variables, make the addresses all be disjoint (taking account of the lengths of the variables, dependent on their types). This prevents physical addresses causing aliasing.
3. Declare sub-programs (in packages) *outside* the scopes of packages in which they are used, relying on the context clause to gain access to them. This ensures that actual parameters are out of scope, so avoids formal/actual aliasing.
4. Use complete arrays and aggregates in preference to individual elements and slices. When individual elements and slices cannot be avoided, use a uniform style for the expressions in them. Check the relationship between the index values, and write the program so that it does not presume that the values are different.
5. Whenever *access* values are used, aliasing may occur. Write the program so that it takes account of the possibility that distinct access variables may refer to the same referenced variable.

Note that aliasing is intrinsically possible with array elements and access types; hence some authors recommend that they be absolutely forbidden in safety-related programming. The present recommendation is to forbid aliasing only in category 1 packages.

Defensive programming

An algorithm, in its primitive form, implicitly assumes certain properties about its input parameters and the other variables on which it depends. Defensive programming is a style in which such assumptions are made explicit, and innocuous actions taken when the assumptions turn out to be wrong.

Thus if *PRE* is the predicate that is assumed to hold on entry to a sub-program (for it to work properly), and *POST* is the predicate that is claimed to hold when the algorithm completes (if it does), we can make the program defensive by building into the algorithm a check that *PRE* actually does hold, with an alternative action (avoiding danger) if it does not. The pre-condition of the defended algorithm is then *TRUE*, and its post-condition is

   POST *or* DANGER_AVOIDED

(where *DANGER_AVOIDED* is the predicate that holds on completion; if *not*, *PRE* holds on entry). Exceptions in Ada are based on this idea.

Issues to be considered in designing programs defensively are what level of detail to defend and what kinds of alternative action to take. Although the issues are logically distinct, the pragmatic solution is to work backwards from the second to the first. The fact that a pre-condition does not hold may be detected within the body of the algorithm: although we state the assumption at the beginning, it is feasible to check it there only in simple cases. (Thus in matrix inversion, the assumption is that the matrix is non-singular. Discovering whether the assumption holds comes naturally in the middle of the algorithm, when the value of the discriminant has been calculated.)

Useful alternative actions, to be taken when the normal assumption does not hold, might be to close down the plant, send an alarm signal to the operator, open escape valves, start up stand-by equipment, or activate isolation procedures. The procedures to control these could be written as exception handlers, at a position in the program such that when the exception-handling actions have been completed (including all logging and abnormality reporting), normal activities are resumed.

Where there is no useful alternative action, the current action cannot be completed and the pre-condition of the enclosing algorithm is now known to be false. This is the Ada rule for propagating exceptions.

The specification of the formal parameters of a sub-program can imply some pre-conditions (for example, when an input parameter is specified as a sub-type) but there may be further assumptions, such as relationships between one input parameter and another. The type-matching rules of Ada will ensure that actual parameters values are of the right type, but a *CONSTRAINT_ERROR* will be raised if any does not conform to its specified sub-type. Relationships between parameters and/or external variables need explicit checking, raising an exception if the check fails.

The above discussion is presented using the concepts of Ada exceptions; however, there are arguments for not using exceptions in safety-critical software, based on distrust of the generated code. To avoid exceptions, the equivalent testing has to be done explicitly using *if* statements. To avoid *CONSTRAINT_ERROR* exceptions being raised, there must be no sub-types in the package, and each constrained input parameters must have an individual check to ensure that it satisfies the pre-condition. (The difficulty with the exception-free style of defensive programming is that the alternative actions must be closely built in with the checks.) If exceptions *are* used, it is important to make sure that testing covers them, including all the handlers and checks on assumptions.

Defensive programming is always relative. Each alternative action has its own assumed pre-conditions, and no matter how hard we try, there are always assumptions we make tacitly. The greatest danger is in the assumptions about the real-world environment that are true during the development period and initial operational use of the system, but, for completely unconnected reasons, become false later. The difference between an automaton and a responsible person is the reaction to such a situation: awareness of it, and ability to cope with it. It is unreasonable to expect an automaton to cope with an unplanned situation of which it has no means of becoming aware. By deploying an automaton in a safety-critical role, we are taking the responsibility for the continuing validity of its assumptions.

Physical design

The physical design of safety-related software (eventually formulated in executable Ada statements with explicit data constructs) comprises the drivers for the controlled devices in the plant (both the hazardous effectors and the guards), the sensors and the interlocks between them. Of these, the input–output drivers are normally logically simple (depending on their physical characteristics) and the interlocks as complex as the safety logic requires. In addition, when system availability is relevant, the physical design must include alternative executable components to take account of run-time failures.

The most important semantic aspect of design for safety is the relationship between the state of the plant and the safety or danger of each controlled device. The need to know that it is safe to operate a device is fundamental to safe operation, and the way in which this information is obtained must be absolutely foolproof. There are various different circumstances to consider: the safety may be instantaneously determinable from the inputs at specific sensors, or may be some combination (instantaneously determinable) of sensor data and internally stored values. In more complicated cases, safety may depend on some timing relationship between the sensor data, or even between data obtained from distinct sensors in different computers communicating over data-links. The most difficult case is when safety depends on the coordination of actions in distinct computers communicating over data-links.

The state of the plant is determined by sensory signals that are sampled at discrete intervals; the sampling interval must be sufficiently short for the circumstances. The detailed design of the software involves planning the algorithms for the interlocks and the device control. The main information about the semantics of the safety conditions has to be obtained from analysis of the plant controlled by the sensor.

When a desired change involves input–output (as do the raw inout output operations on which safety depends) we have to define the information to be transferred into or out of the computer, and define the partner for the communication. It is good design practice here to separate the physical input–output (for transmission to and from the partner) from the change of representation that is involved (e.g. binary numbers for internal use to sequences of decimal digits externally). The two sub-problems then are to carry out the internal change of representation and to transmit a value across an interface between the target computer and the plant with its environment. The program to change the representation has to be validated by proving that the two representations concerned preserve the value of the data involved. The program to do the transmission has to be validated by proving that it communicates the right data to and from the right partner.

Double insulation

Raw input–output (written as a low-level package) can be protected against interference from the rest of the program by a technique which takes advantage of the visibility rules of Ada. The raw input–output package is written as a sub-unit in the body of an outer package, thus making it logically inaccessible to the rest of the program.

Each critical (potentially dangerous) output device should have a handler which is encapsulated in *two* enclosing packages. The innermost package handles the operations on the device, for all circumstances: normal (including innocuous as well as dangerous actions) and unusual (e.g. maintenance or adjustment) operations; this package contains all the specific device controls. The outer package handles the interlock(s) on the device operations, and makes use of information from relevant sensors; it provides to the rest of the program only the interlock-protected operations, so that any attempt to carry out a potentially dangerous operation when it is not safe to do so would be rejected. Because the inner package is encapsulated within the outer one, no other parts of the program can bypass the interlocks. We call this technique 'double insulation' (Pyle, 1987).

The outer package ensures that the general sequence of operations is sufficient to assure safety, in the following basic pattern:

> apply guard
> (wait for guard to become effective)
> check interlock
> perform action
> (wait for plant to become safe)
> check interlock
> remove guard

The above sequence may be adapted according to the characteristics of the plant: simple electrical systems (where effects are virtually immediate, so latency can be ignored) need no guard; inertial systems (including those with electrical reluctance, as well as mechanical systems) must recognize that timing delays in effects can be significant. On the other hand, it may be more difficult than it appears, if the computer controlling the guard is different from that handling the interlocked operation, or if the plant does not have a safe state. Each of the steps in the sequence may fail, and if this could lead to danger, positive confirmation must be obtained, with substitute steps to be carried out if necessary. In communication systems (including distributed control), failure as well as delay must be considered; and in man–machine systems, the right balance of responsibility must be allocated between those involved. Ada, with appropriate design rules, provides the program structure and analysability that is fundamentally required for safety-related software.

RESIDUAL DEFECTS

The checking of a safety system is vital because of the inevitability of defects in any artefacts. By understanding the kinds of defect which may exist in a carefully designed system, we determine the checks that must be carried out to confirm their absence. These correspond to the sources of danger derived earlier in this chapter. The specification of the safety system and the assumptions about the plant and its environment must be articulated as part of the development work, and must be checked before deployment of the constructed controller to confirm that they are still applicable. This requires comprehensive understanding of the context in which the plant will be used, to avoid unjustified expectations about the role of the control system.

Systematic fault assessment

The fundamental distinction among defects is between random failures (which occur in hardware) and systematic failures (in the design of hardware or software). There is currently much concern about the best way to take account of the possibility of systematic faults in a computer-based system. Techniques are available to determine the system reliability in the face of random faults in the hardware, but it has been found difficult to bring the concept of 'software reliability' into the framework of those techniques. This section suggests an approach based on the random occurrence of operational situations combined with possible systematic faults arising from residual (undetected) defects in software or hardware design.

Reliability requirements are conventionally expressed as an expected period of time before failure, with the connotation of progressive (stochastic) deterioration. Software does not fail like that, so how can we interpret the concept of expected time to failure in a system whose behaviour is determined by software?

The various checks described produce a body of evidence concerning properties of the target computer's behaviour, which gives confidence that the operational behaviour will be safe. But currently we have no way of assessing this confidence to put a figure of merit or probability factor on it. Thus there is a significant intellectual gap between the best available practice and the desired prediction, with scant basis on either side for making the link between them.

Reliability

Conventionally, the reliability of a system is determined from its hardware design, taking account of replication of components to provide redundancy.

There is no room in such a structure for design defects. In a computer-based system, there is the possibility that mistakes have been made during the development, and the certainty that omissions have been made during the pre-release checking. The present approach takes these into account, as an additional mode of failure. It can thus be combined with the hardware reliability elements.

Although the software is constant (at each version during evolution) and therefore already contains any faults that might lead to danger, these faults are latent rather than manifest in the running system, since the actual behaviour depends on the particular part of the software that deals with the operational data, plant states and operational conditions. The defective behaviour depends on the *variety* rather than the *intensity* of use. It is the combination of operational situations and executed software on the target computer that changes stochastically with time, and from this observation we can interpret 'expected time to failure' for software.

The basic contribution of systematic (principally software) faults is given by a three-term formula:

$$S = pC * pV * pD$$

where

pC is the density of faults in the software (as created),
pV is the proportion of stimuli that are not verified before operation,
pD is the rate of arrival of stimuli,

S is the rate of operational data causing execution of a path that contains a fault.

Note that these three terms reflect activities at significantly different periods relevant to the system: its invention; its pre-operational checking; and its operational use.

The error density pC depends on the software development technology and quality control before verification; it can be estimated by determining the proportion of software faults discovered *during* the pre-operational testing, on the assumption that the faults are equally likely to be made in the checked as in the unchecked parts.

Verification can be considered as the software analogue of accelerated life testing in hardware. Whereas it is necessary to find ways of increasing the probabilistic rate of random errors in hardware (by, for example, running the unit at a higher temperature) to establish the raw failure rate, in the case of systematic errors this is no problem: if the error happens once, it will happen every time, and whatever happens with a particular situation will always happen in that situation. Thus the situations that arise frequently need be tested only once, giving time for testing the situations that arise only rarely during operational use. The domain of test data inputs must take account of all values significant for the activity of the system. It is a characteristic of software-based systems that the *variety* of behaviour is too great for exhaustive testing. Verification (including factory tests) covers some proportion of this domain. The proportion of operational situations that are exercised during pre-operational checking is (usually) intended to be completely representative. Various techniques are available for estimating the proportion of paths in the program that are exercised by a particular test set. If a particular situation exposes a fault in the software, it can be corrected before operational deployment. Sources of such faults are (1) deficient or ambiguous specification, (2) unjustified assumptions and (3) bad logic in the development. The faults are likely to occur in any part of the design. Verification gives both an estimate of their density, and the feedback for exposure of a proportion of them. The result of the combination is that the software contains a (static) proportion of undetected faults.

The quality of a computer-based system can be interpreted as an indication of the presumed residual error density in the delivered system. Since errors in software are independent of operational time (but are exposed by specific operational circumstances), any errors that remain are those that were either detected and not properly corrected or were not detected by any of the checks before deployment. Much of the management effort and evidence required for certification focuses on the first of these, to ensure by audit trails and cross-reference lists that all detected errors have been properly corrected. The residue are then those errors that were not expected at all, not looked for, so not detected, but nevertheless made during the creation of the software. This accounts for the two time-independent terms in the quality formula, which are the first two in the reliability formula. We can take this as the measure of the software quality.

Operational conditions generate data and situations at a certain rate, covering a range dependent on the elapsed time of exposure. When an operational situation arises that is outside the verified domain (in other words, was not anticipated when the verified situations were prepared), it will execute software which has the original susceptibility to error, without the benefit of the verification exposure. Thus we get a time-dependent probability, which can be combined with the hardware failure rates.

The above analysis applies for a single item of software, without considering its design in any greater detail. As with hardware, a more significant analysis can be carried out after the system has been designed. The impact of software fault-tolerant design, with exception detectors and handlers, is to qualify the above analysis for individual software units, and indicate how the static measures for each unit should be combined according to the pattern of data and situations which it has to handle. Significantly, a software-intensive system makes use of *layers* of facilities, which the higher layers depend on the proper functioning of the lower layers (see Figure 8.2). Although there is useful disjunction of functionality among the program units within each layer (Ada packages), there is a strong dependency through the use of common facilities from one layer to another. This characteristic is very important for the checking of software (see Pyle, 1988).

Safety checking

HSE (1987) identifies the key elements which contribute to safety: hardware failure rate, configuration and quality. Checking for random hardware failures

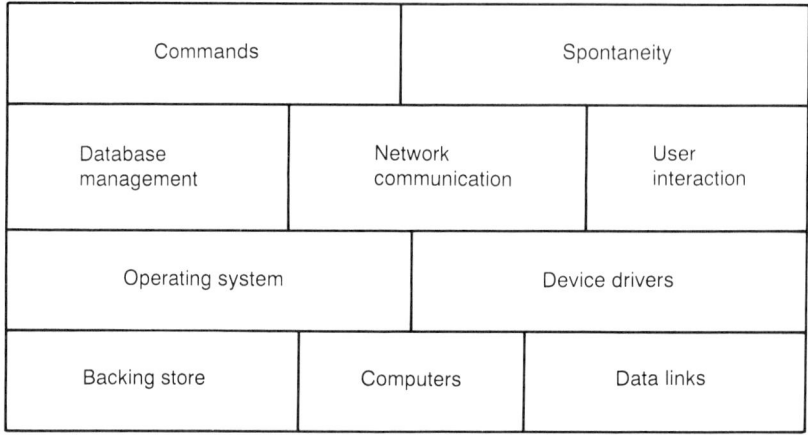

Figure 8.2 *Layered software structure*

within the control system must be done on-line by the control system software being self-aware. There are aspects of this both before and during operation.

The configuration of a protection/safety system must be checked to ensure that safety is assured even in the event of random failure in the control system itself – for example, by supplementing programmable electronics with alternative technologies such as non-programmed protection and physical containment. This includes the provision of redundant devices and resources to compensate for random failures during operation.

A predeployment check must be made to ensure that the specification of the software does cover all the modes of random hardware failure, with suitable detection (needing sensors aware of the controller itself, not only the equipment under control) and reaction to preserve safety (for example, using other elements of the total configuration of safety systems protecting the plant).

An important check which must be made when there are multiple devices of the same type is of their distinct identities, to avoid the danger of confusion (e.g. a fire in the port engine being detected, but reported as in the starboard engine, and the wrong fire extinguisher applied).

Software checking

Given the virtual certainty of errors in the specification, and the likelihood of errors in the underlying assumptions about the context of use, it is important to check complete control loops, by a combination of analysis and testing (i.e. static and dynamic checks). Each kind of check rests on certain assumptions, which other checks confirm.

Static checking confirms the relationships within a single layer of software (e.g. the body of a procedure), assuming that the layers below it (software and

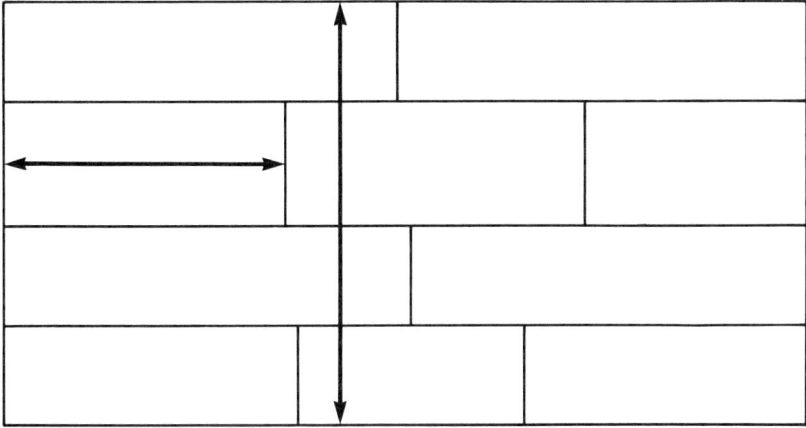

Figure 8.3 *Complementary checking by analysis (horizontal arrows) and testing (vertical arrows)*

hardware) behave as specified (see McGettrick, 1982). This is indicated by the horizontal arrows in Figure 8.3. Dynamic checking confirms the behaviour of the system in a single situation (e.g. an event in a particular operating mode), assuming that similar events elicit similar behaviour. This is indicated by the vertical arrows in Figure 8.3.

Static checking exposes the regions of continuity in the situations to which the software responds: the collection of situations in which the behaviour is determined by a particular path in the software (so together would or would not be handled as expected). This then determines which tests must be carried out for each module of the software.

Each Ada package (in categories 1 and 2 explained above) must be checked, both analytically and by testing. Analytical checks are purely formal, taking no account of the use or infrastructure of the software. They confirm the claim for the package, and indicate that tests are necessary to cover the full variety of situations. The tests are entirely pragmatic, taking no account of the discontinuities in behaviour in adjacent cases. The combination of 'horizontal' and 'vertical' checks leaves only the possibility of omitted discrimination in the specification, and of ill-conditioning; in other words, software where slightly different events give rise to significantly (an unexpectedly) different behaviour.

Residual weaknesses in design in Ada

The strength of a program design in Ada stems from the comprehensive consistency checks provided automatically by the compiler: the human designer is not allowed the luxury of deferring critical decisions or of following several incompatible paths at the same time. (This does not exclude the possibility of exploring several designs to discover the best: it simply ensures that they are *visibly* distinct.)

The residual weaknesses are those aspects of the design that are not automatically checked by a compiler that enforces the rules of the language. These aspects are those the V&V contractor will concentrate on – and be the more effective from having a clear focus of attention.

A comprehensive review of 'insecurities' in Ada has been carried out (Wichmann, 1988). The specific features concerned for safety verification are (1) intercommunication between distinct computers, (2) input–output and the use of representation clauses, (3) exception handling, (4) task termination and (5) mutual exclusion (and shared variables). We discuss each below.

Weaknesses at intercommunication

Since Ada deals with the program in a single computer, there is no check for consistency between programs in distinct computers. (Current research is addressing this problem, but there are no satisfactory solutions yet.) In particular, whenever messages are sent between computers there is no automatic check of type-compatibility or of proper sequencing. Thus the whole issue of intercommunication protocols is beyond the scope of Ada checking, and must be investigated using other methods by the V&V contractor. Specifically, the protocol must be specified and checked. The program (i.e. relevant packages in Ada) can be checked as a correct implementation of the protocol, and the rules of Ada used to ensure that all communication is carried out by means of the operations in the proper package.

Weaknesses in input–output

Low-level packages that drive peripheral devices to carry out input–output operations will use representation clauses to reach specific addresses, with specific record structures, bit-maps and representation codes. While Ada allows these to be specified, there are no automatic checks on them, for consistency, completeness or repetition. The information in representation clauses depends critically on properties of the target computer, particularly on details that computer manufacturers seem cautious about exposing, so the independent check by the V&V contractor will be particularly valuable.

Ada does not prevent several distinct driver tasks from using the same physical address (since the hardware may necessitate this), and a valuable V&V check is to look for repetitions among the addresses given throughout the whole program (not limited to individual packages). A simple tool could be developed to produce the information needed for this check.

A further check at the input–output level concerns safety: where output devices have the potential to be harmful, the package that allows the rest of the program to use them should include the safety interlocks. A raw device handler should always be encapsulated inside a protective package. Similar principles would be applied if information had to be encrypted for transmission over insecure communication channels.

Weaknesses in exception handling

While Ada recognizes that any action in a program might fail, the designer has the responsibility for deciding the level of abstraction at which the failure is handled, so that appropriate repair and recovery can be carried out. The design expressed in Ada will identify the exceptions that are recognized at each level, listing them in the packages with the data types whose operations may be defective.

The basic Ada rule is that an exception is propagated upwards until it is handled: consequently, a failure at some level where there is no handler amounts to failure at higher levels, up to that containing a handler. The usual nesting scope rules apply to the exception names as to all others, so exceptions can be raised deeply within packages in the context of the declarations.

A possible program error is therefore to have an exception declared, and handlers in some (but not·all) of the sub-programs declared at the same level. If the exception is raised in a deep subsidiary procedure that happens to have been called by a sub-group that does *not* have a handler, then propagation will continue upwards to the enclosing task or main program.

The V&V check should relate all exception handling to the relevant declaration and handlers (across packages, taking account of context clauses), and ensure that the protection is complete. In particular, there should be a check that the top level of every task and main program has a handler for *others* as a catch-all.

Weaknesses in task termination

Ada tasks are allowed to abort one another and voluntarily to terminate, as well as to reach a natural end. The program designer will have to make particular choices as to the use and disposition of tasks, with no automatic checks for coherence.

The scope rules ensure that only tasks within the same computer can abort one another, so one task is assured of survival. Tasks containing a *select terminate* construct have a clean end, but any execution of *abort* can leave the referenced task with variables in an inconsistent state, and any structure containing a task with *loop select* and *select terminate* will never reach completion. All these problems can be detected by the V&V contractor examining the task termination relationships in the program.

Weaknesses concerning mutual exclusion

Ada provides the mechanism for mutual exclusion (by selective entries in a passive task), but also permits re-entrant use of procedures in a package. It is the designer's responsibility to specify mutual exclusion (as opposed to re-entrance) when necessary; there are no compiler checks.

If the facilities of a package are only used by one task, there is no problem. The V&V contractor will therefore locate any use of a package by more than one task at a time, and investigate such usage carefully to determine whether the operations interact (e.g. by using shared variables). The same principle will be applied to any variables or procedures in the same declarative part as the task declarations, since these also may be improperly accessed without mutual exclusion.

Other Ada features

Certain other Ada features need particular attention because they may impact on the complete behaviour of the target computer, thus influencing the safety of the plant it controls. In addition to representation specifications (which are central to the present approach) and certain task interactions, these are the facilities introduced in particular sensitive packages, namely *LOW_LEVEL_IO, SYSTEM, UNCHECKED_CONVERSION, UNCHECKED_DEALLOCATION* (or application-specific packages making use of their features), and, of course, *MACHINE_CODE*.

In addition, where timing is important, the software must be checked for adequate performance. Only a few Ada constructs can lead to unbounded (i.e. context-dependent) timing, beyond the general dependence on the speed of the target computer. The timing for control loops relevant to safety must be analysed in terms of data values and task interactions, taking account of any unbounded constructs that might be present.

Apart from the timing constraints, the structure and checks advocated in the present approach give sufficient protection to ensure that any of the above category 3 constructs *outside* the double insulation (of category 2 and category 1 constructs) will fail-safe rather than fail-to-danger. The proscribed features should not be used directly or indirectly *inside* the double insulation other than as advocated by the given design rules. In other words, keep the checks and controls simple.

Software/hardware interaction

The residual source of danger in an Ada program written according to these guidelines arises from the software/hardware interaction. Ada cannot check that representation specifications are given correctly, or that they are restricted to specific parts of the program. It is therefore necessary to carry out a comprehensive syntactic check of the complete program to ensure that the elements in each package satisfy the design rules. In particular, the checks must locate all representation specifications and analyse them in an integrated way. The program in Ada expresses the logical structure of the system, which has no significance for representations.

It is particularly important to verify those packages that handle application-specific devices. The above 'concept definition' guidelines should allow the verifier to focus clearly on these; in addition, for safety-critical output devices the verifier must confirm that the designer has specified:

(a) The circumstances under which it is safe to operate the device;
(b) The safe closed-down condition of the device.

The most important check to apply is on the device address specifications. The address of each input–output device should be distinct and in a distinct package. This can be checked by preparing a list of all address specifications sorted by address, identifying the package and device name.

For each type of device there should also be a control and status word format. The use of packages declaring these should be checked for congruity with the categorization of the devices into device types.

The verification consists of checking the data structures and representations for control registers, and the operations on the device. The verifier should:

1. Confirm bit pattern interpretations in control registers, by reference to the hardware specifications;
2. Confirm addresses for access to control registers, by reference to the configuration specification;
3. Check that device operations can only take place when it is safe to do so (by rule a);
4. Check that safe close-down and safe operation are the only operations possible (rules a and b).

It should be always borne in mind that logic is not the prime influence on I/O device checking, because the attributes are highly specific and application-dependent, usually put together in rather *ad hoc* ways. The verifier has to rely on the information provided about the device by its supplier, which must be cross-checked against information from other sources (e.g. tests carried out on the actual device).

Summary

This section has reviewed the fault modes to which software in Ada is susceptible, so that the designer, verifier, checker and assessor can ensure that sufficient attention has been given to it for the level of safety integrity required.

CERTIFICATION OF ADA SOFTWARE IN A SAFETY-RELATED SYSTEM

An automatic control system which is responsible for safety has to be certified by a responsible body to give public assurance that the work has been done properly. From this analysis, the design rules and checking criteria have been formulated for software developed in Ada.

Safety integrity analysis

The HSE Guidelines require the safety-related system to be analysed to ensure that the required level of safety integrity has been achieved, according to the criteria set for the particular plant. This means investigating all possible influences that could affect the ability of the plant to perform its required functions in the desired manner on the occasions when it is required to perform them, under all the relevant conditions. There are basically two steps in this analysis: (1) identifying all the influences and (2) delimiting the functions, conditions and occasions in which the performance could be affected. Hardware failures are explicitly to be included in the safety integrity analysis (for example, communication between sub-systems in a distributed control system).

With regard to the software, the HSE Guidelines recognize that the safety integrity cannot be quantified, but can only be considered qualitatively. The Guidelines give an example in which there are two independent channels contributing to safety: one programmed in BASIC, the other a Programmable Logic Controller, in which the real program is independent of the application, with parameters defining the particular protection logic used.

The qualitative method of analysis given in the HSE Guidelines uses lists of questions covering the requirements, hardware, software, operations, maintenance and common cause failures. Each question is formulated to take an answer 'yes', 'no' or 'not applicable', where the 'yes' answer is the good one. The analysis is completed by summarizing the percentage of questions to which each answer is given: values around 80% of 'yes' answers may be required for the safety of a petrochemical plant. Each of the 'no' answers has to be investigated further to determine how serious it is. (Note that this way of summarizing the answers gives equal weight to all the questions. This is not absolutely justified, but is a basis for comparison, and establishes a common framework of assessment for all safety-related systems.)

The questions in the HSE checklists are mainly unaffected by the decision to program in Ada, but some of the software questions can be further amplified in this case, either by giving a direct answer now or by showing how the question is to be interpreted for software in Ada. Each checklist has a number, and each question has a number which starts with the checklist number. We give the specific Ada-related questions in the Appendix with appropriate comments.

Formal checks

Formal techniques are fundamental to computer-based systems, as all information handling in a computer is formal, being based entirely on its form (ultimately as bit-patterns) regardless of any intended meaning or interpretation. Formal analyses may be carried out by a person (with logical/mathematical skills) or by an automaton. In general, a check by an automaton (for that is the best way to think of automatic checks using software tools) is an exhaustive application of the individual checks deemed appropriate by the human inventor of the software tool. It thus eliminates the risk of unintentional or resource-imposed omission or incomplete coverage which is common in human checking, but loses the application of natural intelligence to any individual peculiarities of the software under test. Extensive software tools already exist, and more are being developed, to carry out formal checks on software in Ada. These have significant advantages, but also some drawbacks, in comparison with other kinds of check.

Checks based on static analysis of the program text also have benefits and shortcomings in relation to tests of the dynamic behaviour of the system under particular conditions, whether carried out automatically or by intelligent inspection. They presume a perfect execution of the program in terms of the semantics defined by the language, thus assuming a perfect compiler, linker, run-time executive, library routines, processor, memory and peripheral hardware. Testing, on the other hand, does not rely on such assumptions. Checks based on static analysis are best for 'negative' checks: those that show the absence of particular features, in either all units or a selection of them. Testing can only show the *presence* of particular features.

Formal proof of a program (with respect to its specification) means a logical demonstration that the program satisfies its specification, without reference to its intended meaning or interpretation. Thus a package in SPARK (Carré and Jennings, 1988) or in Ada annotated in Asphodel (Hill, 1988) would be formally proved by giving the logical steps to show that the specification holds from the program text. This demonstration must be completely logical, so may be carried out by a human logician or an automaton. The steps are usually so many and tedious that it is preferable to use an automaton to carry out the logic, with a human to guide it and determine the strategy. The evidence that an automatic control system behaves as it should is best presented in this way, supported by evidence that the specification and assumptions are adequate for its intended use.

Intelligent inspection

Another human mind, distinct from that of the designer, can locate many flaws in a design. The main problem is that the inspector, properly seeing a different way of designing the system, is tempted to be constructively critical, and thus to suggest changes to the software that do not solely eliminate mistakes. This is not necessarily bad, but it makes the responsibility of the inspector clear: there are likely to be many ways of designing satisfactory packages, of which the designer has chosen one. It is not the role of the inspector to select a different one (whatever its merits) but to identify potential safety risks with the design that has been chosen.

This search for potential problems must not be restricted to the formal program text, but must encompass the whole context of intended use: the adequacy of the interlocks and guards, as well as the stated intention of each operation provided by the critical packages. There are opportunities for formal notations other than Ada to be used to express intentions, against which appropriate parts of the Ada program can be checked. The evidence for certification should focus on the adequacy of the specification and assumptions, including those related to the software handling of the random hardware failures and reconfiguration.

Inspection is so important for safety systems that organizations are structured to facilitate it. Verification and Validation (known as 'V&V') is often the specific responsibility of a distinct company or group, which is independent of the design organization. The activities may include testing as well as inspection, extending the initials to 'V,V&T'.

Testing

Notwithstanding all the checks of the software provided by automata and intelligent inspectors (accompanied by the use of formal methods where inferences can be formally derived from the program text), testing is essential to produce evidence that the software causes the target computers and plant to behave as intended. The real world of the plant is not formal, and the input–output devices perform operations whose formal descriptions must be checked. This raises two problems: how an Ada program should be tested in general, and what special steps should be taken for safety-related systems. (Perhaps the more general matters could have been left out, but, given the present dearth of experience on testing Ada programs for embedded-computer systems, it was decided that the material would be useful to readers.)

Tests exercise the binary code and the hardware that executes it, thus confirming the code generated by the Ada compiler, the run-time system and the underlying computer together with its peripherals. These dynamic checks complement the static semantic analyses described in the previous section. Testing has to cover both the algorithms and the data representations. Traditional analyses have concentrated on testing the algorithms, without explicit attention to the mappings between abstract data and their representations. Data typing is a central concept in Ada, and the adequacy of the mapping (e.g. variants for compound types, range for scalar types, precision for numerical types, size for dynamic types) must be tested.

Safety is a negative property – so testing can confirm the presence of interlocks and guards but not the absence of danger. A suitable module testing strategy is to plan tests for all the operations which each device is capable of performing (the potentially dangerous ones as well as the safe ones) and all the modes of operation available (typically, a normal mode and a maintenance mode, when external guards are used to keep victims out of danger). Testing must cover the individual program units that drive each input–output device related to safety (and the others as well, for full confidence in the program), particularly the combinations that give interlocked protection.

By analysing the tests with respect to the requirements at each level of design (i.e. performing a requirements coverage analysis), we can relate each test case to the software requirements it confirms (individually and in combinations), and thus identify which test cases are essential to demonstrate that the software adequately complies with the functional requirements.

The claim that the system is fit for its intended purpose must include

1. Demonstration that all individual parts of the software have been tested; and
2. Reasoning and evidence of the overall accomplishment, linking statements of the software produced with the requirements.

The fault incidence rate depends fundamentally on the separate influences: the source language (which limits the faults that can be articulated), the checking strategy (which determines the probability of residual defects), and the operational utilization of the system (since an error will show when the input data stimulate a residual fault in the program that was not detected by previous testing or operational use). Fault seeding is useful at the end of conventional testing to estimate the number of errors remaining undetected, but it cannot relate them to operational utilization. Mutation testing is valuable for estimating the effectiveness of test data as representative of the input data space. Random data testing is particularly useful with Ada (and other strongly typed languages); it has the advantage that different samples from the data space avoid any bias by the tester about operational use, and give rarely occurring data equal probabilities of being tested.

Evidence for certification

The award of a certificate of safety for a computer-based system depends on the regulatory body being satisfied that all proper steps have been taken. The assurance activity demonstrates to the regulatory agency that the development and the subsequent verification (analysis and testing) have been carried out in a manner appropriate to the software risk factor to give a tolerable residual fault density. In general, evidence must be produced for each distinct unit of software (i.e. Ada compilation unit), depending on the risk factor of the software unit concerned. The evidence produced to give this assurance may include assertions of compliance with published standards, reports by witnesses, historical records, and information generated by verification analyses such as cross-reference matrices and test coverage calculations. For airworthiness certification of avionics systems or equipments, a Statement of Compliance with a documented software development process is needed for all steps in the development of risk factor 2 software, implying that the developer accepts the responsibility for the checking. All documentation and results must be independently inspected for software of risk factor 1 (which requires formal documentation, maintenance, control and retrieval procedures). In addition, for risk factor 1 software there must be analyses to assess the coverage of the design requirements from the software requirements, and of them from the system requirements.

Tests have to be verified as well as performed satisfactorily. Where particular criteria are set for safety-related software, it is important to verify that they are met in the software produced, and to ensure that all infringements of the criteria are identified and justified.

Thus the acceptability criteria (e.g. acceptable system error rates, with software detection and corrective actions) should have been agreed as a constraint in the initial requirements. The development procedure should include production of documents to show that these criteria are met, with complete audit trails. The verification should be carried out by qualified people independent of the developers.

DO-178A (RTCA, 1985) does not call for any specific evidence about dependencies between software modules (because it does not recognize layering in the software). The analysis suggested here is therefore supplementary evidence of the software accomplishment.

Defence Standard 00-55 (MoD, 1991) lays down responsibilities for safety management concerning in defence equipment by having individuals nominated to specific roles. The certificate of suitability for service is an unambiguous, clear and binding statement by accountable signatories from the Design Authority, countersigned by the Independent Safety Auditor. Having the software written in Ada and checked as described here will be a significant contribution to the dependability of the target system behaviour, and thus to the total system safety.

APPENDIX: ADA-RELATED TOPICS IN HSE GUIDELINES

HSE Checklist 10A: Software Specification (Ada program unit semantics)

10A.4 'Is use made of a formal specification language or some other means of ensuring a precise and unambiguous specification?' The example in the HSE Guidelines shows that pseudocode is considered adequate to answer this question 'yes', so the recommended style of using claims would also be satisfactory.

10A.9 'Are automated tools used as an aid to the development of the software specification in (i) documentation; (ii) consistency checking?' An Ada compiler would count as such a tool, treating the annotated package specifications as the documentation of the software, and noting the automatic consistency checking between compilation units.

HSE Checklist 11A: Software Design (Ada program unit specifications)

11A.4 'Is use made of a formal, structural program design language or some other means of ensuring a clear and unambiguous statement of functions to be coded?' Ada satisfies this.

11A.5 'Is use made of a suitable graphical representation of programme [sic] flow control (e.g. flow chart) and programme data flow or other means of assuring that the programme operation is clear and easily understood?' With Ada it would be normal to rely on the 'other means' in the question – specifically the readability of Ada and the use of claims.

11.A.6 'Are there guidelines for constraining the control flow of the programme by the use of acceptable flow control structures?' The question does not define which flow control structures are 'acceptable'; the design rules given in this book (about the use of *go to* and exceptions) satisfy the question.

11A.7 'Are automated tools used as an aid to design in regard to (i) documentation; (ii) control flow analysis; (iii) data flow analysis; (iv) information flow analysis: (v) semantic analysis?' An Ada-specific editor would satisfy point (i), and the SPARK examiner (Carré and Jennings, 1988) or MALPAS (Webb, 1990) would satisfy the others.

11A.8 'Are there guidelines for the design of data structures?' Some are given in ARINC Paper 613 (ARINC, 1987), but there is little relevance to safety. The guidance to avoid access types could be considered as satisfying this question, but it is not clear what purpose such guidelines are intended to serve.

Use of Ada in safety-critical systems   183

11A.15 'If a concurrent processing philosophy has been adopted rather than sequential task execution: (i) has the need for this been established; (ii) have suitable concurrent processing methods been adopted; (iii) has the use of interrupts been kept to a minimum?' Suitable concurrent processing methods are provided by Ada run-time environments. Minimization of interrupts depends on the timing analysis, to determine whether polling is an acceptable alternative.

11A.16 '(i) Are separate software modules used to implement the safety-related functions; (ii) Is the data used by them protected as far as possible from write access by other modules?' The recommended structural design satisfies the first point. The scope rules of Ada ensure that the second is satisfied.

11A.18 'Does the software contain adequate error detection facilities allied to error containment, recovery or safe shutdown procedures?' The style of defensive programming, possibly with Ada *exceptions*, satisfies this.

11A.19 'Are safety-critical areas of the software identified?' This point underlies the categorization of packages described above.

HSE Checklist 12A: Software Coding (Ada program units which are proper bodies)

12A.9 'Is an appropriate high-level programming language used where speed considerations allow?' Ada is currently the most appropriate such language.

12A.10 '(i) Is a well established compiler/asembler used; (ii) Does it have a good error detection capability; (iii) Is it certified to recognize standards?' A validated Ada compiler is assured to be sufficiently well established to satisfy the validation tests, which include tests of the error-detection capability, and certify that it conforms to the standard definition of Ada.

12A.11 'Does the programming language: (i) encourage the use of small and manageable modules; (ii) allow access to certain data to be restricted to defined modules; (iii) permit operations to be carried out on variables of the expected type; (iv) allow the definition of variable type sub-ranges?' Ada strongly satisfies these.

12A.12 'Is the code written in a form which helps comprehension by (i) adequate use of comments; (ii) sectioning of functions or modules etc.; (iii) the consistent use of acceptable control flow structures; (iv) the use of different levels of indenture for associated statements?' Ada satisfies this by its concern for readability, although the necessity to use comments (in any language) must be regarded as a weakness: information that cannot be formalized in the programming language itself is not so strongly checked for consistency.

12A.13 'Are automated tools used as an aid to development in regard to (i) documentation; (ii) control flow analysis; (iii) data flow analysis; (iv) information flow analysis; (v) semantic analysis?' (Note the similarity of this question to question 11A.7, illustrating the fact that design and development are not distinct steps in software engineering.) Depending on the interpretation of 'documentation', the first point could be satisfied by an Ada compiler (treating a package specification as its documentation) or the SPARK examiner (treating the annotation as documentation). The SPARK examiner would satisfy the others.

12A.14 'Are there guidelines for limiting the size of program modules to avoid over-complexity?' The design rules to facilitate verification avoid over-complexity, but not explicitly by limiting size. General guidelines (not specific to safety) limit the size of individual compilation units (e.g. to 200 lines).

12A.15 'Are safety critical areas within the code identified?' (This is like question 11A.19, again confirming the similarity of design and development.) The recommended categorization of program units would satisfy this.

HSE Checklist 13A: Software test

13A.10 'Is each software module tested individually as fully as possible before incorporation onto the full program?' This will be satisfied if the present recommendations are followed.

13A.11 '(i) Are there specified criteria for the coverage of tests (for example, is each control flow path through the program tested to ensure that each statement is executed at least once); (ii) If not, is the coverage of the tests known; (iii) Are test results analysed to reveal any areas of the software which show an unexpectedly high rate of failure in test; (iv) If so, are the reasons for the high rate of failure established?' The recommendations deal with the coverage of the tests. The points about an expected rate of failure seem to imply possible acceptability of a safety-related system in which tests have exposed failures. The coverage analysis should show that these cannot lead to danger.

13A.12 'Have arithmetic functions been tested with the sets of input values which give the maximum and minimum computed results to ensure that no overflow conditions are reached?' This would be satisfied by extreme-value testing (data on boundary values) and Ada exception detection for range constraints.

NOTE

The views expressed in this chapter are those of the author, and do not necessarily reflect those of SD-Scicon.

ACKNOWLEDGEMENT

The material in this chapter is extracted from the author's book *Developing Safety Systems – a Guide using Ada*, Prentice Hall International, 1991.

REFERENCES

Bennett, P. A. (1984), *The Safety of Industrially-based Controller Incorporating Software*, PhD thesis, Open University

Carré, B. A. and Jennings, T. J. (1988), *SPARK – The SPADE Ada Kernel*, Dept of Electronics and Computer Science, University of Southampton

EWICS (1985), 'Safety related computers – software development and system documentation', European Workshop on Industrial Computer Systems, TC7: Systems Reliability, Safety and Security, Verlag TUV Rheinland

Goldsack, S. (ed.) (1985), *Ada for Specification and Design – possibilities and limitations*, Ada Companion Series, Cambridge University Press, Cambridge

Gordon, A. M. (1988), 'Introducing Ada at GEC Sensors Ltd', *Ada User*, 9, No. 3, 127–128

Helps, K. A. (1986), 'Some verification tools and methods for airborne safety-critical software', *Software Engineering Journal*, 1, No. 6, 248–253, November

Hill, A. (1984), 'Asphodel, An Ada compatible specification and design language', *Proc. 3rd joint Ada Europe AdaTEC Conference*

Hill, A. (1988), 'The formal specification and verification of reusable software components using Ada and Asphodel', *Ada User*, 9, 113–123

Holzapfel, R. and Winterstein, G. (1988), 'Ada in safety critical applications' in *The Use of Ada in High Integrity Systems*, Cranfield Information Technology Institute, and in Heilbrunner, S. (ed.), *Ada in Industry*, Cambridge University Press, Cambridge

HSE (1987), *Programmable Electronic Systems in Safety Related Applications* (2 vols), HMSO, London
Volume 1: *An Introductory Guide*
Volume 2: *General Technical Guidelines*

IEC (1989a) *Software for computers in the application of industrial safety-related systems* (Proposal for a standard); SC65A(Secretariat) 94

IEC (1989b), *Functional Safety of programmable electronic systrems* (draft), SC65A (Secretariat) 96

Jennings, T. J. and Carré, B. A. (1988), 'A subset of Ada for formal verification (SPARK)', *Ada User*, 9, Supplement, 121–126

Luckham, D. C., von Henke, F. W., Krieg-Brueckner, B. and Owe, O. (1984), *ANNA, A language for annotating Ada programs (Preliminary Reference Manual)*, Technical Report No. 84-248, Stanford University Computer Systems Laboratory, June

McCormick, F. (1988), 'Ada scheduling in integrated civil avionics', Position paper for the Second International Workshop on Real-Time Ada Issues, Moretonhampstead, Devon, UK

McGettrick, A. (1982), *Program Verification using Ada*, Cambridge University Press, Cambridge

MoD (1987), *The development of safety-critical software for airborne systems*, Interim Defence Standard 00-31/1

MoD (1991) *The procurement of safety critical software in defence equipment*, Part 1, Requirements, Part 2, Guidance, Interim Defence Standard 00-55, Issue 1

NCC (1987) *The STARTS Guide – A guide to methods and software tools for the construction of large real-time systems*, 2nd edn (2 vols), NCC Publications, September

NCC (1989), *The STARTS Purchasers' Handbook – Procuring software-based systems*, 2nd edn, NCC Publications

Pyle, I. C. (1984), 'Limits on the use of Ada for specifications', in Teller, J. (ed.), *Proc. 3rd Ada Europe Conference*, Brussels, pp. 251–260, and Cambridge University Press, Ada Companion Series (1984), p. 761

Pyle, I. C. (1987), 'Designing for safety using Ada packages', in Daniels, B. K. (ed.), *Achieving Safety and Reliability with Computer Systems*, Elsevier Applied Science, Barking

Pyle, I. C. (1988), 'Safety implications of integrated avionics systems', in *Military avionics architectures for today and tomorrow*, ERA Report 88-0437, ERA Technology Ltd, Leatherhead, Surrey, UK

Pyle, I. C. (1991), *Developing Safety Systems: A Guide Using Ada*, Prentice-Hall International, Englewood Cliffs, NJ

Rex, Thompson & Partners Ltd (1987), *The capabilities of MALPAS – a software verification and validation tool*, RTP/4002, April

RTCA (1985), *Software Considerations in Airborne Systems and Equipment Certification*, Document No. RTCA/DO-178A, prepared by SC-152, Radio Technical Commission for Aeronautics, March

Webb, J. T. (1990), 'MALPAS and Ada', *Ada User*, **11**, No. 1, 14–20, January

Wichmann, B. A. (1988), *Insecurities in the Ada programming language: an interim report*, National Physical Laboratory, Report DITC 122/88, August

9 Fault-tolerant control for safety
Iain H. A. Johnston

INTRODUCTION

Modern control systems frequently involve the use of complex algorithms and extensive empirical data to implement their control strategy. Often digital techniques using Programmable Electronics Systems (PESs) are employed to implement these control strategies. It is in the nature of man's endeavour that the systems he constructs are not perfect. In the physical (analogue) world small inaccuracies rarely have catastrophic consequences provided appropriate margins are allowed in the design. In the digital world small inaccuracies can often affect performance and results in unexpected and significant ways.

There is a need, therefore, to accommodate the imperfections which are built into systems. It may be that the consequences of failure resulting from the imperfections are insignificant and the accommodation is therefore automatic. For applications where safety is a potential concern it is unlikely that this will be the case. In these circumstances it is necessary to incorporate some mechanism to offset these inevitable imperfections; in other words, to reduce the risk associated with the application.

There are two principal approaches:

1. *Fault prevention.* The application of fault prevention recognizes that faults will occur during the development of the system, but tries to prevent their inclusion in the operational system.
2. *Fault tolerance.* The application of fault tolerance accepts that faults will be included in the operational system, but tries to restrict the effects of any failures which result.

These two approaches are complementary. Fault prevention is necessary to a greater or lesser degree for any system. It minimizes the number of faults, and hence failures, which must be handled by fault tolerance. Fault tolerance provides a means by which the system can continue fulfilling its function when a failure occurs. In other words, the failure of part of the system does not necessarily mean the failure of the whole system. There are a number of possible reasons for building fault tolerance into a system. Typical are the desire to increase the reliability, availability or dependability of the system as perceived by its users. The importance of user perception should not be underestimated.

In most cases the perception of the service provided by a system is, in the end, the criterion by which a system will be judged. There may be objective means of measuring reliability, particularly where hardware is concerned. Nevertheless, reliability is, by its nature, a non-deterministic quantity. Once a system is in operation the empirically determined reliability is therefore more persuasive than any theoretically determined value. Furthermore, the perceived reliability is what will influence the users' opinions of the system.

SAFETY

This chapter discusses fault tolerance specifically with respect to safety. It must not be forgotten that in many cases there are two different and, to some extent, competing reasons for applying fault tolerance. Typically, high availability is required for commercial reasons with fault tolerance ensuring that operational capability is maintained in the presence of failures. In contrast, for safety reasons it may be that fault tolerance is required to ensure that a process is shut down if a failure occurs. Depending on the application, therefore, it may be that the goals of safety are in direct conflict with those of overall system availability, dependability and reliability.

Safety is a concept which is related to risk. Bennett (1984) defines a situation to be safe if the level of risk is 'judged to be acceptable'. This concept of the acceptability or tolerability of risk is discussed at length by the HSE (1988). Risk is defined by Bennett as a description of 'the probability of a hazard materializing' and by the IEC (1991) as 'the combination of the frequency, or probability, and the consequence of a specified hazardous event'. In order to improve safety, risk must be reduced. This can be done either by reducing the probability (increasing reliability) or reducing the severity of the consequence (possibly by taking some emergency action). Using fault tolerance to improve reliability may therefore be, at least in part, consistent with improving safety. The reliability concerned, however, is reliability with respect to failures which will realize the hazard if they occur.

THE NEED FOR DETECTION AND REPAIR

Fault detection is of crucial importance to the implemenation of fault tolerance (Anderson and Lee, 1981). There are two different reasons why this is so. The mechanism by which the fault tolerance is implemented may require some action to take place in the event of an error occurring. This is particularly the case for tolerance of software faults or for systems where passive redundancy is used. In any event, a failure usually requires some form of maintenance if the required level of fault tolerance is to be maintained. In order for a repair action to be initiated it is necessary for the fault to be detected and reported.

Active and passive redundancy are typical approaches to providing fault tolerance. The distinction between them is important. Passive redundancy typically involves the provision of a stand-by system or sub-system. When a failure is detected the standby system is switched in, either manually or automatically. Active redundancy typically involves the provision of duplicated or triplicated systems or sub-systems which are used all the time with a voting mechanism. Active redundancy therefore provides a means of detecting faults, whereas passive redundancy requires that faults are detected in order to operate successfully.

For real-time control applications it is likely that there will be constraints on the time available to react when a fault occurs. Typically, this will mean that passive redundancy is not acceptable except under very tight constraints. For tolerance of faults in software this may severely restrict the techniques which are appropriate.

Repair time is also an important consideration. If a failure disables a channel then the fault-tolerant mechanism ensures that the system continues to provide service. 'A fault-tolerant system can, however, only sustain a limited number of failures before one more failure will fail the system' (Harper, 1988). In order to provide continued fault tolerance it is essential that repairs are carried out promptly when the need for them is discovered. What constitutes a sufficiently prompt repair will vary from system to system and from one application to another.

RANDOM AND SYSTEMATIC FAILURES

Providing fault tolerance with respect to random hardware failures is a relatively straightforward process involving the provision of redundant hardware components or systems. Tolerance of systematic failure is more complex.

Random hardware failures involve the physical failure of a hardware component or sub-system. Such failures occur in a random fashion (usually taken to be in an exponential distribution) and may be reasoned about using well-developed statistical techniques. The nature of this type of failure is that it is independent, that is, the failure of one component is no indication of any change in the likelihood of another component to fail.

Systematic failures are 'failures due to errors in design, construction or use of a system which cause it to fail under particular combinations of inputs or under some environmental condition' (HSE, 1987). Systematic failures are therefore failures which result from some common cause (Common Cause Failures or Common Mode Failures, CCFs or CMFs) or from lack of independence between components or sub-systems. Typically, the common cause is a design, manufacturing, installation or operating fault. Such common causes are, in fact, examples of a lack of independence between different components or sub-systems. Typically, systematic failures affect more than one component or sub-system at a time.

Random hardware failures may be protected against by using two or more examples of the component or sub-system. This is conventionally shown in a reliability block diagram as components or sub-systems in parallel (Figure 9.1). Such a structure may be sufficient in itself to protect against random hardware failure, or may require some means of failure detection in order to operate, as discussed above. Where some form of voting is employed this is likely to involve another sub-system, connected in series. Random hardware failures of this other sub-system are not protected against.

190   Safety Aspects of Computer Control

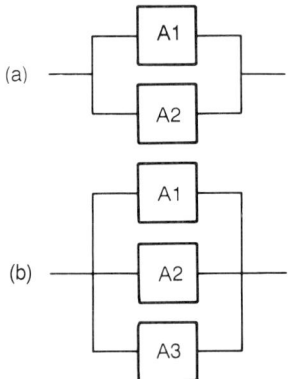

Figure 9.1 *Reliability block diagram for (a) dual and (b) triple redundant components*

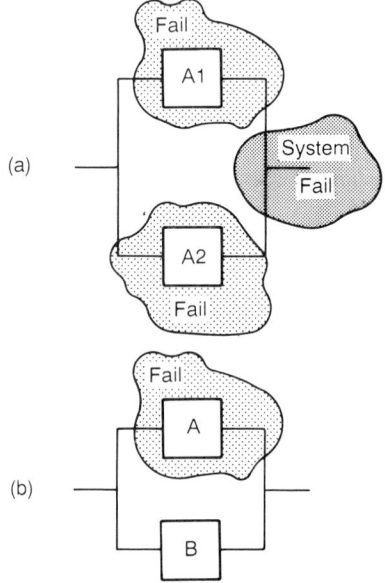

Figure 9.2 *Effect of systematic failure on (a) redundant and (b) diverse sub-systems*

Systematic failures cannot be successfully protected against in the same way. A manufacturing error in subsystem A (see Figure 9.2), which results in a failure in the presence of a particular set of environmental conditions will result in the failure of both of two redundant sub-system As. Typically, such a failure might result from the use of components from a batch which is out of tolerance and which has not been picked up by quality control procedures. Arguably, the error at the root of the systematic failure is in fact a quality assurance failure.

Fault-tolerant control for safety   191

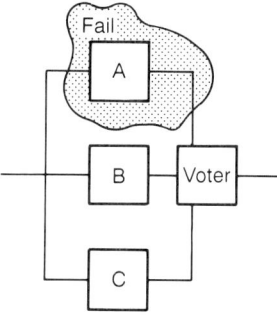

Figure 9.3 N-*version programming with voting*

Such a scenario can be guarded against by using diverse rather than identical redundancy (see Figure 9.3). Such diversity may be implemented in a number of different ways. For failures such as that suggested above it may be appropriate for sub-systems A and B to be sourced from different manufacturers. Alternatively, they may be different systems.

The example of systematic failure quoted relates to a manufacturing error in hardware. While such failures are not unimportant, failures due to design errors are of greater concern. This is of particular importance to PESs, since these are the only errors which affect software. There are many reasons for this and these are discussed elsewhere (McDermid, 1992). Of most importance from the point of view of this chapter is the complexity of the design of software. Design complexity is not, however, the exclusive prerogative of software. Design errors are also recognized as a problem in VLSI and other complex electronic circuit design.

The problem of introducing diversity which is suitable as a defence against such design errors is substantial. Designs are produced to satisfy a specification, making use of the designer's expertise and experience. In order to introduce true diversity of design, diverse specifications design personnel and design personnel backgrounds are required. Clearly, this is impracticable in most cases and any such diversity must eventually come back to a single point of original, high-level, specification. In fact unless this single point is reasonably far down the design path it is likely that the two resulting systems will be so diverse as to be impractical to operate together.

REPAIR AND FAILURE MODELLING

An obvious potential cause for concern, but one which is often overlooked, is the need to maintain fault tolerance while the system is under repair. Typically, a modern fault-tolerant control system provides for active redundancy and the replacement of redundant modules on-line. If only dual redundancy is used then the fault-tolerant character is lost when the one of the modules is removed for replacement. Even where triple redundancy is used the fault tolerance provided is degraded when a module fails or is removed for replacement.

When fault tolerance is used solely in order to improve reliability or availability this may not matter. The repair time may be so short as to have little effect on the overall reliability or availability figure. When fault tolerance is used in order to improve safety the loss of fault tolerance, even for a very short period, may be important. This is why care must be taken in regarding the improvement of safety as relating simply to improving the reliability in the equation:

Risk = Reliability × Severity

The characteristics of the overall system, particularly those of the process being controlled, are important factors in determining the fault-tolerant behaviour required. Harper (1988) lists seven possible objectives of fault tolerance from Goldberg (1985). These are restated here in a modified form and with additions to illustrate the point that different processes may require different behaviour of the fault-tolerant system:

1. No erroneous output;
2. Protection of internal data integrity;
3. Rapid recovery from a system failure;
4. Avoidance of specified non-safe conditions;
5. Safe shutdown in the event of system failure;
6. Infrequent system failure;
7. Low maintenance costs; and
8. Minimum down-time.

The analysis of redundant systems using Markov Models (Alleman, 1989) or Reliability Block Diagrams (MoD, 1983) can be an effective way of identifying the mechanisms of system failure and indicating the weak points of the system design. This can only be really effective if the modelling process and analysis takes account of the possible sources of system vulnerability to systematic and common cause failures. The models can provide an aid to the process of understanding the system, but if no attempt is made to attempt a wide understanding, including systematic failures, the models will not help. Alleman discusses the use of Markov models extensively and introduces a number of alternative approaches to the modelling of systematic failures. He does not, however, address the consideration of systematic failures as part of the Markov analysis. Rather the consideration is a 'bolt-on' modification of the results generated by the analysis.

At this time and to reinforce the preceding paragraph it is appropriate to reconsider the dichotomy of reliability and safety. Markov Models and RBDs can be and are used to model and predict system reliability and availability. Sophisticated analysis can be used to extend these models to take account of the error-detection facilities available in the system and of estimates for CCFs. In the end the result is a non-deterministic theoretical estimate which provides a good indication of what the perceived, empirical, reliability of the system will be.

This does not bear any relation to the perceived or actual safety achieved by the system unless the consequences of failure, with respect to safety, are also brought into consideration. These consequences depend on the process, other system elements and on the objectives set (explicitly or implicitly) for the fault-tolerant system.

HARDWARE AND SOFTWARE

There are important differences between software and hardware which must be taken adequately into account if a fault-tolerant computing system is to be successful. Hardware is subject to both random and systematic failures, software only to systematic failures, and these failures result principally from specification and design errors.

With current knowledge there is no means of knowing that software is error free (Myers, 1976) and there are no 'rules of thumb' which may be used in software development to ensure adequate margins of safety (Gilb, 1977). Software design and implementation does not have the same mature mathematical basis as more conventional engineering. Other branches of engineering use accepted basic measures or relationships as volts, amps or Ohm's law (Bennett, 1984). There are no such generally accepted software equivalents.

There are a number of reasons why software is different from hardware:

1. Software does not fail randomly through ageing, all failures are systematic and result from design faults;
2. Reliability models do exist for software but the nature of software failures means that real questions remain as to their validity and appropriateness;
3. The discontinuous nature of software means that small changes in inputs can result in unexpectedly large changes in output values. This means that meaningful testing is much less straightforward than for conventional analogue systems;
4. Any non-trivial software is extremely complex and unlikely to be understood in its entirety by a single individual;
5. Software is deceptively easy to change and small changes can have unexpectedly far-reaching results; and
6. Software is conceptual rather than physical, though it can be represented physically.

A number of software characteristics are particularly relevant to the tolerance of faults in software. This is especially true of fault tolerance which is implemented as a means of improving safety (or of improving availability in safety-related systems):

1. The unpredictability of the consequences of design faults makes the tolerance difficult, and only possible through the use of diversity (Shrivastava, 1991);
2. Assessment of the reliability of software, and hence of the utility of fault tolerance, is likely to be problematic (Anderson *et al.*, 1985);
3. The behaviour of the software can vary considerably and unexpectedly through small changes in input values, thus potentially demanding extreme sensitivity in fault-tolerant recovery mechanisms.

In the context it is important to realize that software on its own cannot harm anyone. Software is a conceptual, not a physical, entity which requires additional physical components to realize it. It is these physical components (the sensors and actuators, together with the devices and processes which they monitor and control) which make the PES and its software relate to safety. For the purposes of safety, tolerance of software faults therefore requires that the tolerance is realized in the physical components of the system. It need not necessarily be realized in the software itself.

For example, an anti-lock braking system is not related to safety until it is connected to a vehicle's braking system and that vehicle is used in circumstances where a failure could result in an accident. Tolerance of software failures in the system in order to achieve safety might be implemented physically by a watchdog mechanism isolating the programmable element and retaining conventional braking. Thus some braking system functionality would be maintained in the presence of a software failure detected by the watchdog.

Tolerance of faults in safety-related software cannot therefore be considered in isolation but in the context of the whole system within which the software exists. Much of the trick involved in reasoning about such software is concerned with selecting the correct system bounds within which to consider the specification, design and assessment of the software.

AVOIDANCE OF SOFTWARE FAULTS

The lack of any faults other than design faults as a source of software failure highlights the importance of fault prevention (fault avoidance and fault removal) in the design of software. If faults are not included in the software there is no need to incorporate provision to tolerate them. The more faults that can be prevented, the less is the extent to which fault tolerance is likely to be called upon. Considerable efforts have gone into the development of specification and design techniques and tools designed to prevent the inclusion of faults in implemented software.

Formal methods attempt to discipline the process of specifying and developing a software system in such a way that mathematics can be harnessed to prove the software's correctness and completeness. This is an aproach favoured by many and is directed at providing the certainty that a system complies with its specification (Jones, 1986).

The use of formal methods, however, is potentially costly and time consuming, though this view is not necessarily taken by its proponents. More importantly, the task of ensuring that the formal specification correctly represents the informally expressed and perhaps unclear requirements is not addressed satisfactorily by the use of formal methods (Stokes, 1991). Many problems which arise with PESs result from incorrect or incomplete specifications, which are not recognized as such until late in the development process or until the system is in use. The detection of incorrectness and incompleteness may well be possible only in relation to the physical aspects of the system and not identifiable by analysis of the software specification on its own.

A further problem, at the moment, with formal methods is that they are not yet sufficiently mature to be readily applied to many types of problem (for example, real-time, concurrency) and that there are few people with the experience and training to apply them productively. An alternative approach is to use techniques and tools which provide a structured development path, supported by automation, to assist the designers and programmers. Such methods attempt to divorce the designers from the more mundane and error-prone development tasks, allowing them to concentrate on ensuring that the system is specified and developed in a correct and consistent way.

Quality assurance is an important contributor to the achievement of acceptable levels of safety. Any safety-related system must be designed and constructed to a high level of quality. There are established schemes for achieving and confirming quality which should be applied to the design and construction of safety-related systems. There are indeed standards which are either directly applicable to software (AQAP, 1981) or which are applicable to software via particular assessment guidelines (BSI, 1987).

It is important that the requirement for a consistent approach is not interpreted as a need for rigid uniformity. In different circumstances and for different applications different methods and tools will be appropriate. It is unlikely that a single method will ever be relevant, even for a single application. A carefully chosen set of tools suited to a particular application which enable the PES and its environment to be considered from differing viewpoints is likely to be the most suitable approach.

These fault-prevention methods cannot eliminate software faults, they can only reduce their number (Anderson and Lee, 1981). Even a single fault in software used in a safety-related application can have extremely serious consequences. As a result, fault tolerance, for software faults, is becoming increasingly essential as more software is used in safety-related applications.

TOLERANCE OF SOFTWARE FAULTS

The application of fault tolerance to software must address systematic failures. As discussed earlier, systematic failures cannot be protected against simply by providing redundant components or sub-systems. In order to provide some measure of tolerance of software faults some diversity is required. A number of research projects have been carried out into the provision of software fault tolerance using diversity (Anderson *et al.*, 1985; Bishop *et al.*, 1986). These projects have concluded that there is benefit in using diversity, reporting masking of around 70% of faults.

There are two principal ways in which diverse software can be used to implement fault tolerance: recovery blocks and voting. The recovery block technique uses an acceptance test to determine whether or not the outcome of a software module is acceptable or not. If the outcome is unacceptable then the function of the module is implemented using the original input data by an alternative diverse piece of software. Shrivastava (1991) describes this using the pseudo-code:

196 Safety Aspects of Computer Control

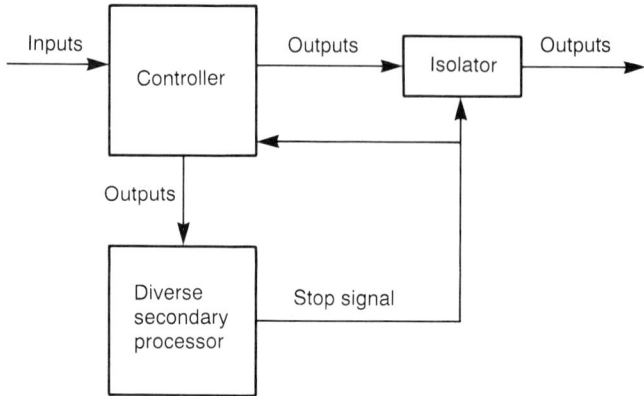

Figure 9.4 *Combined hardware and software diversity*

ensure <acceptance test> *by* P_0 *else-by* P_1 *else* fail

Thus recovery blocks use an acceptance test which is necessarily diverse to detect a failure, then attempt to recover from the failure using a diverse implementation of the desired function.

The use of voting (N-Version Programming) is analogous to hardware redundancy (Shrivastava, 1991; Stone, 1989) (see Figure 9.3). Two or more (N) versions of a program (or module) perform a function, simultaneously or in sequence. The results are then compared to identify any discrepancies and to select the correct result by majority voting. Thus the voting mechanism and the diverse implementations together provide both the detection and the recovery mechanism. If only two versions are used or if there is no majority result some safe action, such as halt or shutdown, is initiated in the event of a discrepancy. This is exemplified by the Airbus A310 slat and flap control system (Shrivastava, 1991).

An alternative approach to providing tolerance of software faults in safety-related applications is to provide some hardware, and hence diverse, protection mechanism. This is particularly relevant where the objective is the avoidance of specified non-safe conditions or safe shutdown in the event of system failure (see above). Typically, hardware interlocks, perhaps associated with an access door, may shut down an otherwise software-controlled process. Such an approach may be used if it is considered that the hardware protection itself provides sufficient risk reduction, making the software non-safety related. The hardware protection may, on the other hand, provide only part of the risk reduction required.

A combination of hardware and software diversity may be used (see Figure 9.4). The example shown in the figure is for a system which can be put into a safe state with the necessary residual functionality if the controller is stopped. Such an approach may also be appropriate for a two – or more version system with voting. Essentially, the approach is to strengthen the software diversity and independence by separating the software onto two or more diverse processors. If the diversity can be usefully extended to the function of the software (as in Figure

9.4, where the secondary processor performs acceptability checks on the outputs) the degree of diversity and independence is even greater.

HARDWARE AND SYSTEMATIC FAILURES

The application of fault tolerance to hardware may, justifiably, address random failures, though systematic failures should not be overlooked. Typical approaches to providing fault tolerance in hardware involve the use of redundancy. Dual redundancy provides a certain amount of protection. As was pointed out earlier, however, dual redundancy does not provide continued fault tolerance while a redundant channel is awaiting or undergoing maintenance. Triple modular redundant (TMR) systems can provide increased protection, particularly during module replacement. Such systems, however, remain vulnerable to systematic failure. Diversity is a means of addressing this problem. Diverse hardware may be provided in a number of ways, from the provision of non-programmable as well as programmable sub-systems to the provision of redundant hardware from diverse sources. The TMR Programmable Logic Controllers (PLCs) which are now available provide an excellent means of incorporating fault tolerance into what may be considered a crucial part of the PES. As with any non-diverse TMR architecture, such systems do, however, remain potentially vulnerable to systematic failure of both hardware and software (see below).

DIVERSITY

The provision of fault tolerance in software requires diversity. Redundant but not diverse software does not provide any fault tolerance except under very restricted circumstances. Diverse software may be associated with diverse or redundant hardware and may or may not run concurrently.

Diversity may be applied at a number of different levels. The preceding sections have suggested several ways in which two systems may be considered diverse. The following list broadly summarizes a number of different kinds of diversity which may be applied:

1. Diverse coding, programming performed by independent teams based on the same (or different) specifications, possibly using different programming languages;
2. Diverse design, software (or hardware) design performed by independent teams based on the same (or different) specifications, possibly using different techniques and tools;
3. Diverse specification, system (or software or hardware) specification generated by independent teams based on the same high-level requirement;
4. Diverse sourcing, hardware components or sub-systems to the same or compatible designs are obtained from different suppliers;

5. Diverse maintenance, hardware (or software) components or sub-systems in different redundant channels are maintained by different personnel and/or with replacement parts from different sources;
6. Temporal diversity, the use of real-time input data at different times may avoid the effects of transient hardware faults on software;
7. System or analytic diversity, the use of different types of sensor or actuator, different methods of calculation or different types of sub-system; and
8. Functional diversity, the implementation of different types of system function (for example, applying acceptability checks).

Diversity, then, may simply be at the coding level or may extend to specification and/or requirements capture. It may even extend to diversity of function, with one software channel providing monitoring and protective functions rather than direct control. In order to extend the level of diversity it may be necessary to explicitly introduce diversity in the methodologies and techniques used during design and development. It can be argued persuasively that the diversity of this nature is an essential element in the avoidance of faults.

LIMITATIONS ON DIVERSITY

There are, of course, limitations on the extent of the diversity which can, or should, be applied in any particular case. As was suggested earlier in this chapter, complete diversity of design and specification is impossible, since at some point there must be a single high-level conceptual specification or requirement which is not diverse. In any case, practicality dictates that there is a common specification at a sufficiently low level to allow the diverse components or sub-systems to be compatible with each other.

Diversity, in any case, requires that greater resource is required in order to achieve the same functionality (Anderson et al., 1985; Bishop et al., 1986). Possibly twice as much resource (Bishop et al., 1986) is required to develop and incorporate the diverse components and sub-systems as is required for the equivalent simplex system. There is a trade-off to be made between the benefit of applying the additional resource to providing diversity and applying it to avoid the inclusion of faults in a simplex system.

The implementation diversity results in possibly different outputs being produced. Some single component or sub-system is therefore required to determine which (if any) of the diverse outputs to accept. This single component or sub-system is the voter (for N-Version Programmable or TMR systems) or the acceptance test (for recovery block methods). The importance of this voter or acceptance test should not be overlooked. It may be a complex piece of hardware or software, and may depend considerably on the designers' understanding of the system being controlled. Diversity does not, therefore, avoid the possibility of a single design error causing a system failure. Properly implemented, however, it does reduce the number of parts of a system where a single error is likely to have such an effect.

STANDARDS AND GUIDELINES

Currently available standards and guidelines which address PESs and safety are the HSE Guidelines (HSE, 1987) the IEC draft standards (IEC, 1991, 1992) and the UK MoD interim standards (MoD, 1991a,b). All these documents recommend a variety of fault tolerance and fault-prevention methods and techniques. Perhaps the most important point is that in no case is there a recommendation of a single method or technique to the exclusion of others. Diversity to an appropriate level should be used in all things. The HSE require that single channels of failure should be avoided in both hardware and software. This is a direct general requirement for provision of some form of fault tolerance.

COMMERCIAL FAULT-TOLERANT SYSTEMS

Purpose-designed fault-tolerant hardware is available which is intended to act as the basis for a high-integrity or fault-tolerant implementation in a variety of application areas. Typical of such commercially available systems are high-reliability TMR Programmable Logic Controllers (PLCs). These systems use identical triplicated hardware modules for processing with single, duplicated or triplicated input and output modules. Typical configurations are shown in Figure 9.5. Sophisticated diagnostic and voting techniques are used to provide extremely high reliability as a result of a high degree of tolerance of random hardware failures. The processors and, in some cases, other hardware modules contain operating system or embedded software. Identical hardware redundancy is used. As a result, TMR PLCs do not provide tolerance of systematic hardware or software failures. This is not to denigrate TMR PLCs, but simply to point out the limitations of such TMR architecture.

High-quality design and implementation of the hardware and of the embedded and operating system software reduces (but does not remove) the likelihood of systematic design faults. No tolerance of such faults is provided. Typically, there is provision for outputs to be deactivated or held at their current values if failures which the PLC cannot tolerate are detected. If the controlled system is susceptible to such an approach then this can provide a degree of tolerance of systematic faults, provided that the application software and the system architecture are such as to take advantage of it.

For any particular application there is therefore a potential for the provision of tolerance of systematic faults by appropriate design of the overall system architecture and the application software. If tolerance of software faults is to be provided it must be done in an application-specific way.

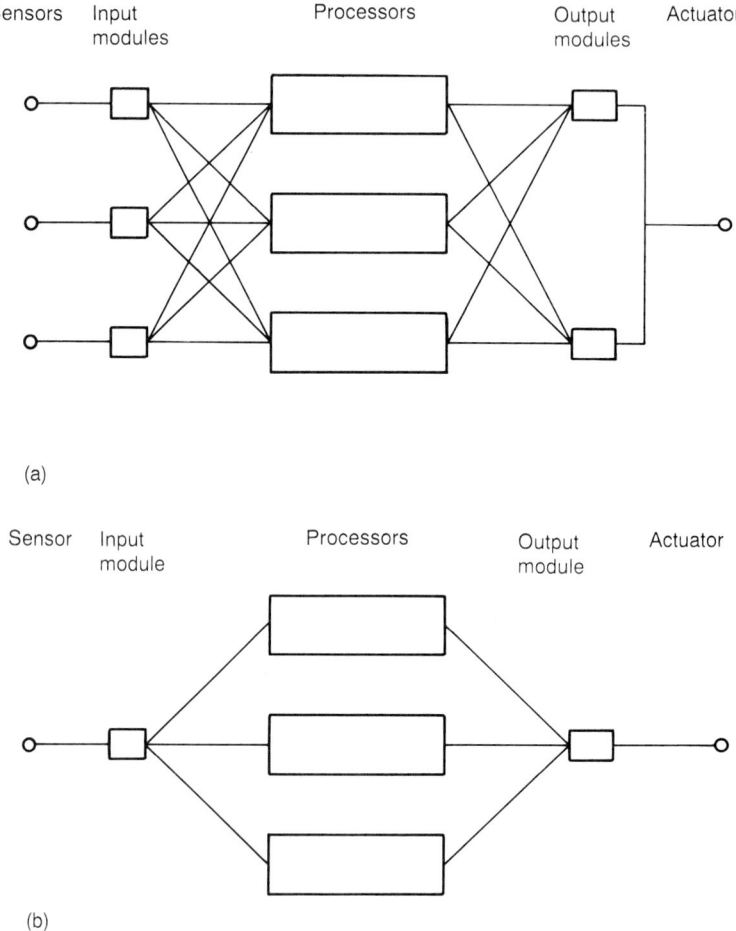

Figure 9.5 *Typical configurations of TMR PLC. (a) Triplicated input and duplicated output modules; (b) Simplex input and output modules*

FAULT TOLERANCE USING NON-FAULT-TOLERANT HARDWARE

There may be a need to use a fault-tolerant hardware system specifically design for a particular application. This may be the case for a range of applications from embedded controllers which will be used in large volumes to single instances of complex control mechanisms for systems associated with possible catastrophic accidents such as process control in petrochemical plants. In the latter case general-purpose fault-tolerant hardware such as TMR PLCs may be employed as part of the system. More generally, a fault-tolerant system will be designed, based on standard non-fault-tolerant components and sub-systems.

The design of fault-tolerant systems, whether they are based on standard components and sub-systems or whether they incorporate general-purpose fault-tolerant hardware, is based on the principles discussed in the earlier sections of this chapter. Four points emerge which are of particular importance:

1. The objectives of incorporating fault tolerance must be clearly defined for each application;
2. Redundancy is required to tolerate random hardware failures;
3. Diversity is needed to tolerate systematic failures, particularly those resulting from design and software faults; and
4. The toleration of systematic failures, particularly those resulting from design faults, requires an overall fault-tolerant design for the system which is specific to the application.

DEGRADATION MODES

Fault tolerance involves the continued fulfilment of a system's functions when a failure occurs (see above). It is not necessarily essential that all functions continue to be fulfilled in the event of a failure. The objectives to be achieved by fault tolerance (see above) determine what functions it is necessary to continue to provide.

A variety of degraded modes of operation are possible, depending on the application concerned. For safety-related systems it is likely that the provision of a degraded mode of operation which is safe in preference to a fuller and perhaps less safe mode of operation will be the required objective of fault tolerance. There may, of course, be competing requirements for increased reliability or availability for commercial reasons.

For a safety-related system it is important that system failures or combinations of failures for which fault tolerance does not enable continued full or partial operation do not result in a dangerous state. To this end, the system must effectively be shut down in some way in appropriate circumstances. Such a shutdown is not necessarily possible for all applications. Typically, the need for such a shutdown is detected and the shutdown implemented by watchdog mechanisms. In more complex cases, where a shutdown is not straightforward, it may be that the objective of fault tolerance is to put such a shutdown into operation whenever certain combinations of failure have been detected, and while the system retains much of its functionality.

THE ROLE OF SOFTWARE IN THE PROVISION OF FAULT TOLERANCE

Software can be used to advantage in the provision of diagnostics for detecting hardware failures and in the provision of mechanisms for reconfiguration to recover from such failures. The ability of software to implement sophisticated algorithms to test equipment, perform trend analysis and manage networks makes it particularly suitable for such purposes. The use of such Software Implemented Fault Tolerance (SIFT) does not, however, provide tolerance of faults in software unless provision is explicitly made for this. There is therefore little direct difference in the fault tolerance provided by SIFT or HIFT (Hardware Implemented Fault Tolerance) systems with respect to systematic and design faults. The sophistication of software diagnostics algorithms may, however, provide early warning of potential system failures which are more related to design faults than to random hardware failures.

If tolerance of software faults is to be provided this must be done, at least in part, on an application-specific basis. Provision of fault tolerance as part of systems which include software, particularly tolerance of software faults, is a non-trivial task. Careful consideration is required at an early stage in the design process. There may be other, more appropriate, ways of improving safety.

For a safety-related system fault tolerance may be advantageous but is not necessarily so. Much depends on the explicit objectives which the fault tolerance is intended to fulfil. The case for and against the use of a fault-tolerant system and fault-tolerant software should be explicitly argued and documented for each particular safety-related application. It is possible that in some cases relatively simple mechanisms such as hardware interlocks may provide better means of achieving the necessary safety.

CONCLUSIONS

Fault tolerance and its associated and complementary techniques of fault avoidance and fault masking involve the recognition that it may not be possible or desirable to design or construct a system which is perfect. Nevertheless, there are situations where system failures are not tolerable. A fault-tolerant system is a system which continues to provide service even when subject to failures.

There are a number of possible reasons for building fault tolerance into a system. Typical are the desire to increase the reliability, availability or dependability of the system as perceived by its users. In applications where a failure of the system may have harmful consequences fault tolerance may be used as a means of improving safety by reducing the probability of failure.

A crucial requirement for successful implementation of a fault-tolerant system is the detection of faults and/or failures. Depending on the mechanism used to implement fault tolerance, it may be necessary to detect a failure in order to continue to provide service. For example, a system may incorporate a stand-by processor which is switched in when a failure is detected in the active processor. Even when this approach is not used, a failure must normally be detected in order to initiate the maintenance actions required in order to continue to provide fault tolerance.

Providing fault tolerance with respect to random hardware failures is a relatively straightforward process involving the provision of redundant hardware components or systems. Tolerance of systematic failure is more complex.

Systematic failures are multiple failures which result from some common cause. Typically, the common cause is a design, manufacturing, intallation or operating fault.

An obvious potential cause for concern, but one which is often overlooked, is the need to maintain fault tolerance while the system is under repair. Typically, a modern fault-tolerant system provides for active redundancy and the replacement of redundant modules on-line. If only dual redundancy is used then the fault-tolerant character is lost when one of the modules is removed for replacement. When fault tolerance is used in order to improve reliability or availability this may not matter. The repair time may be so short as to have little effect on the overall reliability or availability figure. When fault tolerance is used in order to improve safety the loss of fault tolerance, even for a very short period, may be important.

There are important differences between software and hardware which must be taken adequately into account if a fault-tolerant computing system is to be successful. Hardware is subject to both random and systematic failures, software only to systematic failures, and these failures result principally from specification and design errors. The application of fault tolerance to hardware may, justifiably, address random failures, though systematic failures should not be overlooked. The application of fault tolerance to software must consider systematic failures.

Typical approaches to providing fault tolerance in hardware involve the use of redundancy. Dual redundancy provides a certain amount of protection. The triple modular redundant (TMR) systems becoming available can provide increased protection, particularly during module replacement. Such systems, however, remain vulnerable to systematic failure. Diversity is a means of addressing this problem. Diverse hardware may be provided in a number of ways, from the provision of non-programmable as well as programmable sub-systems to the provision of redundant hardware from diverse sources.

The provision of fault tolerance in software requires diversity. Redundant but not diverse software does not provide any fault tolerance except under very restricted circumstances. Diverse software may be associated with diverse or redundant hardware and may or may not run concurrently. Diversity may simply be at the coding level or may extend to specification and/or requirements capture. It may even extend to diversity of function, with one software channel providing monitoring and protective functions rather than direct control. For both hardware and software architectures the most important characteristics are that single channels of failure should be avoided (independence) and that there should be provision for functions to detect and correct failures (recovery).

Purpose-designed fault-tolerant hardware is available which is intended to act as the basis for a high-integrity or fault-tolerant implementation in a variety of application areas. It is important to realize that both software and hardware implemented fault tolerance in such general-purpose systems provides tolerance only of hardware faults. If tolerance of software or other systematic faults is to be provided it must be done in an application-specific way.

Provision of fault tolerance as part of systems which include software is a non-trivial task. Careful consideration is required at an early stage in the design process. There may be other, more appropriate, ways of improving safety.

REFERENCES

Alleman, G. B. (1989), *Fault-Tolerant System Reliability in the Presence of Imperfect Diagnostic Coverage*, Triconex Corporation, Irvine, CA
Anderson, T., Barret, P. A., Halliwell, D. N. and Moulding, M. R. (1985), 'Software fault tolerance: an evaluation', *IEEE*, **SE-11**, No. 12, 1502–1510
Anderson, T. and Lee, P. A. (1981), *Fault Tolerance, Principles and Practice*, Prentice-Hall International, Hemel Hempstead
AQAP (1981), *AQAP-13, NATO Software Quality Control System Requirements*, NATO International Staff Defence Support Division
Bennett, P. A. (1984), *The Safety of Industrially-based Controllers Incorporating Software*, PhD thesis, Open University
Bishop, P. G., Esp, D. G., Barnes, M., Humphreys, P., Dahll, G. and Lahti, J. (1986), 'PODS – a project on diverse software', *IEEE*, **SE-12**, No. 9, 929–940
BSI (1987), BS 5750: Part 1: 1987, ISO 9001–1987, EN 29001–1987, Quality systems – Model for quality assurance in design/development, production, installation and servicing, British Standards Institution, London
Gilb, T. (1977), *Software Metrics*, Winthrop, Cambridge, MA
Goldberg, J. (1985), *Challenges and Directions in Fault Tolerant Computing*, FTCS
Harper, R. L. (1988), 'Triple modular redundancy – its impact on fault tolerance in process industries', in *Theatre of Control*, at PC88. Honeywell, UK
HSE (1987), *Programmable Electronic Systems in Safety Related Applications, General Technical Guidelines*, HMSO, London
HSE (1988), *The Tolerability of Risk in Nuclear Power Stations*, HMSO, London
IEC (1991), *Software for Computers in the Application of Industrial Safety-related Systems*, 65A (Sec) 122, International Electrotechnical Commission
IEC (1992), *Draft– Functional safety of programmable electronic systems: Generic aspects*, 65A (Sec) 123, International Electrotechnical Commission, Switzerland
Jones, C. B. (1986), *Systematic Software Development Using VDM*, Prentice-Hall International, Hemel Hempstead
McDermid, J. A. (1992), Chapter 7, this volume
MoD (1983), *MoD Practices and Procedures for Reliability and Maintainability*, Part 2: *Reliability Apportionment, Modelling and Calculation*, MoD Defence Standard 00–41 (Part 2)/Issue 1, Ministry of Defence, UK
MoD (1991a) *The Procurement of Safety Critical Software in Defence Equipment*, Interim Defence Standard 00–55/Issue 1, Ministry of Defence, UK
MoD (1991b), *Hazard Analysis and Safety Classification of the Computer and Programmable Electronic System Elements of Defence Equipment*, Interim Defence Standard 00–56/Issue 1, Ministry of Defence, UK
Myers, G. J. (1976), *Software Reliability, Principles and Practices*, John Wiley, Chichester
Shrivastava, S. K. (1991), 'Fault-tolerant system structuring concepts', in McDermid, J. A. (ed.), *Software Engineer's Reference Book*, Butterworth-Heinemann, Oxford
Stokes, D. A. (1991), 'Requirements analysis', in McDermid, J. A. (ed.), *Software Engineer's Reference Book*, Butterworth-Heinemann, Oxford
Stone, R. F. (1989), 'Reliable computing systems – a review', Research paper 286, YCS110(1989), University of York, Department of Computer Science

10 The problems of an industrial supplier – and how to achieve good quality
Leif Danielsen

WHAT IS SOFTWARE?

Computers and software are taking over control of safety-related applications as in all other types of control systems. The computer hardware itself is relatively simple or at least standardized in its design, which does not differ much between applications. This means that the units used (the circuit boards and peripheral units) can be produced in large quantities and consequently at a lower price than if they had to be produced for specific applications.

This means that hardware costs can be kept at the same level. The high degree of integration in electronic components is keeping costs down. But why, then, is the cost of a control system continually rising? Computers are so easy to program! Of course, it is relatively easy to introduce a new code and to change versions of the software. But the reason for the high cost is that computers make it possible to design increasingly sophisticated and complex functions, and manpower is needed for their design. Most of the cost of a computer control system is moved from the hardware to engineering.

Computer specialists and programmers are, at present, considered to be some sort of magicians and are well paid. They are called software specialists and programmers, whatever type of control system or computerized system they design. Would one call an engineer designing a railway signal system with relays a relay specialist?

What is software? At least, the transforming of a control function into code could be called software engineering or programming, but that is only 10–15% of designing a control system. The rest is analysing the process to be controlled and the machinery involved. It is to structure the system and the related control and protection functions, to configure the system and describe the control function before the program structuring and the coding (the programming) begins. This is a task for a process control engineer who is familiar with the process and who has some knowledge of the software's capabilities. The engineer may need some help from the programmer to construct the code and test it. Then the process control engineer takes over and ensures that the program functions specified are implementing the control function.

This process is illustrated in Figure 10.1. In the figure the circles show the amount of work on the process control application, the computer configuration and the coding. The overlaps also indicate the qualifications needed for the different tasks. The application engineer needs to know a lot about the process, something about computer configurations and how a computer works, but very little about coding itself. The programmer needs to know a lot about coding and computer configurations but very little about the process.

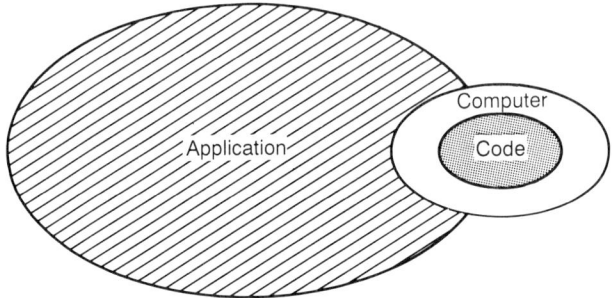

Figure 10.1 *Relations between engineering costs for a control system*

A Swedish communications company has taken advantage of this. They use highly qualified engineers for system analysis and structuring and less qualified engineers to carry out the detailed design work, and let those trained in coding do the coding. This means that highly qualified engineers do not become involved in simple work and staff previously engaged in electromechanical production do not have to be motivated.

WHAT ARE THE SUPPLIERS' PROBLEMS?

Many different organizations are involved in the design of a control system: the customer (the end user of the system), the machinery supplier, consultants, installation companies, authorities and the supplier (or suppliers) of the control equipment. It is not easy to draw the lines of responsibilities.

If the quality standards are followed the supplier should have a requirement specification from the customer. The reason for building a new system is often that a customer wants a more sophisticated and effective one than those of his competitors. In many cases the customer cannot specify in detail what he really wants the control system to do. He may wish to use new features in computer technology but may not have enough knowledge about them, which results in the requirement specification being rather vague.

Therefore the customer must consult with the system suppliers, machinery suppliers, consultants, etc. to find out what can be done. This implies that the suppliers' application engineers must have a good knowledge of that process. It is very risky to enter a completely new field.

When he thinks he understands the process and what the customer wants, the supplier must transform these requirements into something he can produce with his type of control system. It is important that he supplies specifications of the system and its implementation of the control functions. The specification should be reviewed against the customers' requirement specification by experts with knowledge of both computer control and the process. They must ensure that the specification is consistent and unambiguous. The supplier should obtain a contractual agreement with the customer on the specification where the responsibilities are clearly stated.

During the design period, if the supplier obtains the contract the discipline must be very strong to avoid introducing new functions, making changes without thorough review. In programmable systems, unforeseen reactions are likely when one is making changes. These changes must be documented in the specification and the revised document approved by the customer. This is not only for commercial reasons: changes can result in delays and extra costs, and the customer must share the responsibilities for those changes. Before he signs the contract he will ensure that his advisers have studied the specification and it can be accepted.

National regulations, and national and international standards, can set requirements on safety-related control systems, which can be inconvenient for a supplier. He must ensure that the standard system he develops can fulfil requirements in different markets. It is a heavy commitment to find the relevant standards and regulations, and it is an even greater effort to analyse the different documents and prove that they have been followed.

It can take up to 2 to 4 years to produce a national or international standard, which often leads to requirements being based on old techniques. An IEC standard on software in safety systems for nuclear power plants states that interrupts shall not be permitted in these types of systems and the program shall run in a closed loop. One will not find any microcomputer system today having some degree of flexibility and the possibility to implement sophisticated functions without using interrupt functions for controlling the microprocesor execution. The standard is probably based on a technique using a single cyclic program loop in instances where it is not possible to implement sophisticated functions.

SAFETY ANALYSIS

In safety-related systems it is important that the safety aspects are analysed and the different types of abnormal events are documented. A safety analysis should be carried out and a special section of the specification produced for the safety requirements of the system. This could be a separate document or a part of the normal specification, but should point out the risks, the possible causes of hazards and the consequences. It should also specify the acceptable risk level.

There are different kinds of risks; the risks of injury or death to human beings, directly or indirectly, and economic risks by destruction of machinery, loss of the material processed and environmental damage.

Who should be responsible for making the safety analyses? The final responsibility lies with the end user, the operator of the system. But he needs help, and where does he start? If we exclude the possibility that the electrical part of the system can harm the people installing or maintaining the system, we have only the machinery itself and the material processed that can cause damage. So we must start our discussion with the machinery.

The following questions must be addressed:

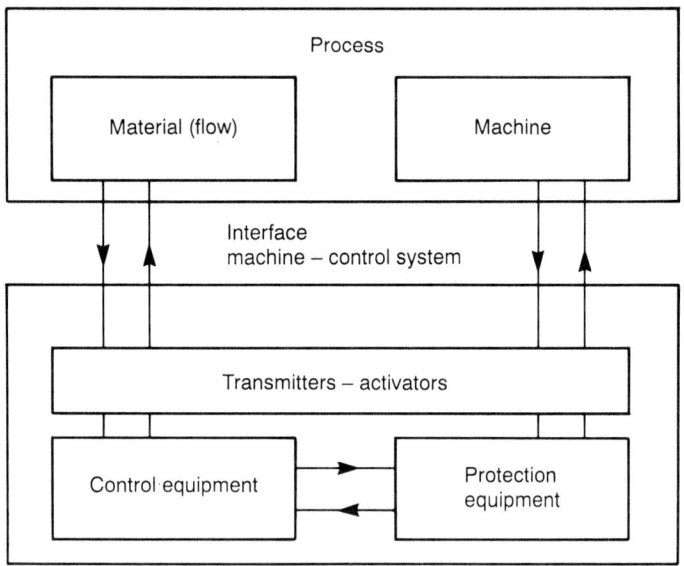

Figure 10.2 *Safety analysis structure*

1. What parts are critical if there are defects in the machinery?
2. What parts of the machinery can be damaged by abnormal process material?
3. What damage can be done by exceptional process flow?
4. What parts of the machinery can be damaged by uncontrolled functions of the control system?

The next question to be asked is, what damage will these defects cause?

The first two types of problems are obviously not due to the control system, but the control system can be used to detect problems. The last two are probably caused by the control system, so the next step in the analysis is to determine the consequences of uncontrolled material flow or damage to the machinery. How serious is it? What actions have to be taken to avoid or limit the consequences?

This procedure seems quite straightforward, and there should be no great difficulty in deciding who should carry out the analysis. Who has the knowledge? In real life there would be problems. One defect could result in a chain of consequences with branches which, in complex systems, can be quite difficult to analyse in detail. Skilled people are needed.

Until now, the control system supplier has not been involved in the safety analyses. As long as the control system is behaving normally, it cannot cause any harm. But what is normal behaviour? As long as the system is behaving according to the requirement specification (or any other agreed description) it is behaving normally. Therefore the question is whether the requirement specification is giving a complete and unambiguous description of the expected behaviour. It must be complete in the sense that it covers how the system should respond to all combinations of inputs. In a complex system this is impossible. Here the supplier of the control system must help in structuring the analysis and ensure as a good coverage as possible.

No control system is perfect. Components in the control equipment may fail and there may be software errors. Therefore we must also be able to handle these abnormal situations.

Failures in the control system lead to abnormal output to the operator of the system or the process machinery, and the consequences must be analysed. If a proper analysis of the machinery had been carried out in the specification some of the answers would be given in that document. Additional analyses should, however, be done by considering the consequences of combinations of abnormal outputs.

We have now defined the abnormal situations that can cause an unsafe situation. How do we detect these abnormal situations, when the system fails to take proper actions? Modern computer systems have sophisticated on-line fault-detection functions for the hardware. Some of the faults can be detected quite quickly, therefore remedial action can be taken without any harm. Other types of faults (e.g. memory faults) can take some time to detect. One has to analyse the consequences of a delay in the detection of a fault. Too long a delay may require other hardware solutions (e.g. to use a read-only memory with parity control instead of a memory with only checksum calculation). This will add to the cost of a system.

What actions can be taken when a fault is detected? In some cases this is easy. The process can be shut down without any damage. This means that the control system can normally be turned off when a fault is detected, leading to a halt in the process. Another alternative could be that only a part of the control and of the process must be shut down. However, this again leads to a more complex analysis and specification of what is and what is not acceptable.

In other cases the process must be shut down in a controlled manner, to a complete halt or a safe state. This means that the control system has to be duplicated in some way, by a redundant control system or a special protection system taking over the controlled shutdown.

High reliability will reduce the risk of failure and will thus improve the safety of the system, but it is important to distinguish between the need for high reliability and high safety. When the system fails we have the same risk of an unsafe situation.

One way to achieve high reliability is to use high-quality components and to implement a good quality system during development, design and production. Redundant system configurations can be used to further improve system reliability. The process can be controlled by one of the systems if the other fails. However, if the requirement is to maintain the level of safety when one system is failing, the non-failing part of the redundant control system can only be used to obtain a controlled shutdown.

A high level of both availability and safety would require a two-out-of-three redundant configuration. This, however, often results in complex diagnosis functions, which, in turn, can lead to low total mean time between failure figures. However, the failing system can be repaired while one of the other two is controlling the process.

We also have the kind of processes that cannot be shut down in a short time. High availability is needed, and two-out-of-three or two-out-of-four configurations are probably required for a sufficient level of safety.

Redundant systems or parts mean that they are doing the same thing; they can replace each other. It is obvious that a fault in the requirement specification will lead to the same fault on all the redundant parts of the system and will not be detected.

What of software failures? The nature of these failures is that they are systematic, they are results of faulty or insufficient specification or faults introduced in coding. Specification faults cannot be detected by testing, and coding faults can be difficult to detect by testing the system. Redundant software will have the same faults. Another method is diversified programming, i.e. the design and coding of the software are done in different ways in the redundant software. The two systems outputs can be compared. However, with two systems only, with different programs, it is normally not possible to determine which program is the faulty one, so the process has to be shut down. With diversified programming there is still a risk of introducing the same kind of faults into the two systems. Programmers have a tendency to commit the same errors when they implement the same function.

A better solution is to give the two systems completely different tasks, one of them performing the control and the other being used as a protection system. The task of the protection system is to supervise the process, to detect unsafe situations and to turn the process off in a controlled manner. In this way, the two systems will have completely different functions. The likelihood of introducing the same type of faults is smaller and that of introducing faults in both systems in the same situation is even less. This means the supplier must have solutions and configuration possibilities for all these types of systems.

One disadvantage with a separate protection system is that the functions and outputs used for the controlled shutdown of the system are normally not 'active', but they must operate without failure when they are activated after days, months or even years. It is necessary to build fault-detection functions into the hardware circuits for a continuous fault diagnosis. In high-risk processes special types of hardware are probably required for the protection systems.

From this discussion it should be clear to the reader that safety analysis and safety specification is not an easy task. The problem increases when the control system is brought into the analysis. Analysis must be an iterative process, with the operator of the system, the machine builder and the control system supplier involved. It is difficult to specify exactly the safety requirements and the consequences of different situations. Different possibilities in control system configurations need to be discussed.

The customer (the operator of the system), of course, normally obtains bids from more than one supplier. This means that he should have the same type of discussion and analysis with all suppliers. Normally, this will not be done in detail, which leads to incomplete specifications. Both the customer and supplier must appreciate that a system can become considerably larger following a thorough analysis.

After commissioning, the system will enter the operation and maintenance phase. Regular maintenance is normally not a great problem in electronic equipment. Moving mechanical components in the system may need regular maintenance, but it is easy to isolate these during the maintenance period. They are often not involved directly in the safety-related part of the system.

Some types of processes may have problems with delays, perhaps caused by maintenance and repair, and the safety analysis should also cover this situation. What types of long shutdowns can cause a hazard? How can long shutdowns be eliminated? Are stand-by service personnel needed? What spare parts are required to reduce mean time to repair?

Sensors, transmitters and activators in the process machine may cause problems if they need regular maintenance. The safety aspects of the maintenance situation need to be analysed and solutions selected to minimize risks. Maintenance personnel are also a risk factor. Clear maintenance instructions must be documented and staff training carried out.

SOFTWARE STRUCTURES

In the early days of computer control one had to start from a basic position when designing the software for a control system. The systems were unsophisticated and there were no standard software available. The concept of making software in modules was not accepted in the same way as with hardware. The re-use of software involved searching one's own files or asking a colleague whether he had a similar code.

Coding is expensive and time consuming. The risk of introducing errors in the code is high and the chance of finding all the errors by testing is low. This means that one has to put in a lot of effort to minimize the numbers of errors in the code (and in the specifications). This has led to the basic software in a standard process control system being highly standardized. Figure 10.3 illustrates a common structure of such a software.

The central parts of the figure contain the system software with the operating system. These are the basic functions needed for the computer system itself. There is normally only one main processor unit in the computer – and even if there are several with different tasks, each can only handle one task at a time. The different tasks have different priorities, so when a task with a higher priority needs the central processor due to some external event in the process the execution of the task with a lower priority (e.g. a printout) must be interrupted. The real-time operating system handles this time-sharing administration.

Other tasks of the operating system are:

1. Communication with the computer operator (not the process operator) for maintenance
2. Computer diagnostic functions
3. Database access – standardized way of updating and retrieving databases with access control functions
4. Basic I/O functions (e.g. device drives for printers, monitors and disks)
5. Mechanism for process communication
6. Mechanism for communication with other computers

212   Safety Aspects of Computer Control

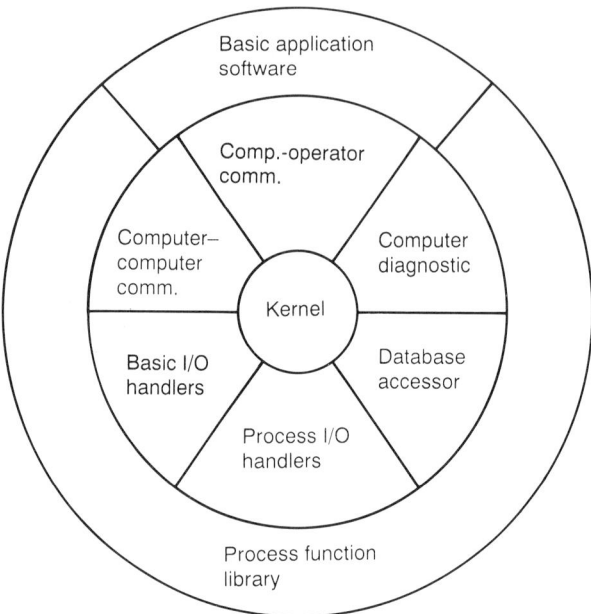

Figure 10.3   *Software system structure*

The next level in the software structure is the basic application software.

A process control system can be reduced to a limited set of basic functions, sequential and logic functions such as AND, OR, EXCLUSIVE OR and FLIP-FLOP memory. Analogue control contains standard arithmetic functions. Therefore if the system contains a library of modules with codes for these basic functions it is possible for a process control engineer to design the control functions for a process using his own familiar process control functions. He selects the right module, sets parameters, defines where to select the inputs and where to put the results as done by hardware modules. For logic control this is a common level of standardization, but for analogue control it is too low a level. The system library would, for example, normally contain modules for complete PID regulators making programming less time consuming.

In the same way, the basic application level contains functions for man–machine and computer–computer communication. The process control engineer selects the appropriate functions; for example, the type of picture for displaying the different measured values and set points for a control loop, with the data to be transferred by a communication bus to a distributed process station as a set point for a loop.

The basic application software also contains interpreter functions that will execute the application programs. Figure 10.4 shows an example of such a programming with standard process control elements in a library. The code for each element is available in the processors' function library. The process control engineer selects elements from that library by making a 'parts list', assigning

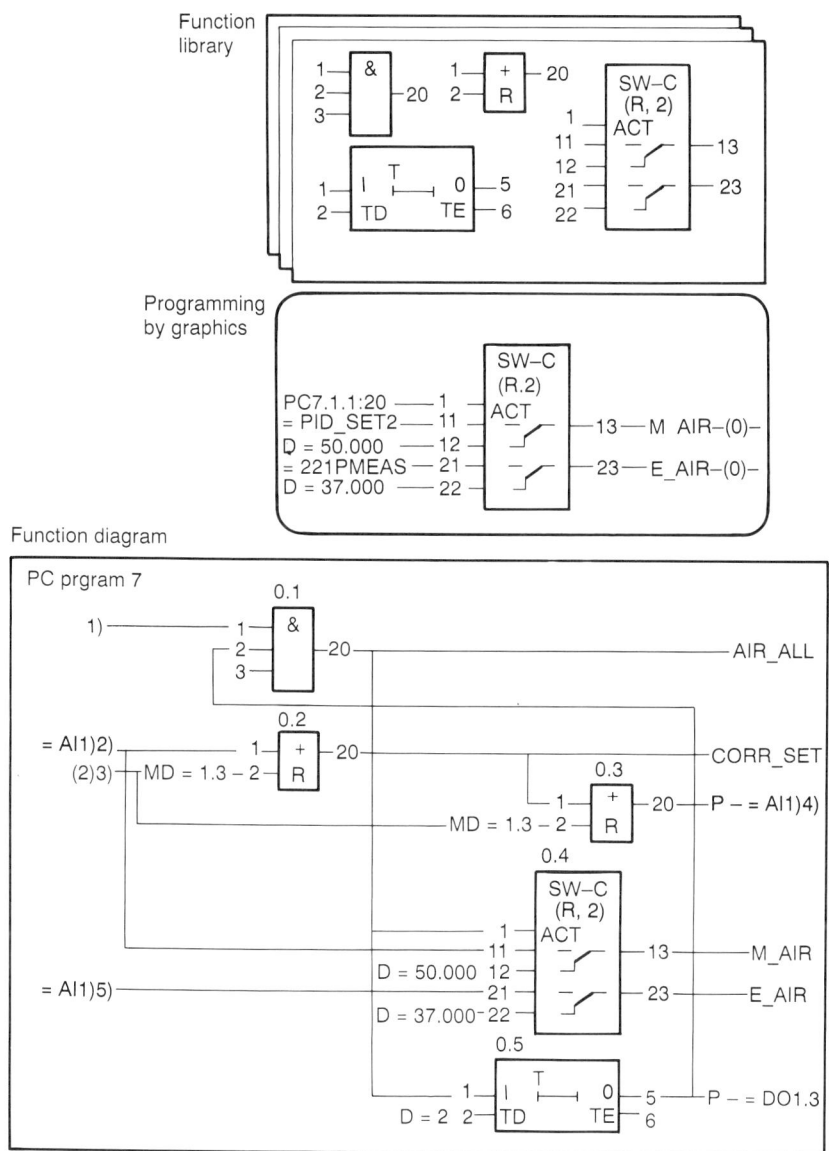

Figure 10.4 *Example of programming by means of library functions*

input signals to each element from the database or other elements and assigning the outputs to the database. He then makes a 'cable list'. In a similar way, he will declare where to put data (signals) coming from or going to the process, parameters set by the process operator or coming from or going to other process control stations or a total plant control system coordinating the different sections in the plant.

The signals can be given meaningful names which can be used as references in the program. Each element in the library has a type designation by which it can be called on, similar to selecting a specific circuit board by means of the type designation. Each input and output has an identification, a 'pin' number. The program with the control functions can be structured according to the process structure. Each part is given an item designation in a hierarchy according to the IEC standard for item designations, which was originally intended for implementations in hardware. This means that every part is identified and in a similar way as if they were realized by means of hardware. It is possible to see the link between the software and the hardware, to follow the process signals.

The programming of the process control functions is carried out by means of a terminal, directly on the control system or by a tool, on-line or off-line. Checks are normally done by the system to avoid syntax errors. The result can often be printed out so that documentation of the program – the control functions – can be verified and used as a decription in training, fault diagnosis and maintenance.

There are other types of process control function languages. Using these types of functions, the programming of the process function is in a high programming language, a process control programming language, not a computer programming one. The control engineer need have no knowledge of computer programming languages. He does require some knowledge in the working of computers, the fact that it is using a common central processor in time sharing between the different tasks, which normally leads to organization problems of the software. However, he will not introduce code errors into the code implementing the functions as he has no access to the code in the function library.

Developing this type of basic function and having them as standard functions available for the process control engineers makes process control design easier, less time consuming and with a lower risk of introducing errors in the control functions. The basic functions are relatively simple, and can (or should) be developed in a project for a standard product. Sufficient time should be allowed for verification of the specifications and testing of the functions before delivery. The functions should be tested in non-safety-related pilot deliveries. They should be used in a large number of normal control systems before application in safety-related systems.

There will always be errors remaining, but there are possibilities of eliminating most of them and of claiming proven design when using them in safety-related systems.

GENERAL QUALITY STANDARDS

Good product quality contributes to a safer system. It is also of interest to the supplier of control systems to have good quality to avoid extra costs due to fault-finding activities and replacements of faulty units. Obviously, the supplier must ensure that customers are satisfied with the quality so that they are prepared to buy other systems in the future.

For newly developed products and new suppliers the customer will have no experience, and if he plans to order safety-related systems he should make an evaluation of possible suppliers. The results of such an evaluation should be an important factor in selecting the supplier.

International (and national) standards on quality systems and quality assurance are tools to be used in such an evaluation. The quality standards can be used as a checklist in assessing the suppliers' quality systems. This means that the assessment is based on the same criterion for all suppliers and the results can be compared.

The ISO 9000 Standard series is now well-established worldwide standards on quality systems. They are not yet in force in all countries, but this is not because of any objections to them. They are also accepted as a European Normalized Standard, EN 29000. The 9000 series consists of the following parts:

ISO 9001 Quality system – Model for quality assurance in design/development, production, installation and service
ISO 9002 Quality system – Model for quality assurance in production and installation
ISO 9003 Quality system – Model for quality assurance in final inspection and test

ISO 9002 and 9003 contain parts of 9001. There are also the ISO 9000 and 9004 guidelines which are more or less explanations of how to use the 9000 series.

SOFTWARE QUALITY STANDARDS

The present ISO 9000–3 series of quality standard is very much focused on the production of hardware. One frequently hears that it cannot be used for software, but an ISO working group has prepared a standard in the ISO 9000 series on *Guidelines for the application of ISO 9001 to software*, which will probably be published in 1990. There is a great interest in this standard, and the group consists of experts from 20–25 countries, of which the author of this chapter is one.

The group's terms of reference were not specifically that the outcome should be a guideline on how to implement ISO 9001. Initially, many members thought that a completely separate standard for software had to be produced. However, it was agreed that ISO 9001 could be used for software. There is nothing contradictory in the standard, relative to software, only that some parts are not relevant.

The group agreed that it is an advantage to use the ISO 9001 as a basis. Software development is often highly integrated with other types of development, and one can have only one type of quality system for these activities. So the decision was taken to make it a guideline on how to implement ISO 9001 on software and what elements in this standard should be focused. Many of the members of the working group, especially the European delegates, were of the opinion that one should structure the guideline strictly according to ISO 9001, more or less clause by clause, in such a way that the users could compare and see which elements where relevant for software and the detailed recommendation for each such clause. Other members of the group were of the opinion that 'software people' would not understand this structure, and that the recommendation had to be structured in a way believed to be more familiar to 'software people'. The result was a compromise, and in the proposal for the standard there are cross-reference lists between the documents.

It is obvious that manufacturing, in the sense of reproducing the same code, in quantities, is no problem for the software product. Methods exists where it is possible to check that the code entered into one computer system with a high degree of assurance is the same as the original. This also means that the final test of the code in the system where one has the copy does not have to be a complete functional test as is usually needed for hardware. If the original (the prototype) has been thoroughly tested the copy will act in the same way.

Therefore software quality activities are very much focused on the design and development phases. Design and development must be done in a planned and systematic manner. There must be reliable documentation and there must be identification systematics for all the parts of the software, including version/revision handling, so that the different parts can be traced and one can see the relations between documentation and code/function.

The definition of the term 'quality' used here is in accordance with ISO Standard 8402; 'The totality of features and characteristics of a product, process or service that bear on its ability to satisfy stated or implied needs.' Normally, one would think about how it is fulfilling the technical specifications, but the standard for software also takes cost and delivery time aspects into account. The aspects concerning software will be discussed in the following sections.

PROJECT ORGANIZATION

Development has to be done in an organized manner. Responsibilities and authorities must be defined so that each group or person knows their task. The interface between the different parts of the project organization must be documented so that everyone knows where to expect inputs, when and in what form to present their own results, i.e. outputs.

It is common to build a separate project organization for the development of a product. The relations between the line organization and the project organization must be documented. Who is supplying resources to the project? Who will take the responsibility of the product over the rest of the life cycle, after the development phases? If the product is developed for a specific customer, relations with the customer must be documented. The documentation of project organization is often referred to in standards as a part of a quality plan.

PROJECT MODEL

Software projects have a tendency to go on 'for ever'. Figure 10.5 shows the so-called 95% syndrome phenomenon. After a certain period the project

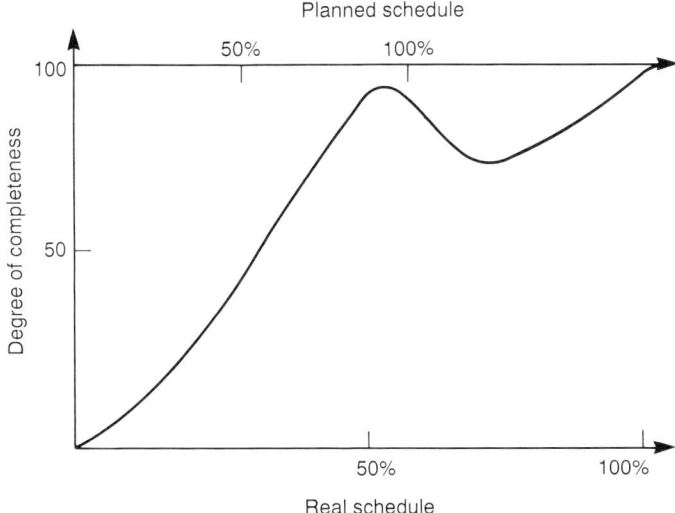

Figure 10.5 *The 95% syndrome phenomenon*

manager reports that 95% of the job is finished, – according to the schedule. Nevertheless, after some further time he returns, saying that 'Well, we discovered some problems during testing, so we have to rewrite parts of the code'. It is also common in development projects for software to plan 'cost per time period', to report the results during the development as accumulated cost and to compare this with planned cost. If they correspond, everyone is happy. No one asks if they have really achieved what they should within this period and to that budget.

The reason for this is bad planning. It is important to put a lot of effort into planning the project, to analyse the different phases and activities in the development and their relation in time. One can estimate the needed resources, time and cost. Now one has a scale of measurement with which one can compare planned time and cost with accumulated time and see if one is on schedule or is delayed. (The author has rarely heard of projects being ahead of schedule.)

This is often referenced as following a project model. One can find different modules in literature and standards, but they do not differ very much. The differences are in the terminology, what the different phases, and activities are called and where they define the 'milestones'. The milestone is the end of a phase when all planned results are available and approved, and can be used as inputs to the following phases.

Common to all models is the job being split into phases. During planning it is defined what are the inputs to a phase, what are the activities and what will be the results. The results will then be used as inputs to the following phases. When this is done one can, based on the available resources, plan the time needed for the activities and fill in the time schedule. Having made analyses of what has to be done and in what sequence, this planning is no different to the planning of a hardware development project. One will make mistakes in the beginning but one will learn by experience.

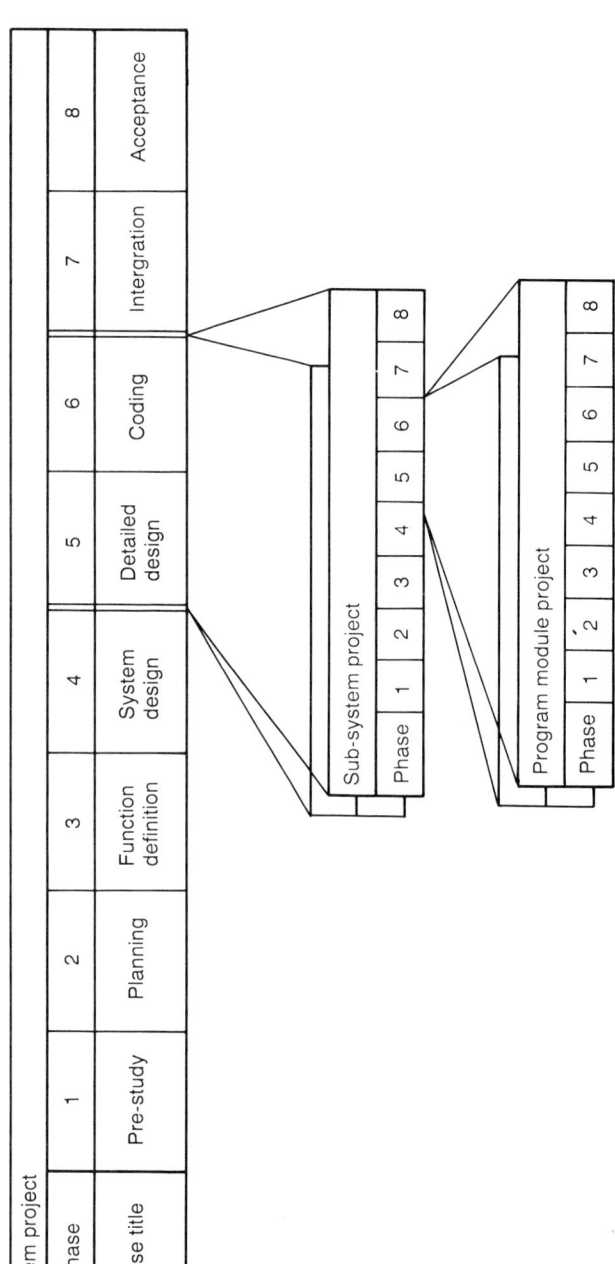

Figure 10.6 *Example of a project model*

Having a plan like this, it is possible to measure the progress of the develoment in small steps. One is able to control the development instead of being controlled by the project. However, to be able to rely on reports it is important to have discipline in reporting of the activities. An activity is not terminated before the result is finished 100%, verified and approved – not to 95%. Then the milestone is passed. Figure 10.6 shows an example of such a project model.

It is common to divide the project into sub-projects, in some cases on several levels, to have control of the development. This is often done according to the natural structure into functions of the product to be developed. The responsibilities for the different sub-projects are to be defined in the quality plan. Each sub-project can be divided into phases and follow the same project model as the main project. It is an advantage to use the same terminology, thus improving communications within the organization.

DOCUMENTATION

The whole development is based on documents. A document does not have to be a piece of paper, it can be any form of information, even code, on any medium – paper, data file or tape. However, it must have an identity and be defined in scope and content so that it can be referred to and can be found when needed. It must allow study, review and approval of the information.

The inputs to a development phase are documents and the results of the activities in a phase, and hence the outputs, are also documents. Different standards define different types of documents for software products, but for process control applications, the content is the same. There is a difference in the terminology, the names of the document, where the different types of information are inserted. Figure 10.7 shows an example of a document structure.

The documents are sorted into the phases where they normally are produced. In the figure there are a main project and a number of sub-projects for software modules. In the main project phase 'Definition of Function' the system's main functions are described, at the interface between the different main functions and how they can be used. This description should follow the requirement specification used as an input to the project, but will normally be more detailed and will be influenced by how the functions are implemented. The Functional Description should not be burdened by describing the 'design', i.e. how the different functions are realized.

Descriptions of how the system should be finally tested (the acceptance test) should be produced in the 'Definition of Function' phase. This may give a lot of input to the Functional Description, making it more clear and complete.

Activities in the 'Definition of Function' phase is a typical task for the engineer who knows the process and has some knowledge of the computer system. It is not the responsibility of the programmer, the code specialist.

The implementation (the solutions) of the functions in code (the program and data structure) is described in the 'System Design' phase in a Design Description. This should be done by a software expert who can use the Functional Description as an input. The program is divided into modules and the function in each

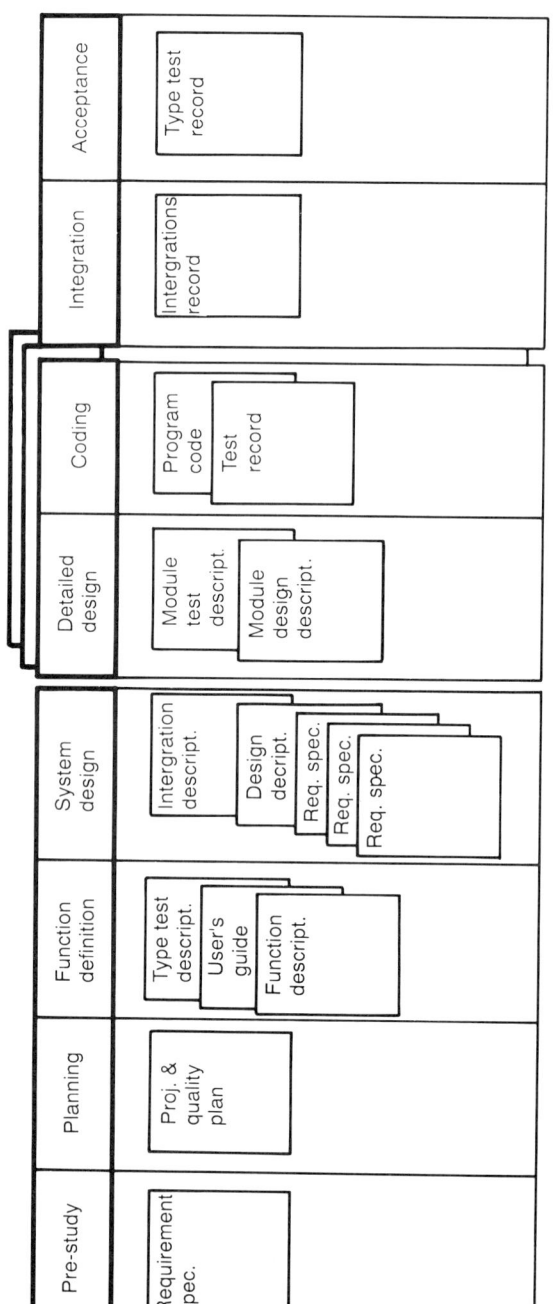

Figure 10.7 An example of a document structure

module described in a Requirement Specification for that module if it is not clear from the Design Description.

An Integration Description must be produced describing how the different modules should be assembled and tested, step by step, until the total system is integrated. It is also likely that extra test code must be produced to simulate the environment for the code tested in each step. The test may be done on host computers, meaning that integration with the target machine must also be carried out.

When there are specifications for each module a parallel design on the different modules can take place. A Design Description should be produced for each module describing their structure. This will be the input to the coding. It is important not to hasten into starting coding before a proper analysis has been carried out and documented. A Test Description for the module test should be produced, decribing the test procedures and test tools.

The code is produced and tested in the 'Coding phase'. It is important that each module be tested to prove that it fulfils the requirements. This will facilitate the test on the next level, the integration test. It is normally done by the programmer, who should produce a Test Record.

When the module tests have been approved, the 'Integration phase' can begin. The modules are integrated in steps and tested with the test tools, hardware and software, according to the Integration Description. It should be done by the system engineers who produced the Design Description and the Integration Description. They will test that the software is working according to how they, the developers, have interpreted the requirements. The test should result in an Integration Record.

The final test, the acceptance test in the 'Acceptance Phase', should be made by persons other than those who designed the system. If the system is produced for a specific customer, he should be represented during the test. Some organizations have special departments for tests. The important point is that the designer should not approve his own design and that a test by a second person or team will improve the quality of the product. The test should be carried out according to the Acceptance Test Description and consequently prove that the functions are according to the Requirement Specification. An Acceptance Test Record must be produced and approved by authorized persons.

VERIFICATION AND VALIDATION

No one is perfect, and system designers and programmers can make errors. In software it is easy to make errors and difficult to detect them. It is difficult to describe sophisticated and complex functions and to detect the abnormal situations in a system that could lead to severe faults and safety hazards.

Quality standards specify that the results from each activity (the specifications and design, including the code) shall be reviewed in review meetings and approved before the next activity, using the results as inputs, begins. The review shall be done by experts in different fields, with knowledge of how the function described is to be used in the total system, coding experts and so on.

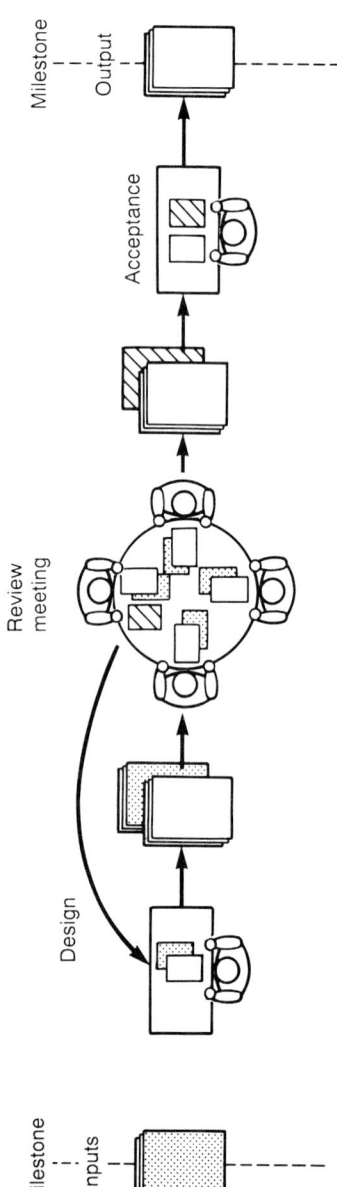

Figure 10.8 Production, review and approval of documents

The results to be examined must be in a practical form, an unambiguous document or code. The review group must have an opportunity to study the document before the meeting. At the meeting the person who has produced the document can present it. It is well known that this often leads to the person discovering errors or problems himself. The experts should analyse the contents of the document to identify such errors and problems and must compare the results with the inputs to the activity. Is the Design Description describing the realization of the function described in the Functional Description? They should not spend much time in finding solutions to the problems, but leave this to the designer or the design team. The errors, problems and decisions taken at the meeting should be documented in a review meeting record that can be used at the next meeting to ensure that all problems have been solved.

IDENTIFICATION

One must be able to identify unambiguously a document that is to be reviewed, otherwise one will not know what was reviewed. Each document must have its own identity and it must be possible to distinguish between the different revisions of the document. When a document is updated (e.g. when errors are corrected) it must have a new revision index.

In the same way, the software must be identified. Each module should be treated as a separate unit. The identity can be a program name as long as it is unique within the environment where it is used. Faults are detected and corrected in the software and each version must have a unique version or revision number.

As discussed earlier, software can be complex. Even in well-structured software there are strong relations between different parts and functions. These have to be tested together to be confident that they will work together in a proper way. Changes in one module will often result in changes in others. They then have to be tested together again. It is often not possible to guarantee that all new versions will operate together with all prior versions. Software is therefore often released in versions, each with its version number. One version contains all the modules for the function and corrections of errors will result in a new release (version) of the total function.

It is necessary to have an exact identity for each version and for each revision of the versions. There must be a complete documentation of what versions and revisions of the different modules are included in the versions and revisions of the total system. It must be documented if (and how) earlier versions have to be replaced. In some cases an error can be tolerated in a system. The system is perhaps not using the function in a way where the fault can do any harm. Changing to new versions, or revisions, is always risky.

FUNCTION AND SOFTWARE STRUCTURES

The software functions (the program) must be understood by those designing, using and maintaining it. The understanding of complex functions is not the best

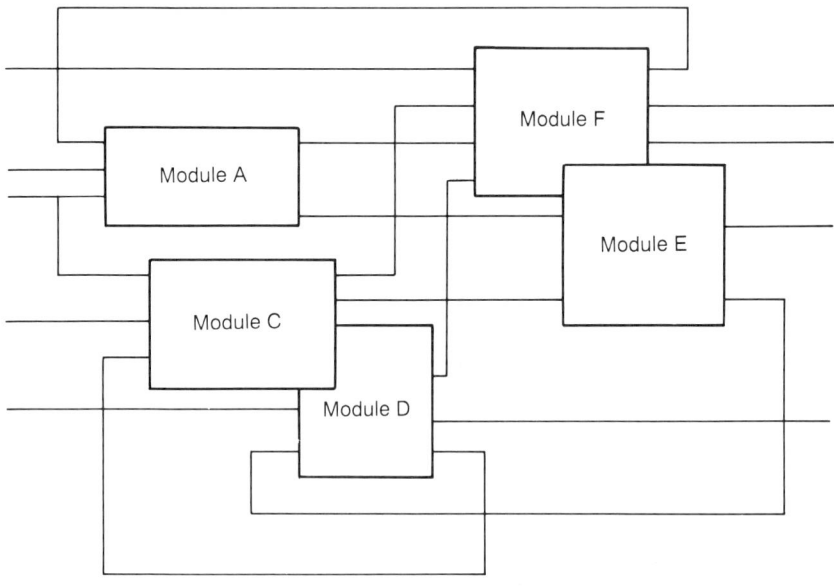

Figure 10.9 *Spaghetti structure*

property of the human being. A software structure of the 'spaghetti type' in Figure 10.9 can hardly work.

Large systems split into smaller manageable parts with a simple interface between them. This also means that it will be possible to divide the development into different groups. As discussed earlier, this is done during the System Design Phase.

Two types of structures can be identified. The first is the functional structure according to the control function, which is how the control engineer sees the system. It could be that this is not the best way to implement the function in the computer, so the second type of structure would be the software structure, the division into modules, adapted to the computer and its operating system. This is how the programmer sees the implementation of the control system. Both structures exist in the same system, and it is an advantage if they correspond.

The structure of the software is essential for the testability of the software. If it is divided into modules with a simple interface between them one can first concentrate on the testing of each module and then test the interface between them. Figure 10.10 is a classical example of a program consisting of modules A and B. Each branch in the figure represents a branch in the code and from the circles the program will continue along one of the branches, depending on the results from the prior branch or branches. To make a 100% test, all combinations of program paths must be tested. If one branch take 1 ms to run through, it would take years to run through all combinations, and it would be difficult to specify the accepted results for all combinations. If the interface between modules A and B is under control one could settle for testing all combinations of program paths in A and B separately. This will take only minutes. In safety-related systems it is of

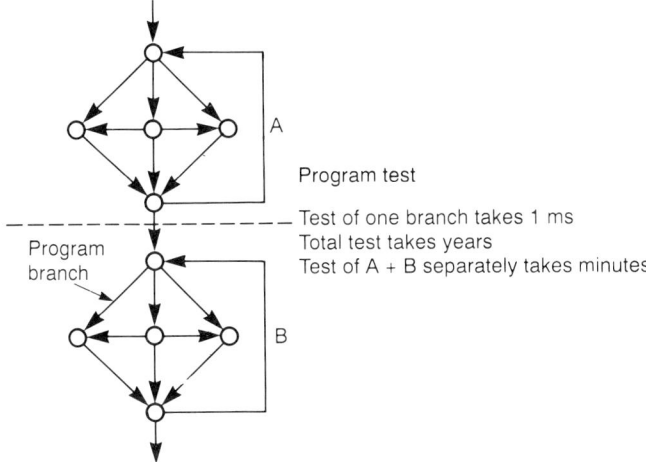

Figure 10.10 *Well-structured program*

great importance that one is not only testing normal situations but also analysing abnormal situations. These must also be tested in a planned and documented way.

PURCHASED SOFTWARE

As discussed earlier, computer systems are becoming increasingly complex and sophisticated. It is time consuming to design and to secure quality, and one has to use standard software as far as possible. The supplier of a control system will not always develop the software completely himself. He will buy standard software from software houses (e.g. operating systems) or let other companies or consultants do the job. Very often he will use sophisticated tools in his development (e.g. assemblers and compilers), tools that will have a great impact on results.

It is clear that the supplier of a control system must ensure that the sub-suppliers are capable of delivering high-quality software. Hence he has to check that the sub-suppliers have a quality system similar to that required for his own work, and should make quality audits to check this.

Sometimes the supplier can settle for 'proven design' if it is known that the software has been used for a long period in many applications. Such analysis of quality systems takes a lot of time and resources. It will be a great advantage when we have an international certification system where the audit is performed by a third party and does not have to be repeated by each purchaser.

SUMMARY

Developing software involves more than producing code. It is often a complex system design (e.g. process control), requiring engineers with process knowledge and who know how to use computers. Coding is a small part of software and can be dealt with by coding specialists.

Designing for safety requires a detailed safety analysis to find solutions to minimize the risks. This has to be done in cooperation with machine designers, process control engineers and control system engineers, regardless of where they belong in the organizations – being customer, process operator, machine builder, control system supplier or consultant. However, their responsibilities have to be defined.

System configuration is dependent on safety requirements, and good software structure will always enhance system safety and quality. Software quality is essential for system safety.

Making software is craftsmanship, and it has to be developed and designed in an orderly manner, where organization and responsibilities are well defined. The development must be carried out in steps according to a project module, where the activities and results are defined so that time, resource and cost plans can be made and the progress of the development measured.

Documentation is essential for software. The results of the activities (the documents) must be reviewed by experts and approved by authorized persons before they are used as inputs. Changes must be introduced in an orderly and documented way, reviewed and approved.

Software modules and documents must have an unambiguous identity, including revision number. One must be able to trace the documents and their status, which revision is valid and which has been used in different deliveries.

The software must have a good structure. 'Smart programming' must be avoided. This will lead to difficulties in maintaining the software. A good quality system will help one to obtain programs with few errors and which will be maintainable during the life cycle of the software.

It is important that management be involved in the quality activities. The quality elements must be considered a natural part of the development, as routines. Difficulties in keeping to schedules must not lead to quality activities being omitted, in the belief that this will lead to a shorter development time. Management must ensure that the documentation is well structured and complete. The documents are the tools to measure progress. The same requirements apply to the quality systems of sub-suppliers of software.

11   Design and licensing of safety-related software
Wolfgang D. Ehrenberger

INTRODUCTION

Safety-related applications differ from other areas of technology through the risk to life and limb of persons. Normally, the usual partnership between manufacturer and customer is supplemented through an independent licenser, who often employs an assessor to make a judgement about the safety aspects of the computer system and its software. It is recommended to have the project structure organized according to this specific configuration.

The following considerations are based on work from the European Workshop on Industrial Computer Systems, related experience from projects in nuclear power, notably in Germany, and two working groups of the International Electrotechnical Commission. For the work of EWICS (see Redmill 1988, 1989). The aspects of nuclear power have been summarized in Bloomfield and Ehrenberger (1987). One of the IEC groups has produced the standard on Software in the Safety System of Nuclear Power Stations (IEC, 1987); the other is currently working on a Standard for Software for Computers in the Application of Industrial Safety Related Systems (IEC, 1989).

The understanding in the software community is that verification questions are to be considered together with development procedures. It is this aspect that this chapter focuses on. The basic idea is to propose software architecture and procedures which specifically qualify for safety-related applications.

LIFE CYCLE AND PRINCIPLES

According to the current state of the art, the software life cycle is grouped into the phases of:

Feasibility study
Development cycle
Operation and maintenance
Decomissioning

Normally, it is the maintenance phase that results in most costs. Unfortunately, very little is known about how to do the related work effectively. Probably the use of tools will provide a sensible contribution to better management and execution of modifications in the future. Some further help may come from object-oriented programming. This chapter deals only with the development cycle and its

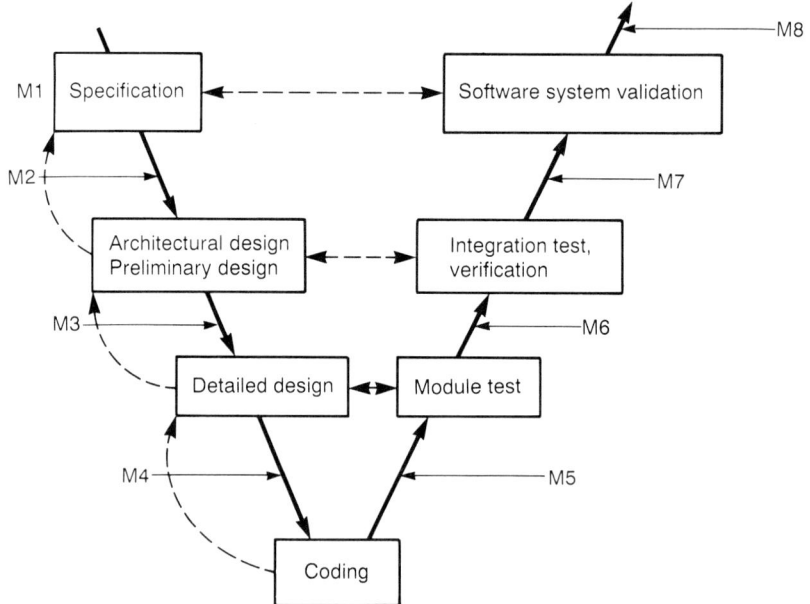

Figure 11.1 *Software system development cycle. M1–M8: milestones – action required by the internal verification team and the assessor; ←— —→ test or verification; ←— — — corrective action if necessary*

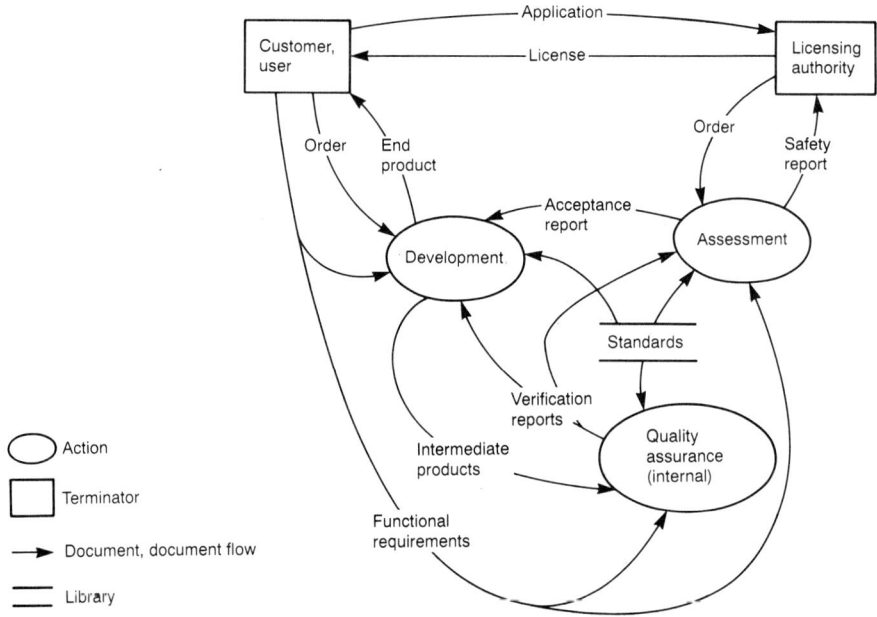

Figure 11.2 *Structured analysis diagram of the interaction between the development process, the internal quality assurance and the external assessment*

Design and licensing of safety-related software 229

Table 11.1 The documents during the first phase of the software development cycle and their producers

Milestone	Customer or sales department	Software developer	Internal verification team	Assessor
M1	Functional requirements specification Reliability requirements specification			
M2		Statement on feasibility	Statement on quality	
				Acceptance report
M3		Software design document		
			Design verification report	
				Acceptance report
M4		Detailed design documents		
			Detailed design verification report	
				Acceptance report
M5		Code		
			Code verification report	
				Acceptance report

architectural design specifically. Figure 11.1 gives an overview. At the appropriate places the milestones are indicated that require definite actions. The information flow between the partners and the major actions required are given in Figure 11.2. Table 11.1 shows the documents that occur during the first phase of the development cycle and their producers.

Because the assessor is very deeply involved in the project it is in the interest of the manufacturer to get an assessor who is competent.

STRATEGIES

Overview

The software system architecture is chosen with a specific verification strategy in mind. Appropriate connection between verification strategy, and development will reduce the necessary cost over the whole project. Figure 11.3 groups the strategies appropriately.

Principally, deterministic and probabilistic verification approaches are to be considered here. The decision about which is to be taken depends on:

1. The required level of safety;
2. The size of the considered product;
3. The professional experience of the persons from the parties involved;
4. The existing software parts;
5. The production facilities and the test environment available.

Regarding the professional experience it is, in particular, knowledge of software verification that is important. In the following, several concepts for safe software architectures are described. It is recommended to adopt one or other of these architectures at the outset of a project with safety-related software. Sometimes it is very expensive if this decision is not taken early enough.

The architectural decision should be agreed with the responsible assessor. The basic principles are (Gorski, 1989):

1. Software shall be structured according to its safety relevance. Safety-related parts shall be separated from non-safety-related ones.
2. The accepted software quality standards shall be met. Safety-critical software shall not be less reliable than conventional software.
3. In any detectable operational failure, safety-related software shall react to the safe side of the technical process.
4. Correct operation of the main safety functions shall be monitored continuously or at least at suitable intervals. (Although this is basically a safeguard against deterioration due to hardware failures or external interference, this principle covers purely software-related aspects as well. In any case, it influences the software system architecture.)
5. A conceptual model of the software system structure should be adopted at the beginning of each software project. The architectural decisions should be taken on the basis of this model.

The following sections are outlines of the work of EWICS TC7, as published in Redmill, (1989).

Design and licensing of safety-related software 231

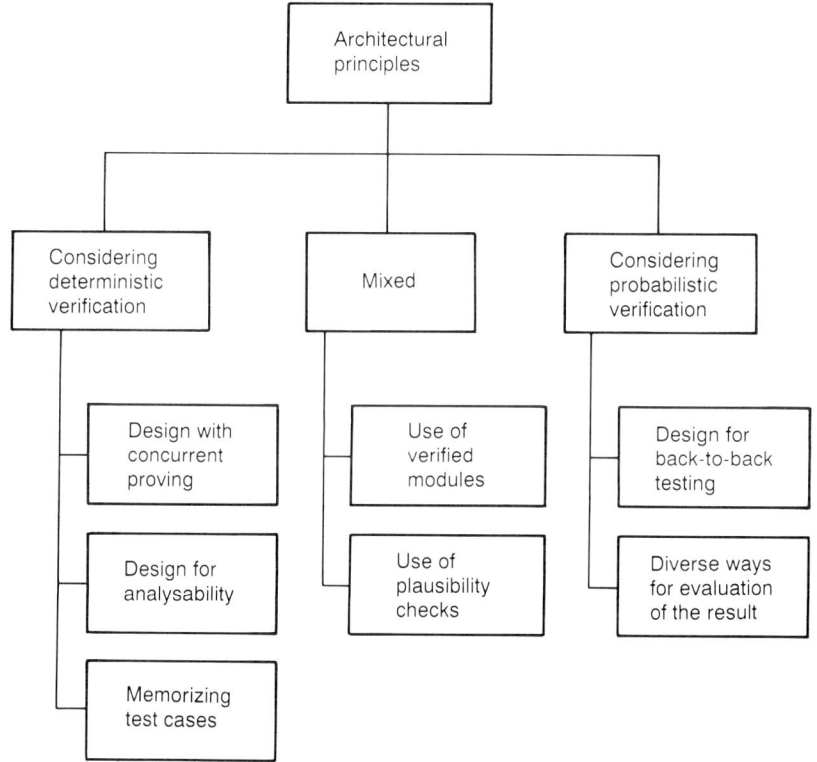

Figure 11.3 *Diagram of methods as seen from the verification point of view*

The strategies in detail

Design with concurrent proving

Aim
Logically correct software at the end of the development phase.

Description
During the development phase the effects on the data area of the execution of any statement are continuously kept in mind. Only statements and statement sequences are used whose effects can be described formally and whose consequences can be completely understood.
The proof of correctness is carried out in parallel with the development.

Conditions
Full knowledge of predicate logic and mathematical proving.
No complex arithmetic.
Sufficient resources in computing power.
Failure-free translations, if the work is to be done at the source code level.

Major advantages
Formally correct program received.
Supplementarily required testing effort very small.

Problems or disadvantages
Considerable restrictions on the problems that can be treated.
Human mental effort required is very large; project progress can be quite slow.
At present, feasible for small programs only.
Language usage to be restricted.

Relationship to other methods
Restrictions of freedom during development at least as severe as for the method on analysable programs.

Assessment
Recommendable for small software parts, if their safety relevance is high and if the other conditions mentioned are fulfilled.

Tools
Program provers exist to a very limited extent.

References
Hoare (1968)
Taylor et al. (1985)
O'Neill et al. (1988)
Baber (1987)

Analysable programs

Aim
To design a program in such a way that program analysis is feasible. The program behaviour must be completely testable on the basis of the analysis.

Description
  Principles
    The rules of structured programming are to be followed.
    The individual program parts have to be designed such that they are decoupled as far as ever possible.
    Mappings and influence on decisions are to be decoupled.
  Details
    Only simple types of decisions about the control flow.
    No pointering over several stages.
    Nesting depth to be restricted; use of sequential structures instead.
    No optimization of the code.

Conditions
The problem to be solved has to be fairly simple.
No complex* calculations as the basis of branching and other types of decisions.
All influences on loop repetitions or branches shall depend in a simple way on input parameters.

Boundaries between different type of mappings shall be simple.
Mappings between input parameters and output parameters shall be as simple as possible.
No interrupts.
Computing time surplus.

Major advantages
Code can be verified completely by testing.

Problems or disadvantages
Considerable restrictions on the problems that can be treated.
Remarkable restrictions on the programming style.
Does not qualify for complex problems, such as some types of sorting, simulation of plant behaviour, Fast Fourier Transform or mathematically demanding tasks.
No real-time features may be explicitly built in; the problem has to be so simple that all time constraints are fulfilled without any specific measures.
No extensive usage of pointers allowed.

Relationship to other methods
To be taken, if the programs are to be verified by program analysis.
All problems that can be described by decision tables can be treated in this way.

Assessment
Recommendable for simple problems and if the verification is planned to be carried out by program analysis,
Recommendable, if the safety relevance is high and systematic verification is aimed at.
Not recommendable in all other cases.

Tools
No specific tools available for preliminary design. The use of general conventional design tools is recommended.
Implementation may use decision table generators.

Reference
Kersken *et al.* (1984)

* Explanation: In this respect 'complex calculations' mean calculations whose sense or meaning or whose possible results may not be initially visible to the assessor.

Memorizing assessed cases

Aim
Switch to the safe state, if a program execution occurs that has not been previously licensed or qualified.

Description
  Principle
    During licensing a record is taken from relevant details of all program

executions. During operation it is checked whether or not the actual case was among the licensed or those already qualified; if not, a safety action is taken.

Details

The record that is to be taken during the licensing or testing phase can regard the sequence of the individual decision to decision paths or the sequence of the individual accesses to arrays, records or volumes, or both. Different methods of storing are feasible: one run can be mapped on one single REAL variable, on a sequence of simple variables or the like.

During operation it is searched whether the executed case is among those stored.

Since the possible combinations of decision to decision paths during a program is very large, it is not feasible to treat programs as a whole. The individual modules are to be taken as supervised units instead.

Conditions

Proper modularization of the supervised code; each module must be independent of any other.

Ample storage is needed for the characteristics of the stored cases; at least three times the storage requirement of the code.

Ample additional execution time must be available during operation to carry out all the searching; the search time normally considerably exceeds the ordinary execution time.

The technical process needs a safe state.

Major advantages

The necessary instrumentation of the code to be supervised can be done automatically; the same applies to the searching and checking during execution.

Only licensed cases may cause actions that are not purely safety related.

In systems that work in cooperation with a human operator, the operator may add new cases among the memorized one, after he has personally checked their correct treatment through the software.

Problems or disadvantages

Additional memory space and computing time.

Prerequisite of independent modules.

No advantage, if complete test or proof have been made already.

Dangerous to availability; availability is lowered.

Not useful, if number of relevant pathes is virtually untestable, because it is too large.

Does not provide any remedy against calculation errors.

Programming errors existing only between modules (distant effects) or in their interfaces may remain undetected if only module supervision is employed.

Relationship to other methods

To be used together with plausibility checks if modules are not completely independent.

Assessment

Safeguards againt hardware failures.

Suitable, if safety requirements are extreme, versus modest availability requirements.

Tools
None

Reference
Ehrenberger (1987)

Use of verified modules

Aim
Avoid redevelopment of the software system from the start, use existing software instead to build the system anew; save costs both during building the software and in verifying it.

Description
The safety system software is composed from existing software modules. These modules may be newly grouped according to the specific needs of the system to be built.

Conditions
The modules are verified through long operating experience or through an earlier program analysis and the related test, or by proof.

Major advantages
No need to verify all the details of the modules again.

Problems or disadvantages
Necessity to carefully investigate the interfaces between the modules, if any part of their mutual composition has been changed.

Relationship to other methods
Complementary to new development.

Assessment
Highly recommendable.

Tools
Generators, configuration management tools.

Use of assertions and plausibility checks

Aim
Check of intermediate results during execution at specific points of the code. In case of incorrect or implausible intermediate results a safety measure is taken.

Description
  Principle
    Intermediate results are checked for correctness, validity or plausibility during execution (e.g. by means of assertions).

Conditions
Only problems whose loss of information content during program execution is not too high qualify for this method.
Careful analysis of the predicates at the different distinct steps of program execution is necessary.
Appropriate actions are to be planned in case of negative outcome of an assertion.

Major advantages
Checks during on-line execution.
Sort problems can be treated.

Problems or disadvantages
No guarantee of correctness can be given in many cases.
Sometimes only very vague predicates can be given that do not mean very much. Derivation of predicates requires full understanding of problem and program; cannot be automated at present. Predicate derivation is possible from the specifications or from intuitive assumptions on program behaviour. Sometimes such assumed conditions do not apply.
Only reasonable, if a safe state exists.
Assertions are meaningless if the program is correct, or if it has been verified by other means.

Relationship to other methods
Checks are the on-line equivalent of program proving.
Relationships to probabilistic verification exist, because the assertions trap execution failures only with certain probabilities, except for simple cases that also qualify for proving.
Adaptive voting may be used, if an assertion is not fulfilled.

Assessment
Recommendable, if no complete test, proof or analysis is feasible, conditions mentioned apply, problem solved by the program is fairly complex.
Provides a certain (however unquantifiable) help against hardware failures.

Tools
Some languages provide means for easily formulating the assertions.

Software diversity

Aim
Check the results of one program through one or several other programs that solve the same problem.

Description
　Principle
　　At least two programs that have been developed independently solve the same problem. Safety actions are taken if one program requires such an action or in case of disagreement of the results of the two versions.

Design and licensing of safety-related software   237

The probability of common failures with identical results of the two programs is considered to be remarkably below the failure probability of one program.

Details
In order to achieve independence during development, different design strategies are recommended for the different versions, different languages and the use of different input data. Strategies could be, for example, JSP versus SADT; different input data could be 'normal' values versus their complements. The most efficient form of diversity is achieved, if physically diverse data are taken as the basis for calculation and the calculations themselves follow different algorithms (functional diversity).

Conditions
At least two independent teams.
Information reduction during compilation is low.
Existence of a safe state of the technical process.

Major advantages
Considerable reduction of dangerous failures.
Possibly reduced project cost due to lower verification expenses.
Can be employed with arbitrarily large or complex programs, verification possible, without considering any details of the code or its structure.
Enables back-to-back testing.
Increases the possibility of finding ambiguous or faulty specifications.

Problems or disadvantages
Normally the probability of common failures is remarkably higher than in the ideal case.
More than double development and maintenance costs and doubling of computer resource needed.
Specification errors may pass undetected into both versions.
Availability is decreased.
Synchronization of the two diverse versions is necessary.

Relationship to other methods
Reasonable primarily with probabilistic verification techniques, in particular with black box testing.
Closely connected to the use of software redundancy.

Assessment
Recommendable after careful planning and execution of independent and preferably forced different development.
Higher degrees of diversity than using two versions are less recommendable in many cases because of the higher costs involved and the comparatively smaller additional safety gains.
For complex parts only.

Tools
Development tools that support the different development methods.

References
Bishop *et al.* (1987)
Knight and Leveson (1986)
Saglietti (1988)
Voges (1987)
Avizienis *et al.* (1987)

Use of redundant ways for the evaluation of the result

Aim
If several ways for the evaluation of the result exist, more than one of these should be used.

Conditions
Software systems in non-procedural languages such as LISP or PROLOG; or systems with databases.

Description
In contrast to normal applications of non-procedural languages, the computation is not stopped as soon as one result has been evaluated, but is allowed to continue until a second or a third or further answer to the related question has been found. A vote is taken among the evaluated results.

Major advantages
Better basis for decisions than in the case of only one result.

Problems or disadvantages
Computing time may become intolerably long.
Knowledge base with enough redundant information required.
In some cases redundant results may be feasible, in others not; difficult to predict this.

Relationship to other methods
Some sort of adaptive voting is required.
Similar to diversity; according to the present state of the art, however, no independency of the gained results may be assumed *a priori*.

Assessment
Recommendable if non-procedural languages or systems with databases are employed. Since such systems are not very reliable at present and since it is impossible to analyse and test them exhaustively or prove their correctness, such methods are to be used with extreme care.
Recommendable, if used diversely to a system in a procedural language.

Tools
No tools available

References
Literature on PROLOG, LISP, artificial intelligence (e.g. Voyer (1987) or Saint-Dizier (1987)

Selection aspects

In many cases it is most suitable to apply a mixture of the above-mentioned strategies, their selection depending on the respective task of the software, including available knowledge, existing parts, etc. The strategies described are considered for software with high safety relevance; for example, if people can be killed in case of failure. If the safety relevance is lower, one may determine not to follow any of the described strategies, but use just the rules of good software engineering, as they are briefly outlined below. They may be sufficient in the case of a sewing machine, where the most dangerous accident is to the operator's finger. Certainly the points in the previous lifecycle should be considered in this connection.

DEVELOPMENT (DESIGN AND CODING) FOR SOFTWARE IN SAFETY-RELATED APPLICATIONS

After the design decisions have been taken, the software development phase starts. The following recommendations provide a guide to good practice for writing software which is as error-free as possible from the beginning and which can easily be verified. They are considered in the context of software written in higher-level procedural languages. The list is by no means exhaustive. Some of the aspects included are well treated in the literature on software engineering. Others are specifically added to facilitate verification, although they may cause considerable overheads during coding. For details see Redmill (1988) or IEC (1987). One problem is that such rules can never be free from contradictions, when they are interpreted literally and rigorously. If contradictions are found the rules shall be interpreted according to the overall principle of understandability of the software for those who are responsible for the safety of the plant. In case of doubt, the assessor should be consulted.

Principles for development (design and coding)

1. Prior to development the functional specification shall be studied carefully. Deficiencies and ambiguities shall be clarified. Particular care should be given to those parts that deal with faulty inputs.
2. The program structure shall be based upon a decomposition into modules.
3. At least two design stages are recommended: the first dealing with the design of the units, packages or modules (preliminary design, architectural design), the second with the sub-programs (detailed design). One design stage may be sufficient if the code comprises less than 20 pages.
4. The program structure should be simple and easy to understand, both in its overall design and in its details. Tricks, recursive structures and unnecessary code compaction should be avoided.

5. Foreseeable changes should be stated; design should be such that they can be implemented by changing one or few modules only.
6. Design should be based on a specific model, e.g. Petri nets, JSP, SA, SADT, etc. It should reflect the problem to be solved.
7. Basic questions should be clarified first, e.g. main data structures, basic functions, time conditions.
8. A top-down approach to software development is preferred to a bottom-up one.
9. Each sub-program shall be readable from start to end. Its function shall be understandable on the basis of its interface.
10. Good documentation shall be provided concurrent to development. It shall be tool based.

Some details of the design

About the product

1. A data dictionary shall be provided.
2. Changes of the databases shall be done only by specialized software parts.
3. The software shall be hardware independent as far as possible.
4. It shall be documented, where hardware properties are being used.
5. Parallel processes shall be avoided, the software shall form only one sequentially working system.
6. Safety functions shall not depend upon time-critical execution.
7. Enough memory space and computing time shall be provided.
8. Real-time influences should be minimized.
9. The use of the operating system should be minimized.
10. The use of interrupts should be avoided.
11. The design shall reflect the problem to be solved both in its data structure and in its execution structure. Possible aspects of grouping are:
    (a) Type of function,
    (b) Adherence to particular devices,
    (c) Operation on certain data,
    (d) Timing aspects,
    (e) Questions of changeability,
    (f) Safety aspects,
    (g) Narrow data interface.
12. In general, each system will represent a compromise between several possible aspects of grouping.
13. In case of failure a well-defined reaction shall be performed.
14. Any re-use of existing parts is to be balanced against the adaptation problems. It is preferable to use library functions against writing new ones.

About the procedures

1. Changes that might become necessary during the development should proceed from the general to the special parts.

Design and licensing of safety-related software 241

2. Concurrent verification such as inspections shall be performed.
3. Project specific rules shall be established, taking into account the capabilities of the persons involved and the organizational environments of their work.

Coding

1. Understandability to other specialists is as important as correctness of the logical function.
2. The code should represent the problem to be solved or the model used of the solution in its validity area.
3. Those language elements should be used that represent the intentions most clearly.
4. Language elements should be used uniformly.
5. Any sub-program should be readable from start to end.
6. No optimization according to run-time or memory space should be allowed.
7. During run-time checks should be performed of:
    (a) Any possible division by 0,
    (b) Variable ranges at the receiving sub-program,
    (c) Array boundaries,
    (d) Possible break of a chain of pointers.
8. All failure messages from standard sub-programs shall be interpreted.
9. Data shall be used for one purpose only. If possible, only one type of addressing should be used for one type of data.
10. Static variables are to be preferred to only part-time present ones.
    ones.
    (a) All interfaces,
    (b) Meaning of variables – if they are not completely self-describing,
    (c) Pointer variables, if the language does not make them visible as such,
    (d) Branch and loop statements,
    (e) Constructs that are possibly unknown to the reader,
    (f) Comments should explain why something has been done,
    (g) Comments shall be selected with care.
12. The rules of structured programming shall be followed. No label variables are allowed. Loops are strongly preferred to recursions.
13. The principles of modularization, information hiding, and narrow data interface shall be respected as follows
    (a) Subprogram size below 50 lines of executable code,
    (b) Only one entrance and only one exit,
    (c) Data transfer between sub-programs only via actual parameters,
    (d) Minimal number of parameters,
    (e) Number of parameters to be restricted, to e.g. seven,
    (f) Complete understandability of the sub-program on the basis of the interface,
    (g) As many local variables as possible,
    (h) Nesting of calls of functions only to a depth of 1.

14. Careful selection of appropriate identifiers.
15. No comparison on equal or unequal with REAL variables.
16. Within one sub-program the number of nestings should be restricted to four. Larger nesting depths should be justified in the documentation. This applies for nesting of control statements, pointers, data structures and brackets.
17. The length of Boolean expressions should be restricted, e.g. to four variables. Within that limit, Boolean expressions shall be preferred to branchings.
18. Brackets should be used, where they clarify relationships.
19. The reason for type conversions shall be explained.
20. With respect to coding style the following points shall be observed:
    (a) Readability is more important than writability,
    (b) Careful indentation,
    (c) Uniform layout,
    (d) Better visibility of key words and standard identifiers,
    (e) Only one statement per line,
    (f) Compact code layout,
    (g) Visibility of standard functions of the language.
21. The language standard shall be observed.
22. The above-mentioned rules shall be appropriately interpreted and clarified for the programming language of the project.

Application of the principles of software ergonomy to user interfaces

The user shall be provided with an interface and, in particular, with output that makes malfunctions due to human error unlikely. This includes in detail:

1. Clear and understandable output, preferably in graphical form, use of the agreed symbols and terms,
2. Appropriate use of lower-case letters and capital letters,
3. Emphasis on the display of safety aspects,
4. Explanation of the detailed meaning of the output on request,
5. Explanation of the dialogue state on request,
6. Different forms of commands for the frequent user and the rare user,
7. Guidance of the operator or user on request,
8. Robustness against human input errors,
9. Consequence prediction of human actions to the system on request,
10. Use of colours according to specific rules,
11. Information diversity (important aspects displayed in several ways).

Language, translator and other tools

Even though a specific programming language cannot be required, the following may be considered as common basic rules for safety system programming languages:

1. Languages with a thoroughly tested translator should be used. If no thoroughly tested translator is employed, additional verification shall show that the result of the translation is correct.
2. The language should be completely and unambiguously defined, otherwise the use of the language shall be restricted to its completely and unambiguously defined features. This applies in a similar way if there is any doubt about the correct translation of a specific language feature or a particular combination of such features.
3. Problem-oriented languages are strongly preferred to machine-oriented ones.
4. A programming language for safety systems and its translator should not prevent by their design:
   (a) Error-limiting constructs;
   (b) Translation-time type checking;
   (c) Run-time type and array bound check, and parameter checking.
5. Automatic testing aids should be available.
6. Automatic development tools should be available.

FURTHER ASPECTS

The above-mentioned list is necessarily incomplete and also in some respects, debatable. It needs interpretation in the practical situation, considering the available skills and tools and the specifics of the software and its task.

Finally, one should keep in mind that the indicated techniques facilitate program verification, if applied appropriately. They cannot, however, replace it. The cost for verification may be lowered but will most likely remain a significant part of the project budget.

ACKNOWLEDGEMENTS

This chapter is based on the discussion of many teams, in particular in EWICS TC7 ('Safety and Security') and in IEC SC65A WG9 ('Safe Software'). Specific thanks are due to the inspiring ideas of the Austrian partners of the IEC group, represented by Mr E. Schoitsch. In Germany it was the groups DKE K714, the Scientific Council of the Gütegemeinschaft Software and the group VDI-GIS 4.1 'Softwarezuverlässigkeit', who dealt with similar problems and whose ideas have been used here. The author thanks all members of these bodies.

REFERENCES

Andersen, O. and Petersen, P.G. (1986), *Handbook of Standards and Certification Requirements of Software*, ECR-182, Report from Electronic Centralen, May

Avizienis, A., Lyu, M. R. and Schütz, W. (1987), *In Search of Effective Diversity*, Technical Report CSD 870060, Computer Science Department, University of California, Los Angeles

Baber, R. L. (1987), *The Spine of Software: Designing Probably Correct Software – Theory and Practice*, John Wiley, New York

Bishop, P. G. et al. (1987), *STEM – A Project on Software Test and Evaluation Methods*, SARSS 87, Elsevier Applied Science, New York

Bloomfield, R. E. and Ehrenberger, W. D. (1987), *Licensing issues associated with the use of computers in the nuclear industry*, Report of the Commission of the European Communities, EUR11147EN

Ehrenberg, W. D. (1987), *Fail-safe Software – Some principles and a case study*, SARSS 87, Elsevier Applied Science, New York

Fagan, F. L. (1976), 'Design and code inspections to reduce errors in program development', *IBM Systems Journal*, No. 3

Gorski, J. (1989), 'Formal approach to development of critical computer systems', *Hawaii International Conference on System Science*, HICSS22

Hoare, C. A. R. (1968), 'An axiomatic basis for computer programming', *Comm. ACM*, **12**, No. 10, October

International Electrotechnical Commission (1987), *Software or Computers in the Safety Systems of Nuclear Power Stations*, Geneva

International Electrotechnical Commission (1989), SC65A, WG9 *Software Safety: Software for Computers in the Application of Industrial Safety Related Systems*, Draft Standard

Kersken, M., Rietsch, L. and Mertens, U. (1984), *Qualification of a Computer System for the Limitation of Power Density in a Reactor Core*, Compsac 1984, 0730-3157/84/0000/0530$0101.00, IEEE

Knight, J. C. and Leveson, N. C. (1986), 'An empirical study of failure probabilities in multi-version software', *16th International Symposium on Fault-Tolerant Computing*, Vienna, Austria, July

O'Neill, I. M., Clutterbuck, D. L., Farrow, P. F., Summers, P. G. and Dolman, W. C. (1988), 'The formal verification of safety-critical assembly code, Paper presented at SAFECOMP '88, Fulda, Germany, November

Redmill, F. (ed.) (1988, 1989), *Dependability of Critical Computer Systems*, Volume 1, 1988; Volume 2, 1989, Elsevier Applied Science, New York

Saglietti, F. (1988), 'Optimal combination of software testing strategies', Paper presented at SAFECOMP '88 in Fulda, Germany, November

Saint-Dizier, P. (1987), *Initiation à la programmation en PROLOG*, Editions Eyrolles, Paris

Taylor, J. R., Voges, U., Puhr-Westerheide, P. and Quirk, W. J. (1985), 'Structural analysis and proof', in Quirk, W. J. (ed.), *Verification and Validation of Real-Time Software*, Springer-Verlag, New York

Voges, U. (ed.) (1987), *Software Diversity in Computerised Control Systems*, Springer-Verlag, New York

Voyer, R. (1987), *Moteurs de systèmes experts*, Editions Eyrolles, Paris

Index

Acceptance phase, 221
Acceptance test, 198, 219
Acts of Parliament (UK):
   Consumer Protection Act 1987, 30, 46–50
   Health and Safety at Work Act 1974, Section 6, 38
   Sales of Goods Act 1979, 39–41
   Supply of Goods and Services Act 1982, 41
   Unfair Contract Terms Act 1977, 46
Ada, 157, 160–9
   aliasing, 164–5
   claims, 164
   defensive programming, 165–7
   design rules, 162–3
   double insulation, 168–9
   other features, 176
   package constituents, 163
   physical design, 167–8
   program structure, 161–2
   software certification in safety-related system, 177–82
      evidence for certification, 181–2
      formal checks, 178–9
      intelligent inspection, 179
      safety integrity analysis, 177–8
      testing, 180–1
   software–hardware interaction, 176–7
   weaknesses, 173–6
      exception handling, 175
      input-output, 174
      intercommunication, 174
      mutual exclusion, 175–6
      residual, in design, 173–4
      task termination, 175
   see also Residual defects
Ada-related topics in HSE guidelines, 182–4
   HSE-Checklist 10A: Software Specification (Ada program unit semantics), 182
   HSE-Checklist 11A: Software design (Ada program unit specifications), 182
   HSE-Checklist 12A: Software coding (Ada program units which are proper bodies), 183–4
   HSE-Checklist 13A: Software test, 183
Administrative law, 31
Airbus A310, slat and flat control system, 196
Aircraft, software in, 33
Algebraic specification techniques, 109
Analysis, 9
Animation, 9, 110
ANNA, 164
ANST-IEE 730: IEEE, 57
Anti-lock braking system, 36–8, 194
Assurance, 101
Automatic development tools, 243
Automatic testing aids, 243
Availability, 157–8, 159–60
Avionics system, 109

Before and after states relationship, 140(fig.)
Behavioural equivalence, 111
British defence standards, 73
British standards, 72–3
British Standards Institute, 24
BS 5750, 44
Built-In Test Equipment (BITE), 159
Byzantine Generals problem, 101

Cable list, 213
Canadian standards, 74
Certification, 6–7, 25–7
Civil law, 29
Codes of practice, 27–8
Coding, 211
Comité Consultatif International Télégraphique et Téléphonique (CCITT), 60
Comité Européen de Normalisation (CEN), 59–60
Comité Européen de Normalisation Electrotechnique (CENELEC), 59–60

Commerce fault-tolerant systems, 199, 200(fig.)
Common cause failures (CCFs), 189
Common law, 30–1
Complementary checking by analysis/testing, 173(fig.)
Completeness, 5–6
Conformance, 7
Constructive approach, 112
Contract law, liability under, 39–43
  action under law of contract, 41–2
  express terms, 41
  extent of contractual liability, 42–3
  implied terms, 39–41
Control system, 205–7
  failures, 209
Correctness, 5
Criminal law, 29

Danger:
  avoidance, 158–60
  classification, 156–7
Danish standards, 74
Defence Standard 00–55 (MoD, 1991), 33, 181–2
Definition of function, 219
DEF STAN 00–55 (UK), 33
Degradation modes, 201
Deontic logic, 127
Descriptions, 105
Design, 4–5
Design description, 221
Diversity, 191, 197–8
Documentation, 219–21, 229(table)
Donoghue v. Stevenson, 43–4

Electricity at Work Regulations (UK, 1989), 38
Errors of commission/errors of omission, 6
ESA PSS–05–0: ESA, 57
ESA standards, 72
European Community:
  Directive (product liability), 46
  liability proposals, 54–5
European Computer Manufacturers Association (ECMA), 61
European Conference of Post and Telecommunications (CEPT), 60
European Normalized Standard EN 29000, 215

European Organization for Quality Control (EOQC), 61
European Space Agency (ESA), 60
European Workshop on Industrial Computer Systems (EWICS), 61, 227
Extended Petri nets, 83–7

FAA–STD–018, 60
Failure:
  random, 189–90
  systematic, 189–91
Failure modelling, 191–3
Fault:
  detection, 188–9
  repair, 189
  tolerance, 187
    using non-fault-tolerant hardware, 200–1
Fault-tolerant behaviour, 192
Fault-tolerant control for safety, 187–203
Fault-tolerant system, 189
Federal Aviation Administration (FAA), 60
  standards, 72
Flow chart, 17
FOREST project, 108
Formal methods, 96–151
  algebraic approaches, 96
  basic concepts, 114
  claim/counterclaim, 150–1
  how to apply, 150
  logic-based approaches, 96–7
  model-based approaches, 96
  model-oriented specification, 113–14
  net-based approaches, 97
  process algebras, 96
  safety example, 120–7
  software development process, *see* Software development stages/process
  strengths, 143–5
  typical specifications, 115–20
  weaknesses, 145–9
  when to apply, 150
  see also Safety-critical systems
Formal verification, 105
French standards, 73

German standards, 73
'Guff-to-stuff' ratio, 147

Guidelines for the application of ISO 9001, 216

Hardware, 193–4
   combined software diversity, 196–7
   hardware interaction, 176–7
   purpose-designed fault-tolerant systematic failures, 197
Hardware Implemented Fault Tolerance, 202
Head-up display, 109
Hierarchical decomposition of systems, 112
HSE guidance on configuration/diversity, 159
HSE Guidelines (HSE, 1987), 199
Human–computer interface, 12

Ideal operation, 3
Identification, 223
Incompleteness, 5–6
Independent software verification/validation, 88–95
   chief software verifier, 93
   interfacing groups/communications, 94
   software verifiers, 93–5
Institution of Electrical and Electronic Engineers (IEEE), 60–1
Integration description, 221
International Atomic Energy Agency (IAEA), 60
International electrotechnical Commission (IEC), 24, 59
   Electrical equipment of industrial machines TC44, 69
   Electromagnetic compatibility between electrical equipment, including networks TC77, 70
   Industrial-process measurement control: IEC TC65, 65–7
   Publication 880, 57
   Reliability/maintainability standardization aspects: IEC TC56, 63–5
   Safety aspects of computer-based systems in nuclear field: IEC SC45A, 61–2
   Safety information technology including electrical business equipment and telecommunications equipment, 69

International Standardization Organization (ISO), 57–9
   Information technology ISO/IEC JTC1, 68
   Quality management/assurance: ISO TC176, 67
   9000 Standard series, 215
Interpretation of formal notations, 143

Knowledge-based systems, 160

Languages, 243
Law of negligence, 43–6
   circumstances of action, 43–4
   extent of liability, 45–6
   practical problems, 44–5
Layered software structure, 171, 172(fig.)
Legal liability, 35–55
   civil 39–52, *see also* Contract law; Law of negligence
   compliance with standards, 52
   criminal, 38
   example (anti-lock braking system), 36–8
   future proposals, 54–5
   identification of risks, 53
   indemnity obtaining, 53
   insurance, 53
   product, *see* Product liability
   records maintenance, 54
   testing of products, 53–4
   trading structures, 53
Legal rate transitions, 122
Licensing, 25–7
'Lift' example, 17
Logic specification, 127

MAL (Modal Action Logic), 127–8
   example specification, 129–35
Malpas, 113
Markov Models, 192
MIL–S–52779, 56–7
Ministry of Defence interim standards (MOD, 1991a, b), 199
Model-oriented specifications, 110
Modularization, 15

NATO Defence Standard AQAP–13, 44
'Natural' way to use cone specification languages, 142
'Non-functional' requirements, 146

Notation, 16–17
  Z, 17

Objective assurance, 11
Objective test, 6–7
Operational research techniques, 142

Parts list, 212
Post-condition, 116
Pre-condition, 116
Predeployment check, 172
Prime numbers, 115
Probabilitic Risk Analysis, 12
Process algebra specification, 135
Process control system, 212
Product liability, 46–52
  causation, 48
  compliance with instructions, 51
  damage, 47–8
  defect, 48–9
  defences, 50
  development risk defence, 50–1
  extent of liability, 52
  persons liable, 49–50
  product, 49
Project model, 216–20
Project organization, 216
Program analysis techniques, 16
Programmable electronic systems, 2
Programmable logic controllers, (PLCs), 160
Programmed digital computer important to safety for nuclear power stations (IEC Publication 987), 62
Programming by means of library functions, 213(fig.)
Proof obligations, 140
'Proof' techniques, 16
Protection system, 210
Prototyping, 9

Radio Technical Commission for Aeronautics (RTCA), 60
  standards, 72
Real-time software requirements specification, 76
  specification language, 81–3
    functions definition, 82
    place invariants definition, 82–3
    places definition, 82–3
    predicate definition, 82

time constraints definition, 83
token environment definition, 81–2
Redundancy, 111
  active/passive, 188–9
Refinement, 15–16, 111
  techniques, 112
Regulation, 19–33
  certification, 6–7, 25–7
  codes of practice, 27–8
  direct, 23–8
  indirect, 23
  industry-specific, 23
  legal 28–31, *see also* Legal liability
  licensing, 25–7
  principles, 22–3
  purpose, 22–3
  software safety, 31–3
  standards, 24
Relay ladder emulators, 160
Reliability, 169–71
Reliability Black Diagrams, 192
Repair, 191–2
Research directions, software, 9–18
  aka 'formalism', 16
  bigger conceptual lumps, 17–18
  bridging the gap, 14–15
  human factors, 11–12
  intent to realization, 14–15
  mathematical logic?, 16
  minimizing change ramification, 15
  software design, 13–14
  structured design, 15–16
  systems or software, 9–10
  technologies, 10–11
  unification, 12–13
Residual defects, 169–77
  reliability, 169–71
  safety checking, 171–2
  software checking, 172–3
  systematic fault assessment, 169
Retrieve function, 140
Rigorous approach, 105–6
Risk assessment requirements and guidelines (Canadian National Committee, 1986), 65
RTCA DO–178A, 181

Safety, 188
  checking, 171–2
  methods of ensuring, 19–22

Safety analysis, 207–11
Safety-critical systems, 13, 32, 98–113
   assurance limits, 101–3
   assurance principles, 103–4
   goals/principles for achieving safety
      integrity, 100–1
   life cycle, formal methods in, 104–13
   software in 98–9
Safety-related software:
   design, 227–43
   development (design and coding),
      239–43
   licensing, 227–43
Safety system, nature of, 154–60
Satisfaction, 140
Sensor, 120–1
Separation of concerns, 11
Simulation, 135
Simple control loops, 154
Software, 193–4, 205–6
   checking, 172–3
   combined hardware diversity, 196–7
   diversity, 197–8
      limitations, 198
   failures, 210
   fault avoidance, 194–5
   fault tolerance, 195–7
      provision role, 201–2
   function, 223–5
   life cycle, 105–6, 227–30
   purchased, 225
   quality standards, 215–16
   safety-related, *see* Safety-related
      software
   spaghetti structure, 224(fig.)
   structures, 211–14
   well-structured program, 224–5
Software development stages/processes,
   106–13
   architectural design, 106, 110–11
   detailed design, 108–12
   implementation, 107, 112–13
   requirements analysis, 106, 107–10
   system specification, 105, 108–9
Software Engineer's Reference Book
   (McDermid, 1991), 106
*Software for computers in the safety of
   nuclear power stations* (IEC
   Publication 880), 62
Software Implemented Fault Tolerance,
   202

Software in the Safety System of Nuclear
   Power Stations (IEC, 1987), 227
Software system development cycle,
   228(fig.)
Soundness, 8
SPARK, 164, 179
Specification execution, 110
Standard(s), 56–74
   applicable to software via assessment
      guidelines, 195
   British, 73
   British defence, 73, 180–1
   Canadian, 74
   Danish, 74
   DEF STAN 00 55 (UK), 33
   directly applicable to software, 195
   ESA, 72
   European Normalized 9000 series, 215
   Federal Aviation Administration, 72
   French, 73
   general quality, 214–15
   German, 73
   history, 56–7
   international, relationship, 58(fig.)
   international organizations, 57–61
   ISO 9000 series, 215
   MoD interim (MoD, 199a, b), 199
   Nato Defence Standard   AQAP-13,
      44
   software quality, 215–16
   United States military, 72
   United States national, 69–70
Standard for Software for Computers in
   the Application of Industrial
   Safety Related Systems, (IEC,
   1989), 66
Structured analysis diagram 228(fig.)
Structured methods, 97
Synthesis, 105
Systematic fault assessment, 167
'System Design' phase, 219
System state, 115–16

Test description, 221
Testing, 8–9
Test Record, 221
Timed Calculus Communication System
   (TCCS), 135–42
Tools, trust in, 149
Tradition, 1–2
Traditional control systems, 154

Transformation, 105
Trends, 1–2
Triple modular redundant (TMR) programmable logic controllers (PLCs) 197, 199, 200(fig.)
Triple modular redundant (TMR) systems, 197, 198, 203

Unavoidable uncertainty, 2–4
Uncertainty reducing techniques, 3–4
United States military standards, 72
United States National Bureau of Standards, 71–2
United States national standards, 70–1

Verification and validation, 7–9, 105 221–3, *see also* Independent software verification/validation

Verification strategies, 230–9
  analysable programs, 232–3
  design with concurrent proving, 231–2
  memorizing assessed cases, 233–5
  selection aspects, 239
  software diversity, 236–8
  use of assertions/plausibility checks, 235–6
  use of redundant ways for evaluation of result, 238
  use of verified modules, 235
VIPER, 151

Walkthrough, 9

Z concepts, 114–15
Z notation, 17
Z specifications, 115–20